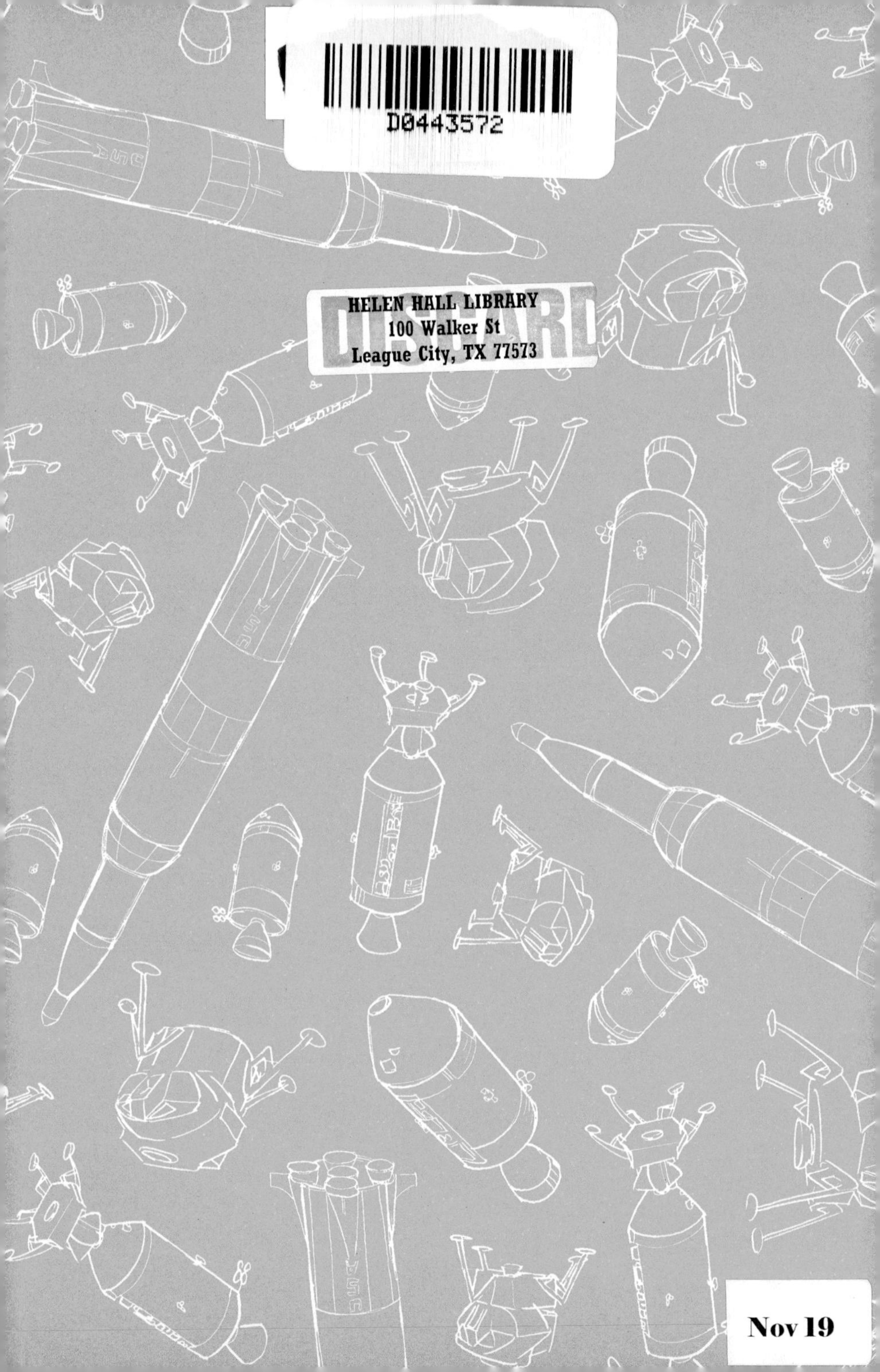

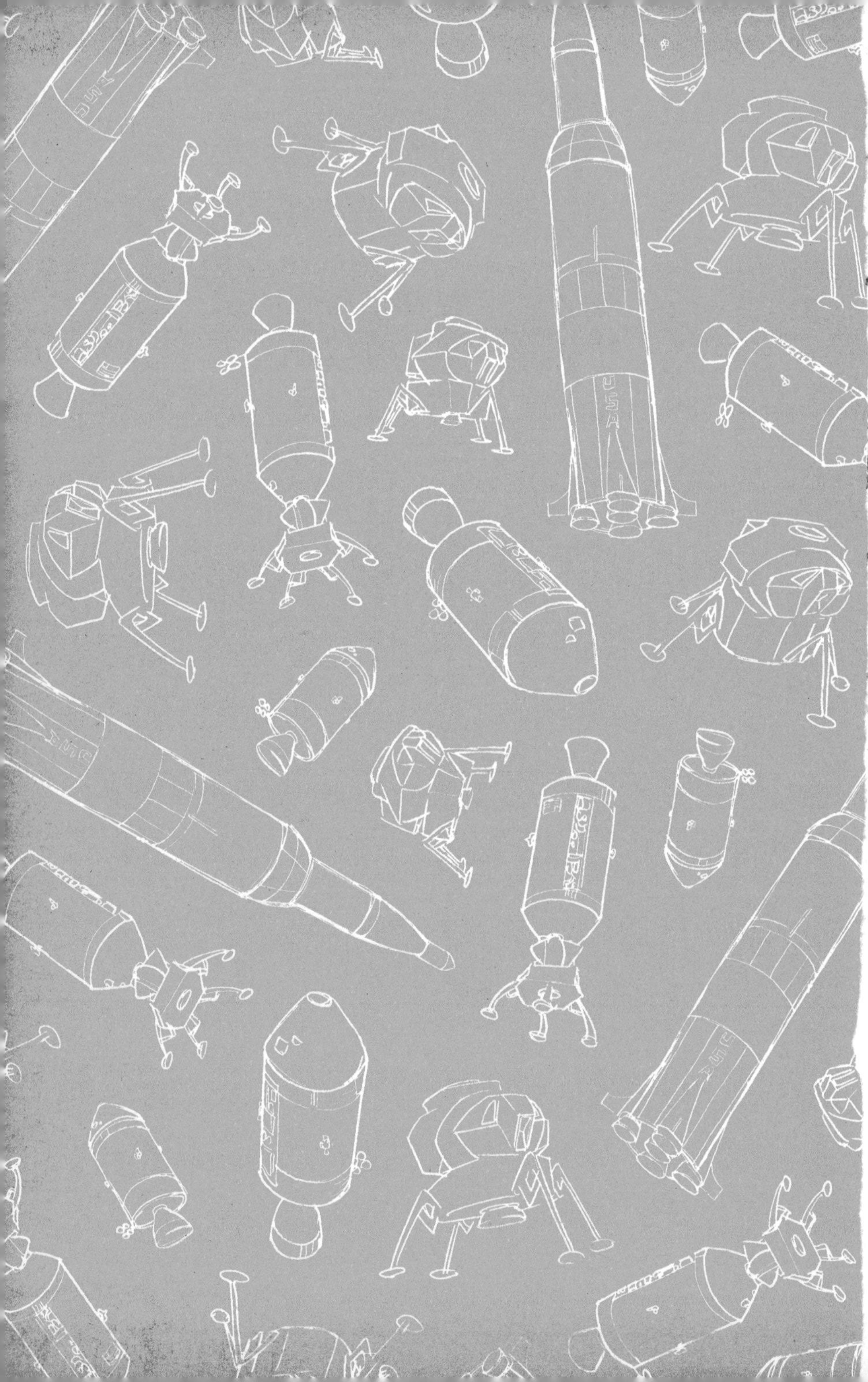

BIG IDEAS THAT CHANGED THE WORLD

ROCKET TO THE MOON!

DON BROWN

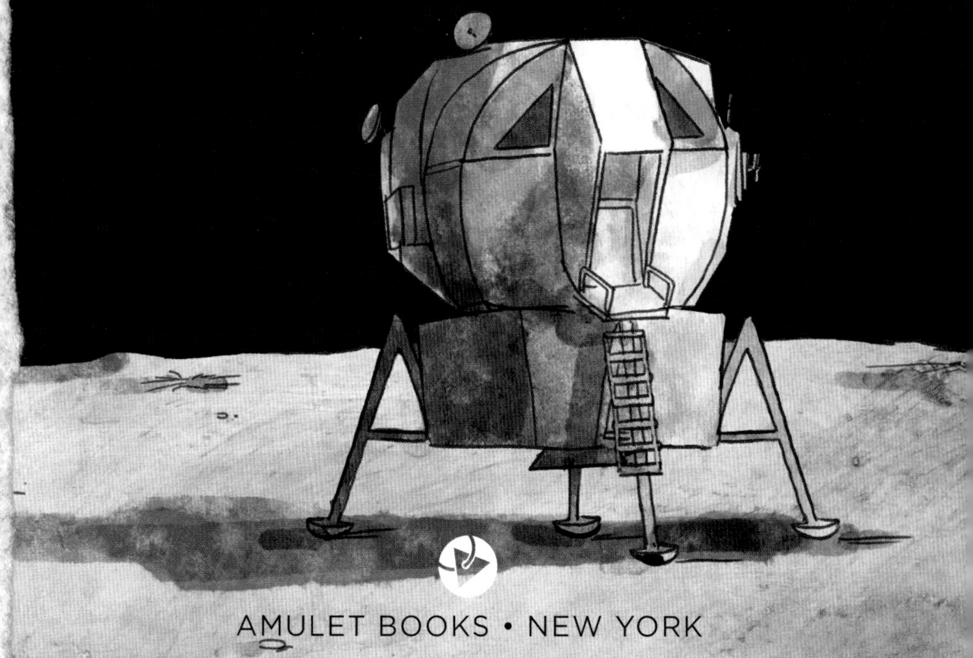

AMULET BOOKS • NEW YORK

The artwork in this book combines hand and digital drawing with digital color collage and painting.

Library of Congress Cataloging-in-Publication Data
Names: Brown, Don, 1949– author.
Title: Rocket to the moon! / by Don Brown.
Description: New York : Amulet Books, 2019. | Series: Big ideas that changed the world ; #1
Identifiers: LCCN 2018022209 (print) | LCCN 2018026295 (ebook) | ISBN 9781683354802 (All e-books) | ISBN 9781419734045 (hardcover)
Subjects: LCSH: Space flight to the moon—Juvenile literature. | Project Apollo (U.S.)—Juvenile literature.
Classification: LCC TL799.M6 (ebook) | LCC TL799.M6 B76 2019 (print) | DDC 629.45/4—dc23

Text and illustrations copyright © 2019 Don Brown

Book design by Max Temescu

Published in 2019 by Amulet Books, an imprint of ABRAMS. All rights reserved. No portion of this book may be reproduced, stored in a retrieval system, or transmitted in any form or by any means, mechanical, electronic, photocopying, recording, or otherwise, without written permission from the publisher.

Printed and bound in China
10 9 8 7 6 5 4 3 2 1

Amulet Books are available at special discounts when purchased in quantity for premiums and promotions as well as fundraising or educational use. Special editions can also be created to specification. For details, contact specialsales@abramsbooks.com or the address below.

Amulet Books® is a registered trademark of Harry N. Abrams, Inc.

ABRAMS The Art of Books
195 Broadway, New York, NY 10007
abramsbooks.com

Dedicated in memory of my parents, Virginia and Milton Brown

Note to reader: Unless otherwise noted, quotation marks signal actual quotes.

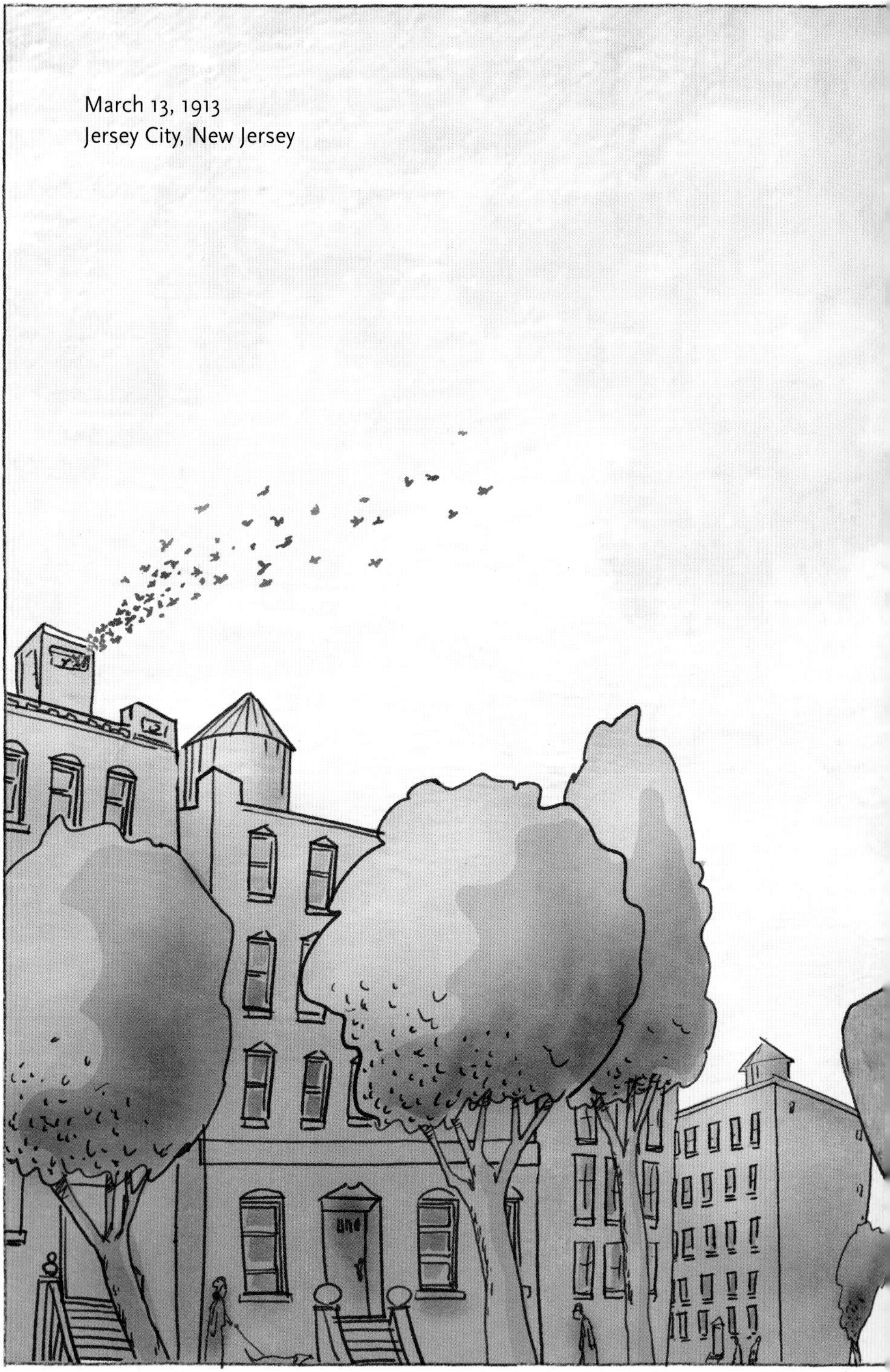
March 13, 1913
Jersey City, New Jersey

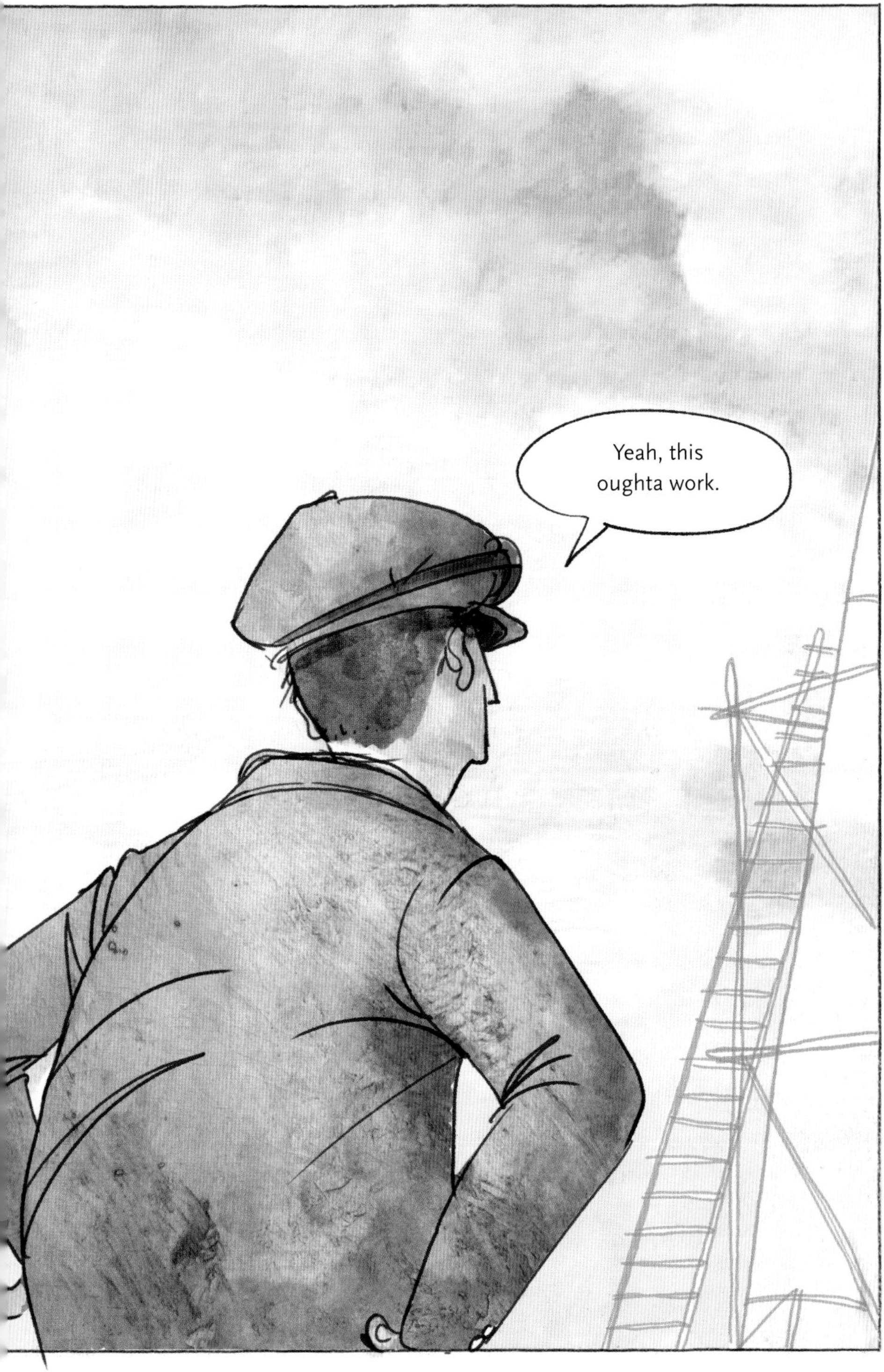
Yeah, this oughta work.

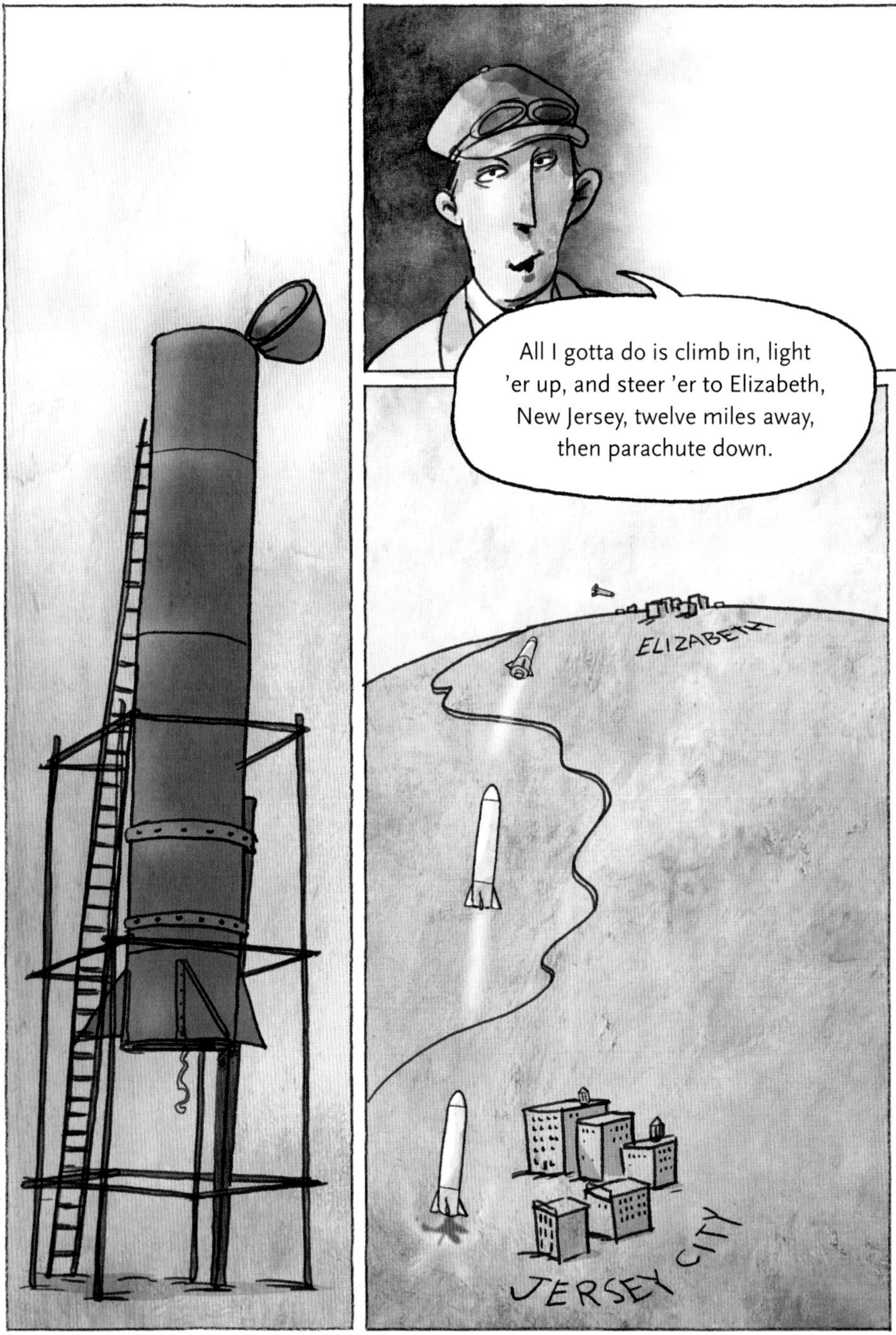
All I gotta do is climb in, light
'er up, and steer 'er to Elizabeth,
New Jersey, twelve miles away,
then parachute down.
ELIZABETH
JERSEY CITY

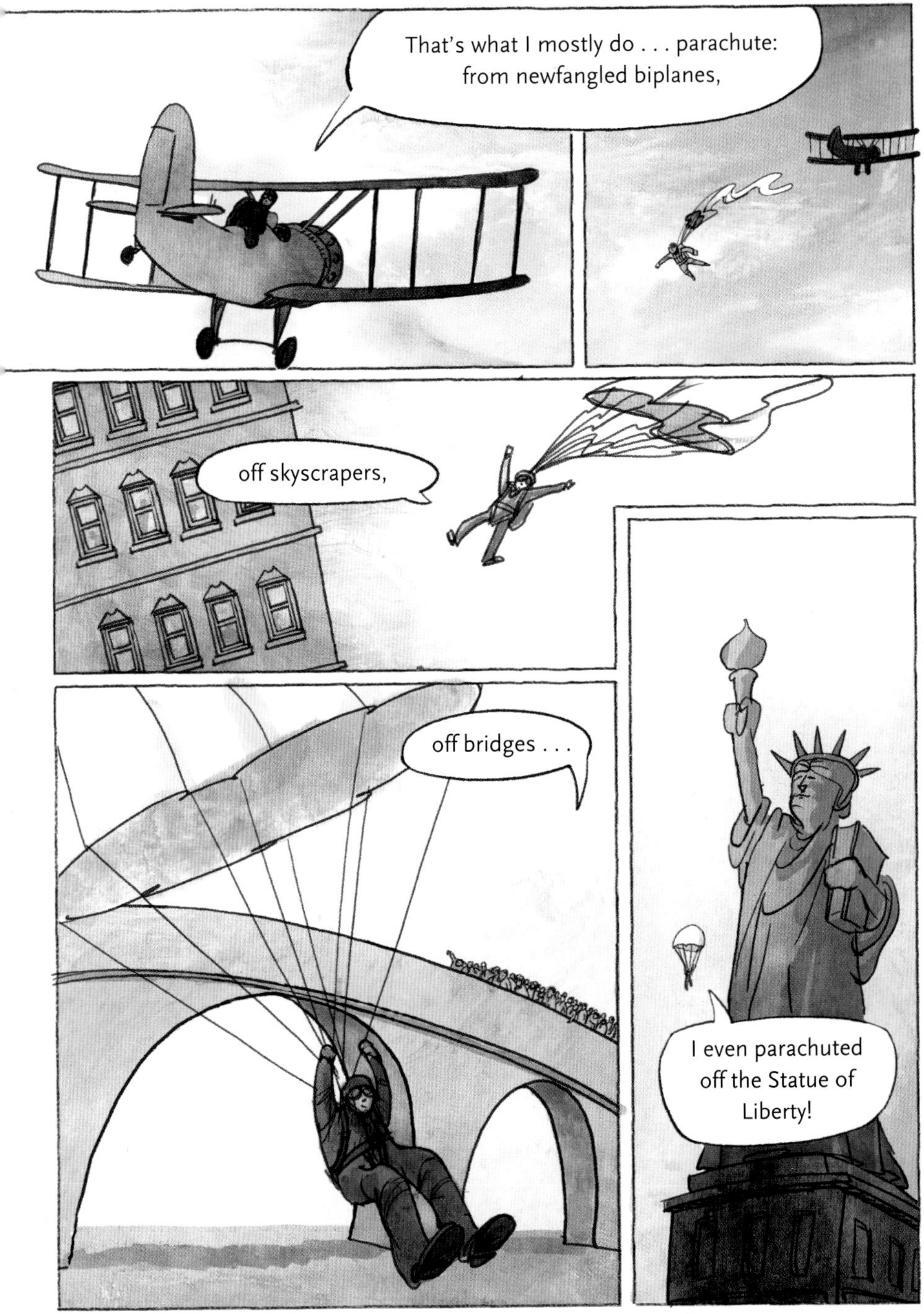
That's what I mostly do . . . parachute: from newfangled biplanes,
off skyscrapers,
off bridges . . .
I even parachuted off the Statue of Liberty!

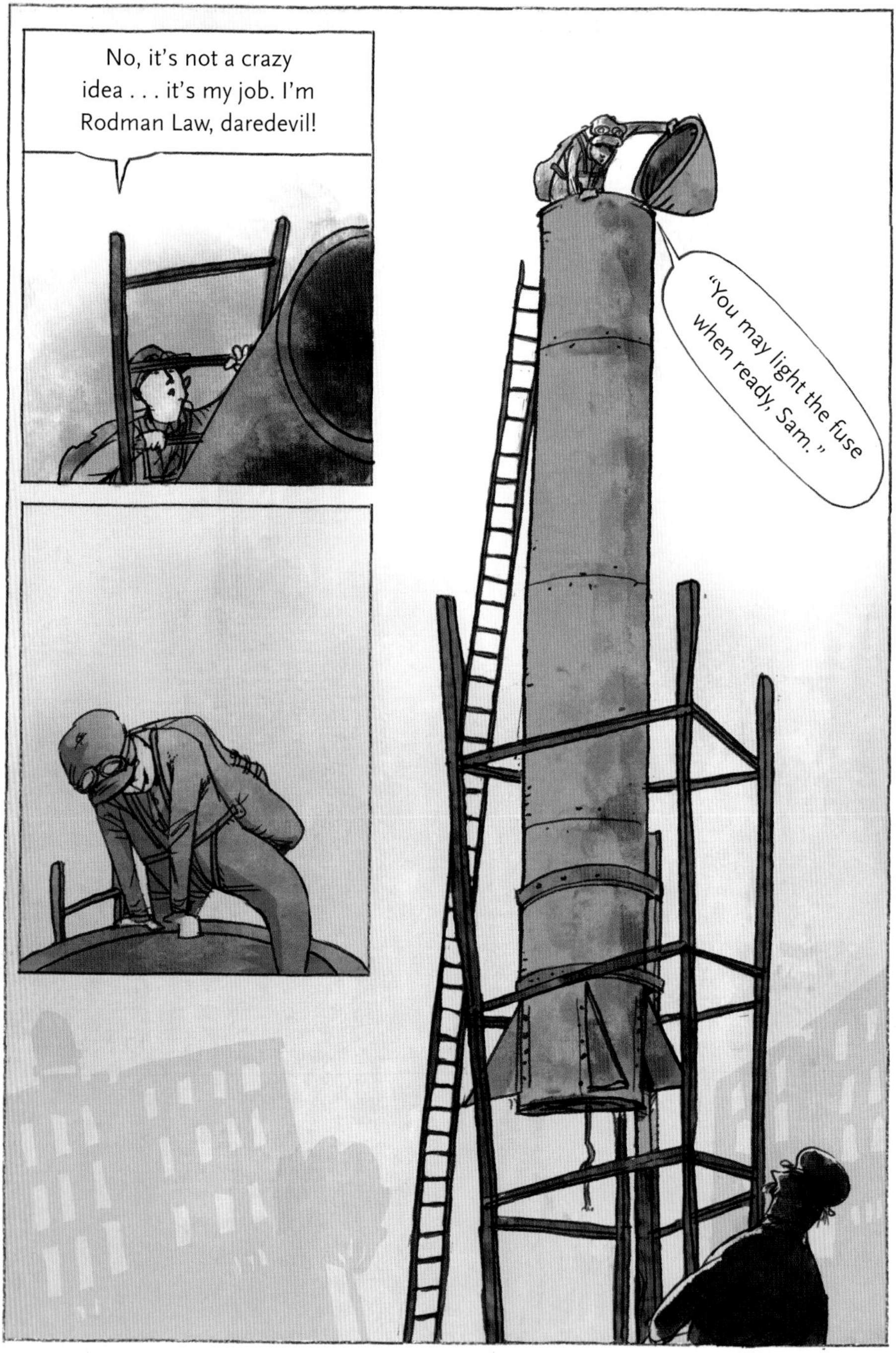
No, it's not a crazy idea . . . it's my job. I'm Rodman Law, daredevil!
"You may light the fuse when ready, Sam."

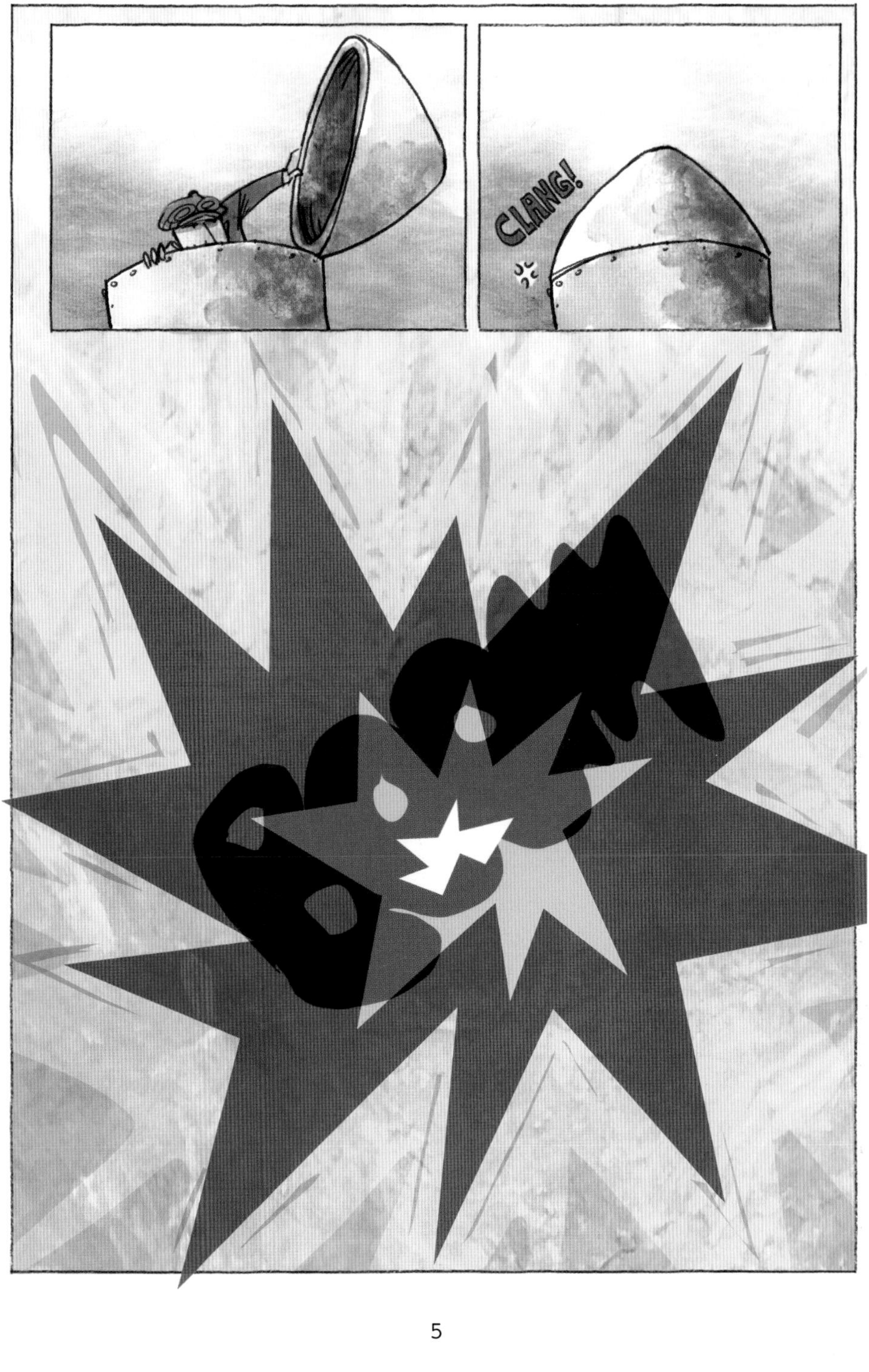
CLANG!
BOOM

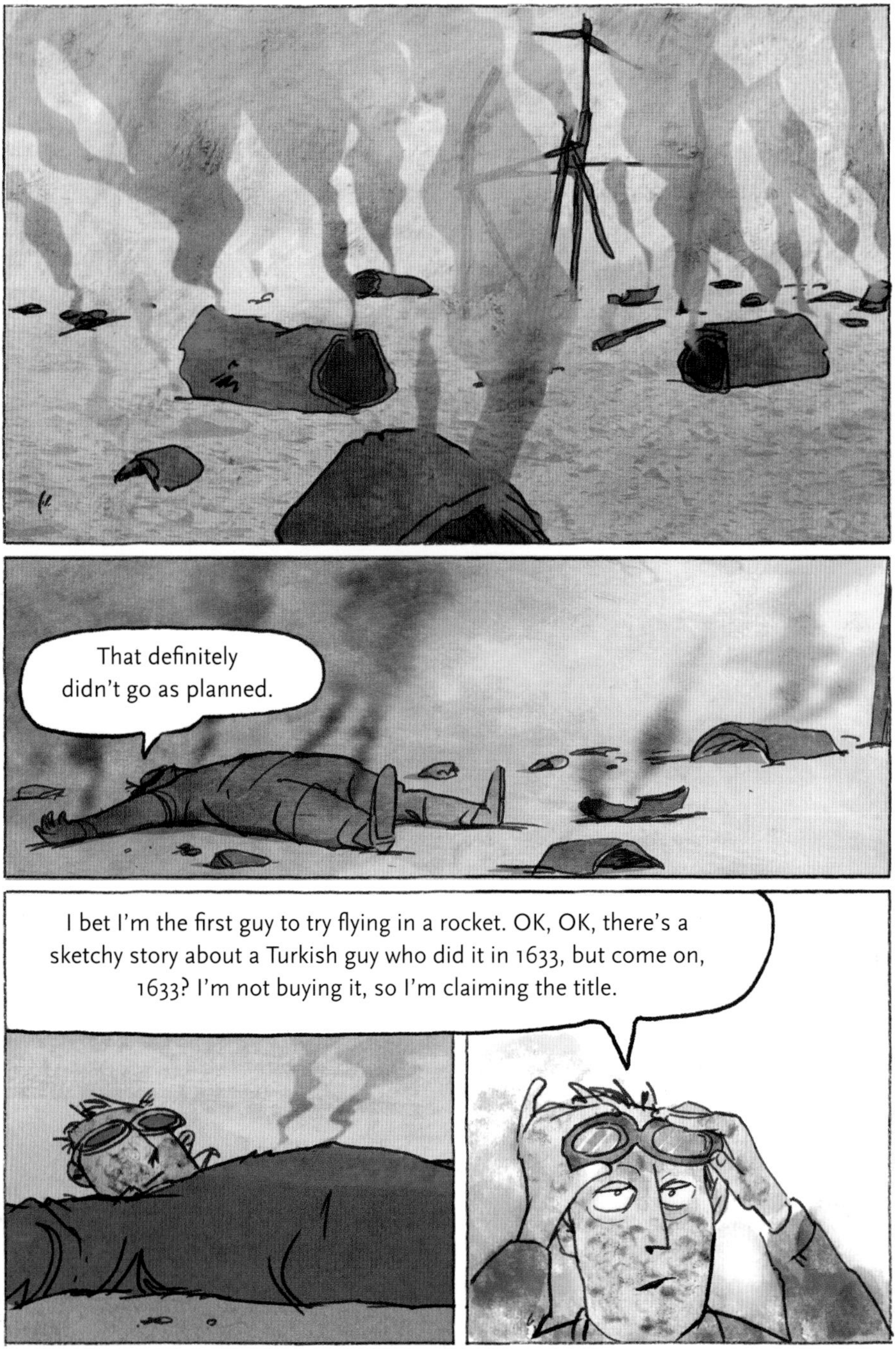
That definitely didn't go as planned.
I bet I'm the first guy to try flying in a rocket. OK, OK, there's a sketchy story about a Turkish guy who did it in 1633, but come on, 1633? I'm not buying it, so I'm claiming the title.

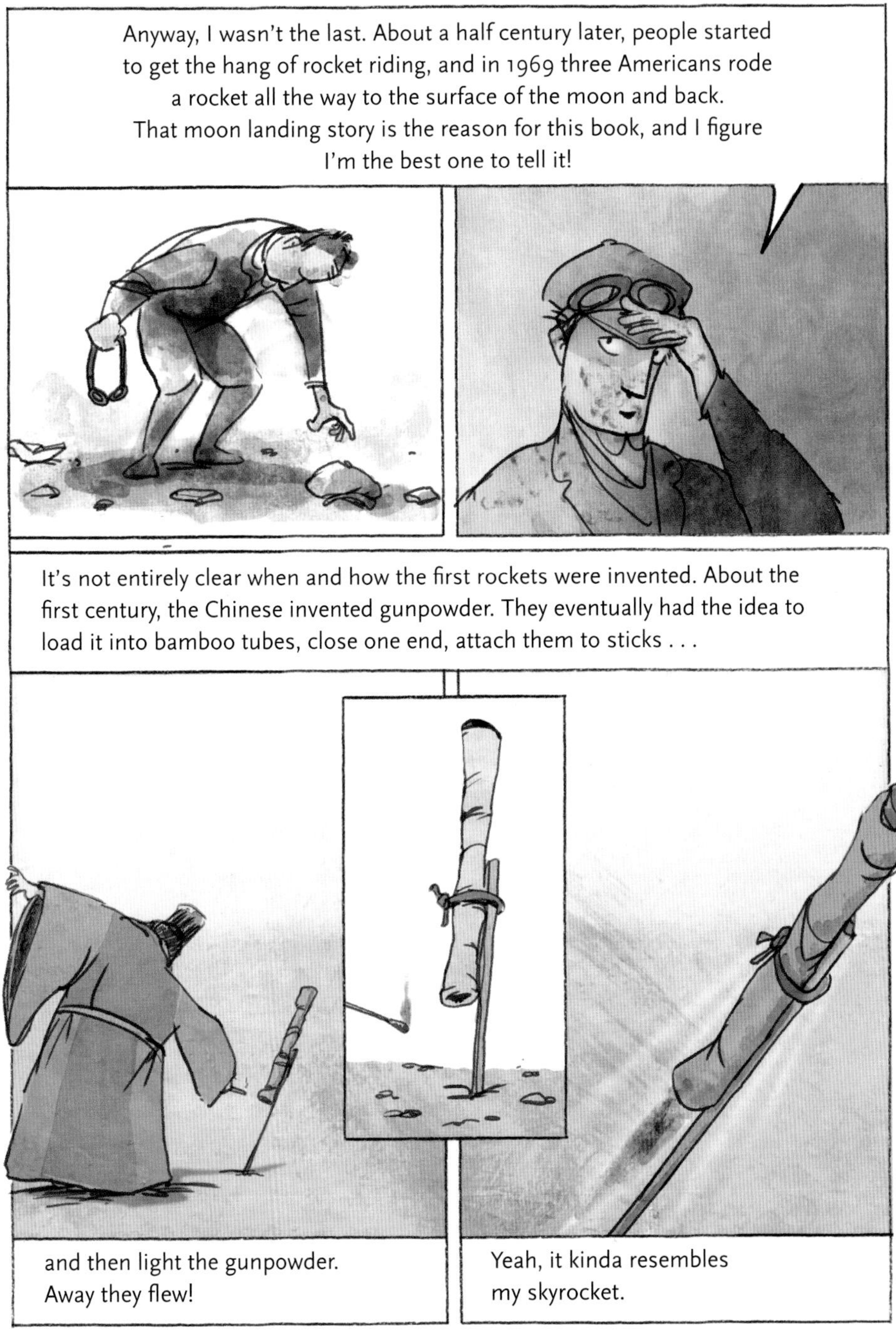
Anyway, I wasn't the last. About a half century later, people started to get the hang of rocket riding, and in 1969 three Americans rode a rocket all the way to the surface of the moon and back. That moon landing story is the reason for this book, and I figure I'm the best one to tell it!
It's not entirely clear when and how the first rockets were invented. About the first century, the Chinese invented gunpowder. They eventually had the idea to load it into bamboo tubes, close one end, attach them to sticks . . .
and then light the gunpowder. Away they flew!
Yeah, it kinda resembles my skyrocket.

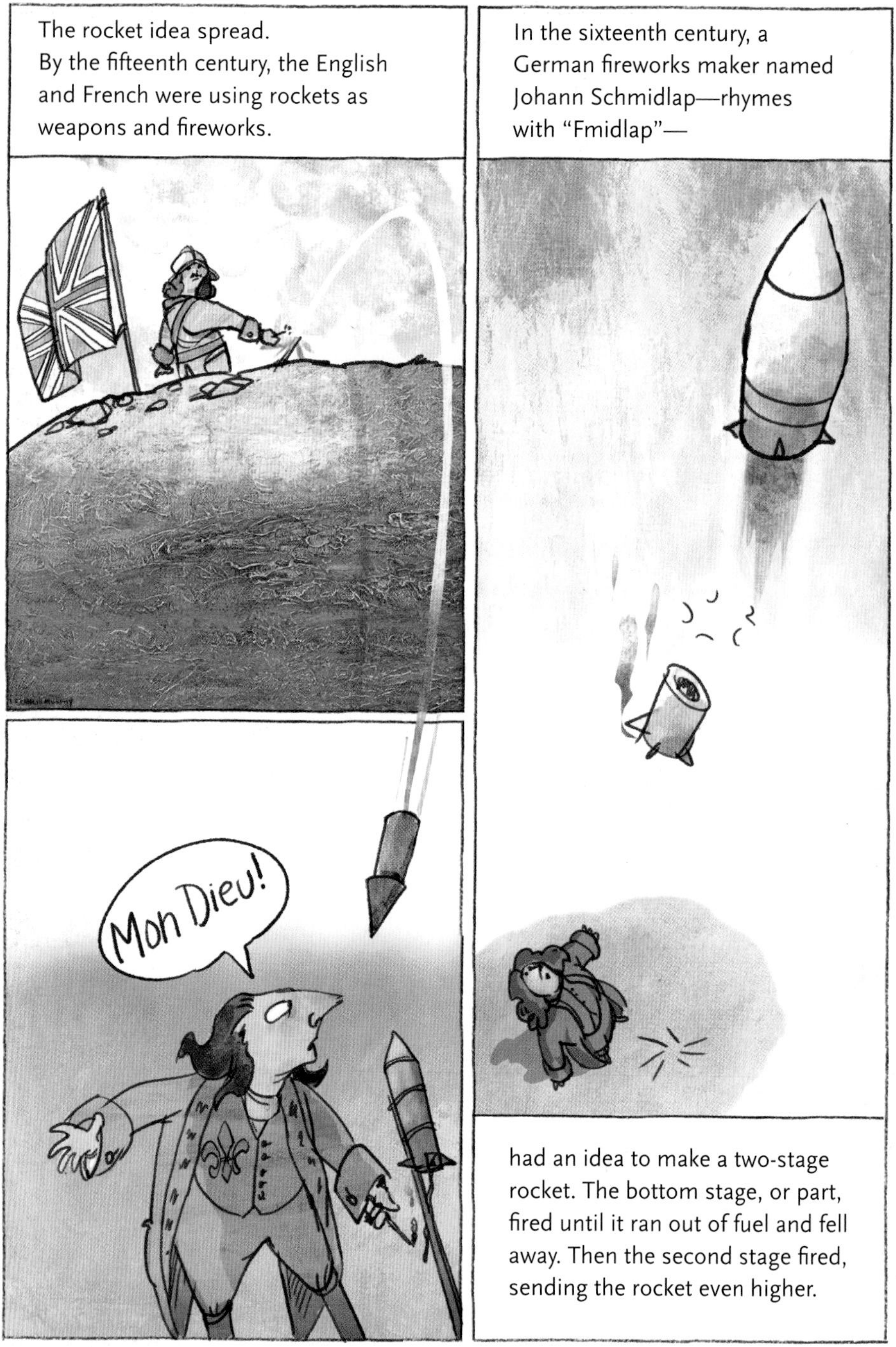
The rocket idea spread.
By the fifteenth century, the English and French were using rockets as weapons and fireworks.
Mon Dieu!
In the sixteenth century, a German fireworks maker named Johann Schmidlap—rhymes with "Fmidlap"—
had an idea to make a two-stage rocket. The bottom stage, or part, fired until it ran out of fuel and fell away. Then the second stage fired, sending the rocket even higher.

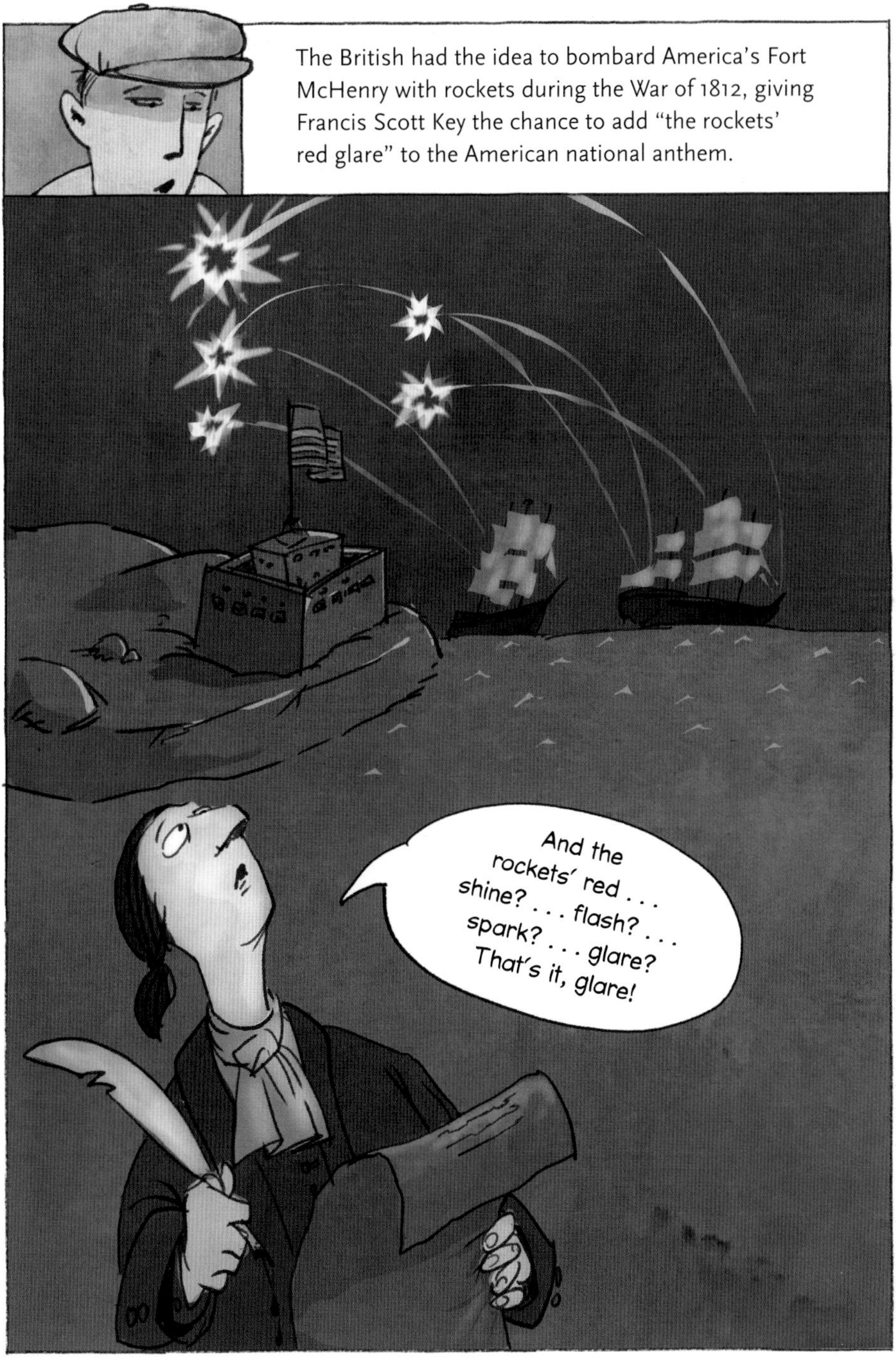
The British had the idea to bombard America's Fort McHenry with rockets during the War of 1812, giving Francis Scott Key the chance to add "the rockets' red glare" to the American national anthem.
And the rockets' red . . . shine? . . . flash? . . . spark? . . . glare? That's it, glare!

Then the ideas dried up, and nothing much happened with rockets until the beginning of the twentieth century, when three honest-to-goodness rocket scientists showed up:

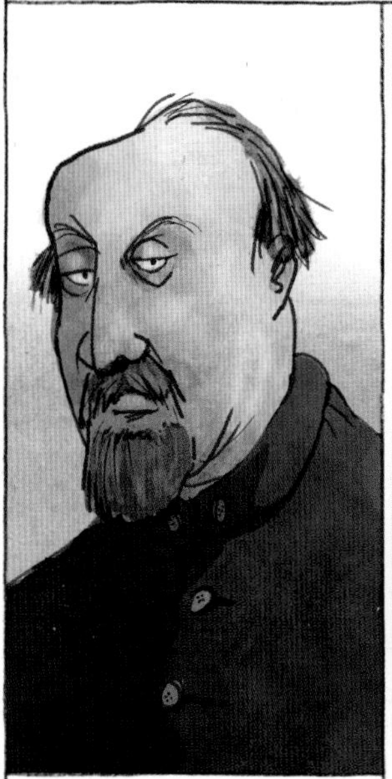

Russian Konstantin Tsiolkovsky,

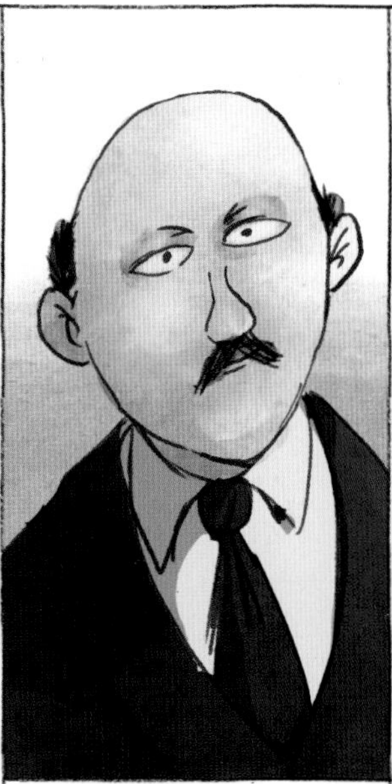

American Robert Goddard,

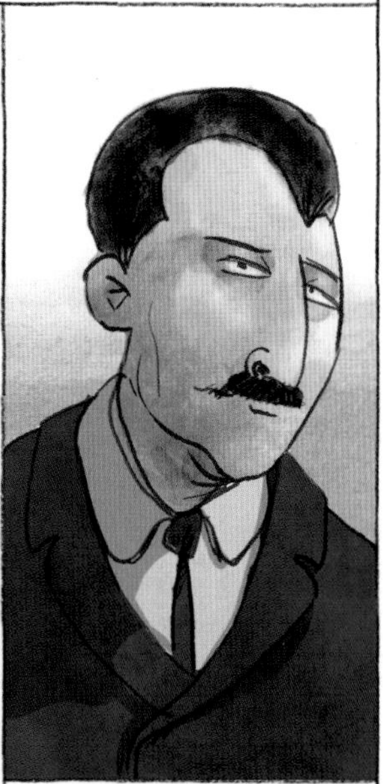

and Romanian Hermann Oberth.

But before we learn about them, I have to tell you what inspired all three . . . a book!
In 1865, French novelist Jules Verne wrote *From the Earth to the Moon*, a science fiction tale of traveling through outer space. The wildly popular book changed Tsiolkovsky's, Goddard's, and Oberth's ideas and the course of their lives.

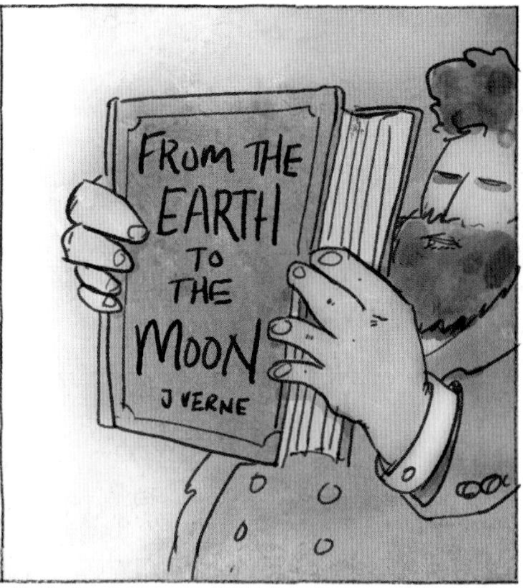
FROM THE EARTH TO THE MOON
J VERNE

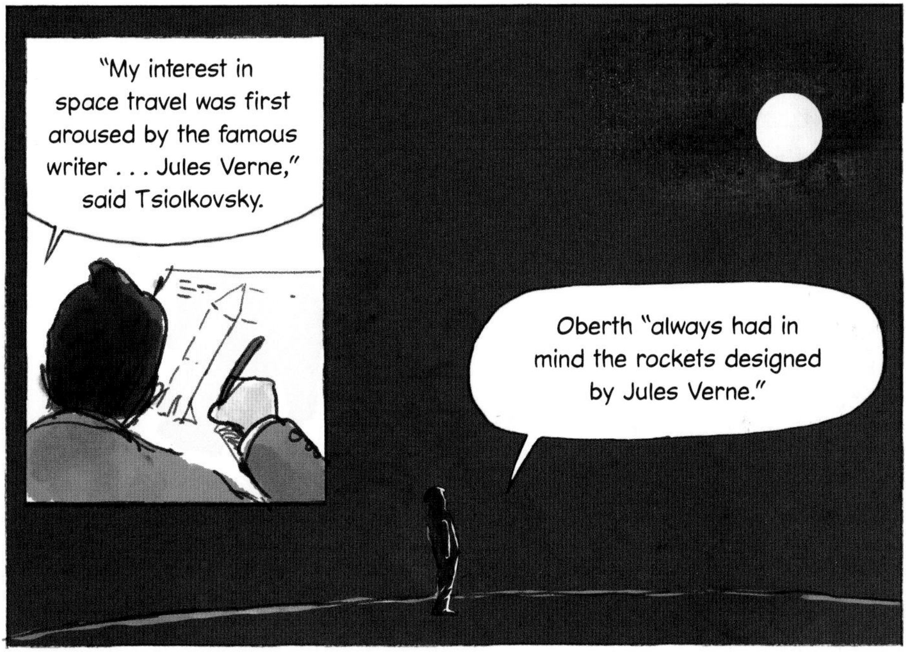
"My interest in space travel was first aroused by the famous writer . . . Jules Verne," said Tsiolkovsky.
Oberth "always had in mind the rockets designed by Jules Verne."

With Verne's story in the back of his mind, young Goddard climbed a tree and looked into the sky.

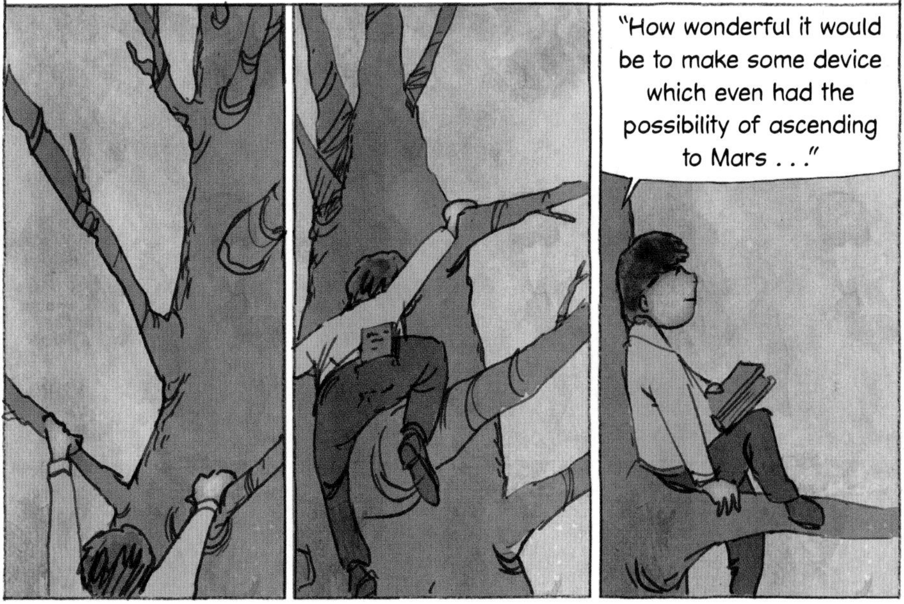
"How wonderful it would be to make some device which even had the possibility of ascending to Mars . . ."

With visions of space flight dancing in their heads, the trio went to work, independently and without personal contact with one another. Tsiolkovsky was hard of hearing, but he wasn't hard of thinking.

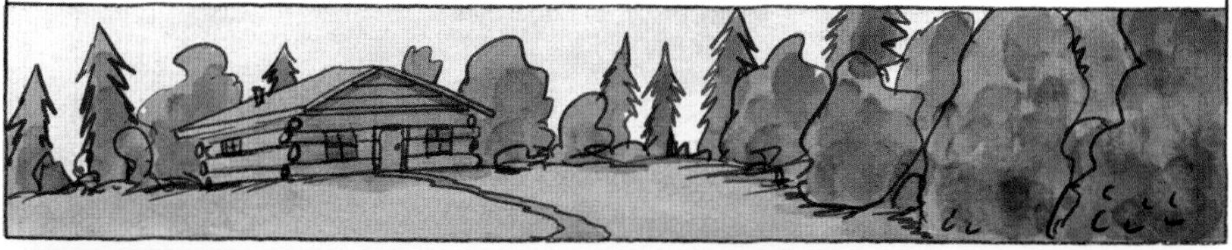

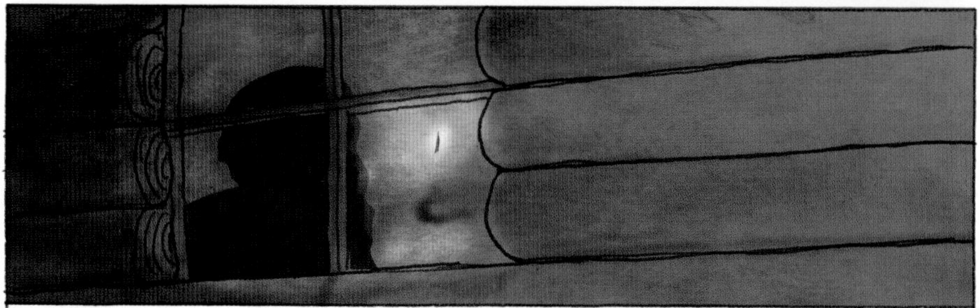

In 1903, he figured the basic calculations for rocket flight. He imagined a multistage rocket that used liquid oxygen and liquid hydrogen to propel two pilots into the heavens.

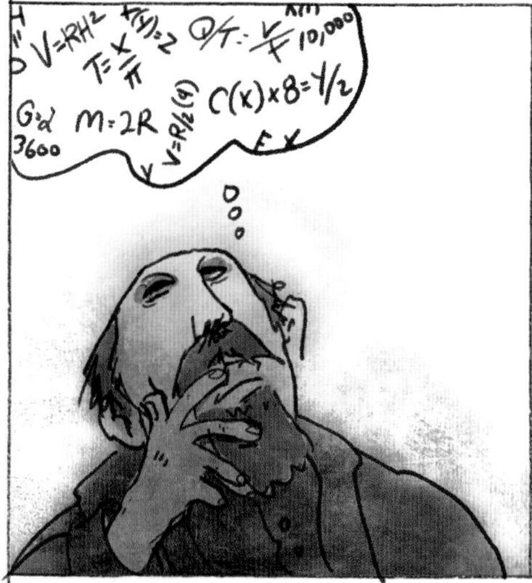

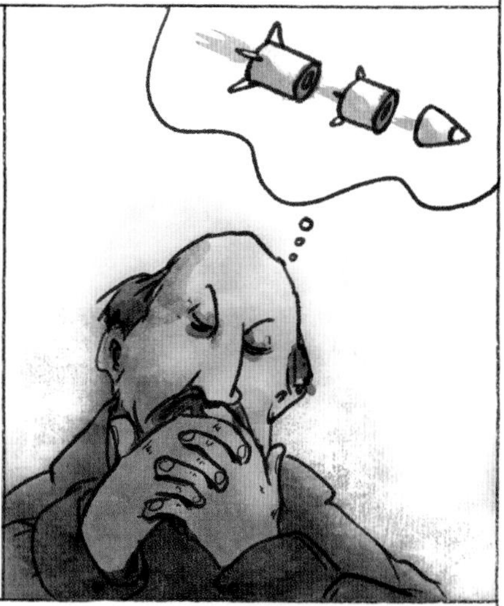

Wow . . . a guy who lived in a log cabin on the outskirts of town and far from universities and academies for much of his life managed to figure out the fundamentals of modern space travel!

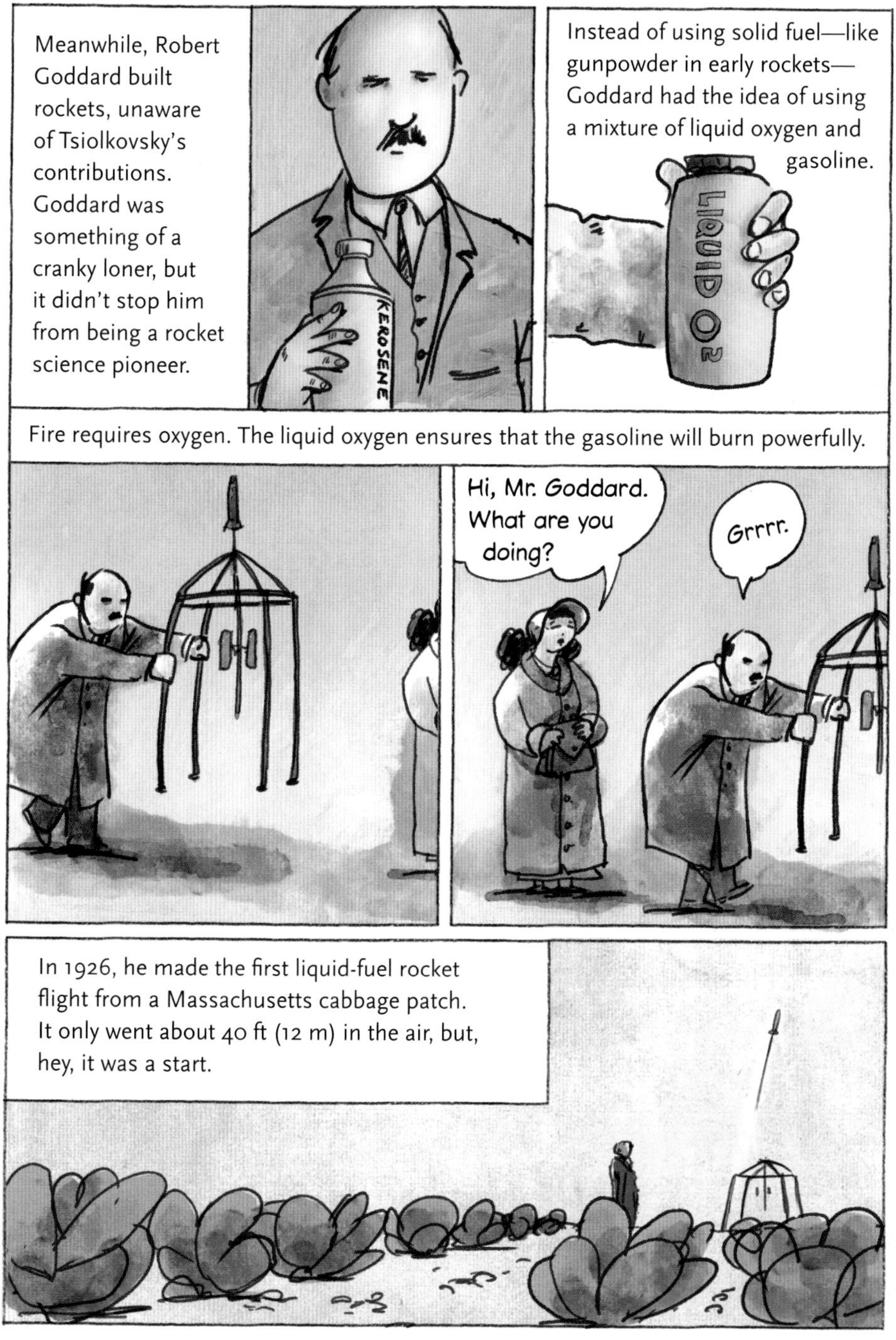
Meanwhile, Robert Goddard built rockets, unaware of Tsiolkovsky's contributions. Goddard was something of a cranky loner, but it didn't stop him from being a rocket science pioneer.
KEROSENE
Instead of using solid fuel—like gunpowder in early rockets—Goddard had the idea of using a mixture of liquid oxygen and gasoline.
LIQUID O2
Fire requires oxygen. The liquid oxygen ensures that the gasoline will burn powerfully.
Hi, Mr. Goddard. What are you doing?
Grrrr.
In 1926, he made the first liquid-fuel rocket flight from a Massachusetts cabbage patch. It only went about 40 ft (12 m) in the air, but, hey, it was a start.

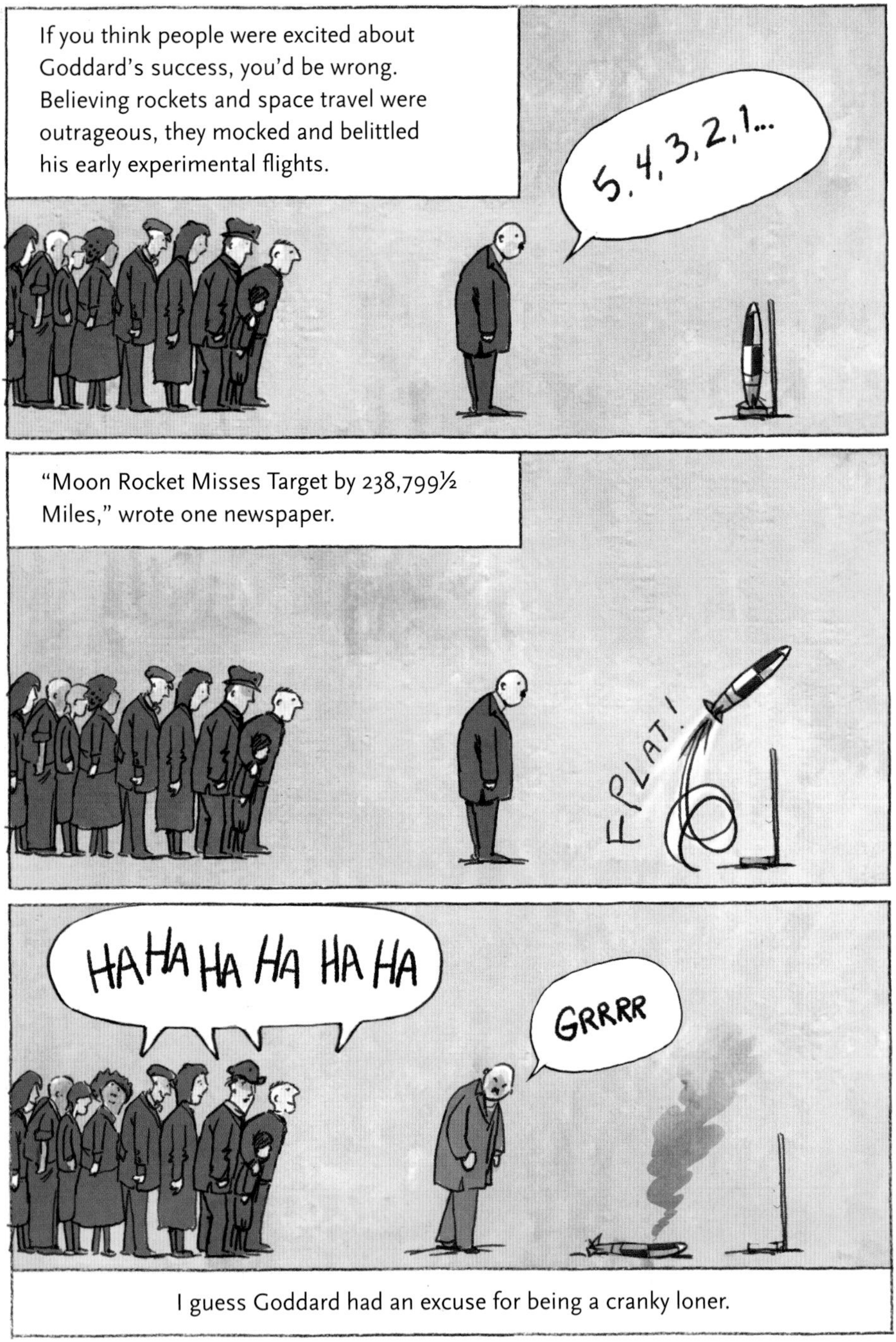
If you think people were excited about Goddard's success, you'd be wrong. Believing rockets and space travel were outrageous, they mocked and belittled his early experimental flights.
5, 4, 3, 2, 1...
"Moon Rocket Misses Target by 238,799½ Miles," wrote one newspaper.
FPLAT!
HAHA HA HA HA HA
GRRRR
I guess Goddard had an excuse for being a cranky loner.

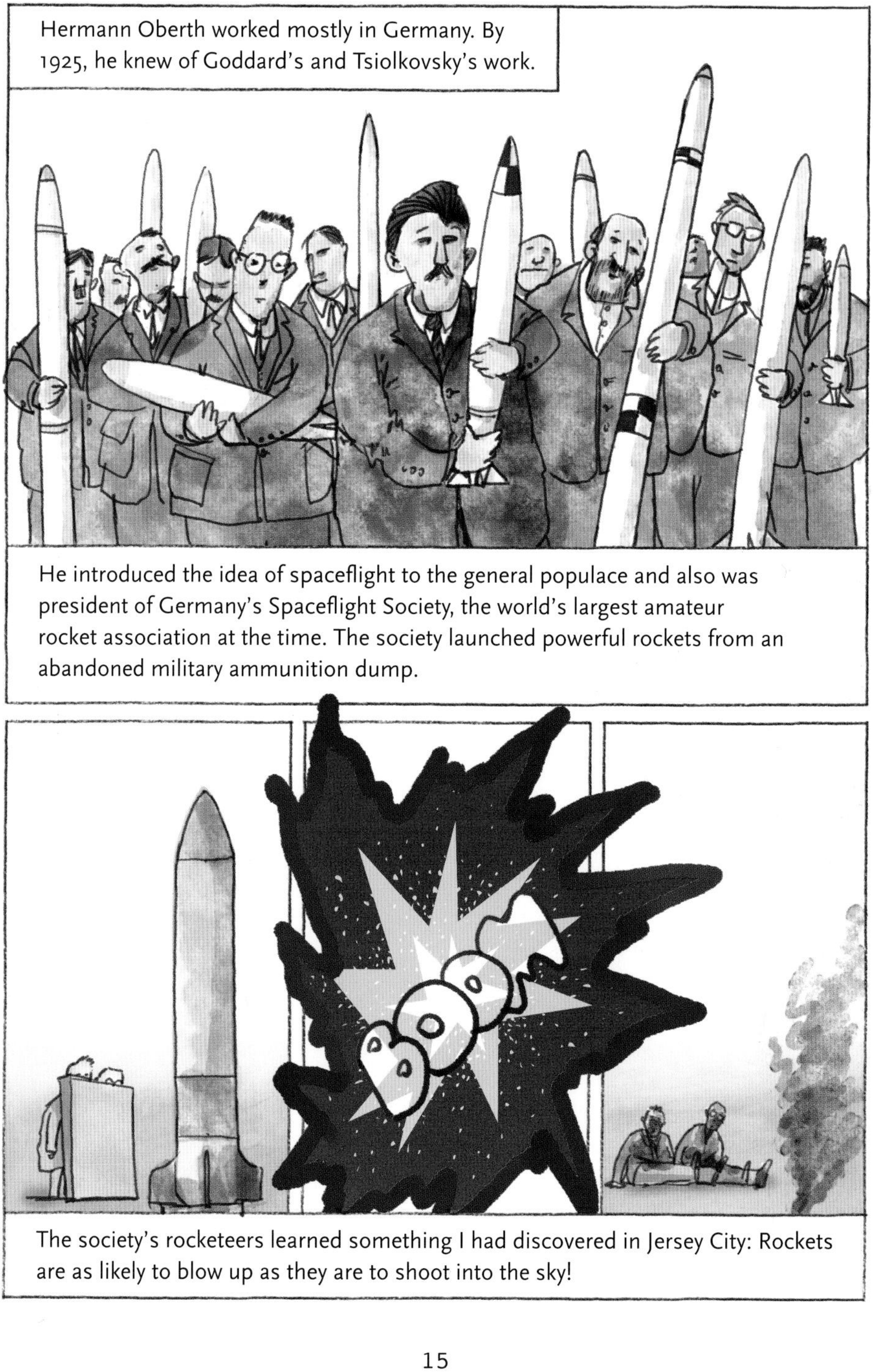
Hermann Oberth worked mostly in Germany. By 1925, he knew of Goddard's and Tsiolkovsky's work.
He introduced the idea of spaceflight to the general populace and also was president of Germany's Spaceflight Society, the world's largest amateur rocket association at the time. The society launched powerful rockets from an abandoned military ammunition dump.
BOOM
The society's rocketeers learned something I had discovered in Jersey City: Rockets are as likely to blow up as they are to shoot into the sky!

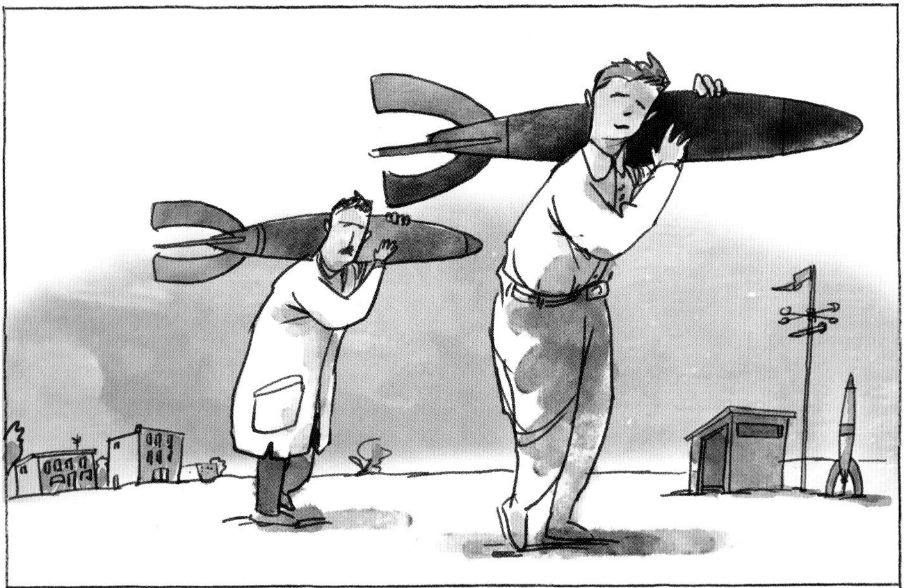

One of the society's most talented members, and Oberth's protégé, was teenager Wernher von Braun. Thoughts of space travel thrilled von Braun.

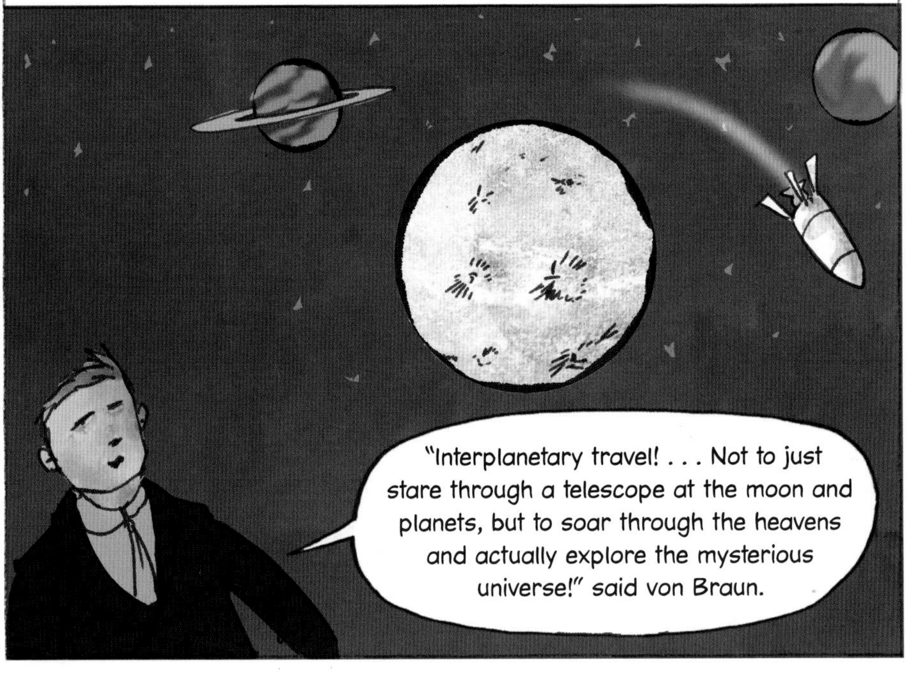
"Interplanetary travel! . . . Not to just stare through a telescope at the moon and planets, but to soar through the heavens and actually explore the mysterious universe!" said von Braun.

Wernher von Braun would eventually become one of the most important characters in America's moon landing story. But that would be later. Before then, von Braun stood with one of America's greatest enemies, Hitler's Germany.

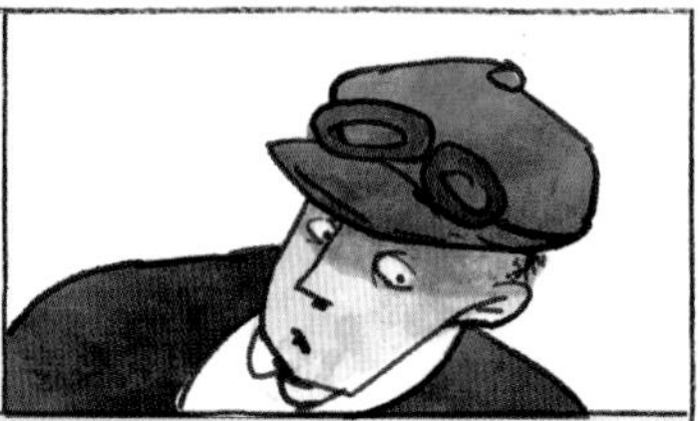

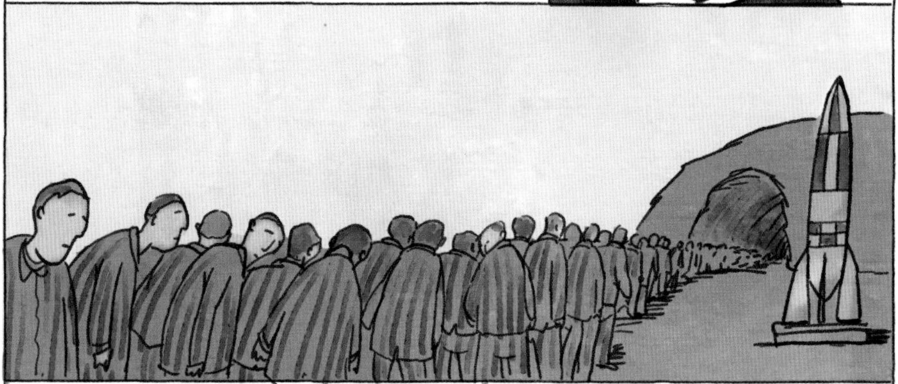

During World War II, Germany used concentration-camp prisoners to build and run a rocket factory. Von Braun—a member of the Nazi Party—and other German scientists helped rain explosives-loaded V-2 rockets on England, France, and Belgium.

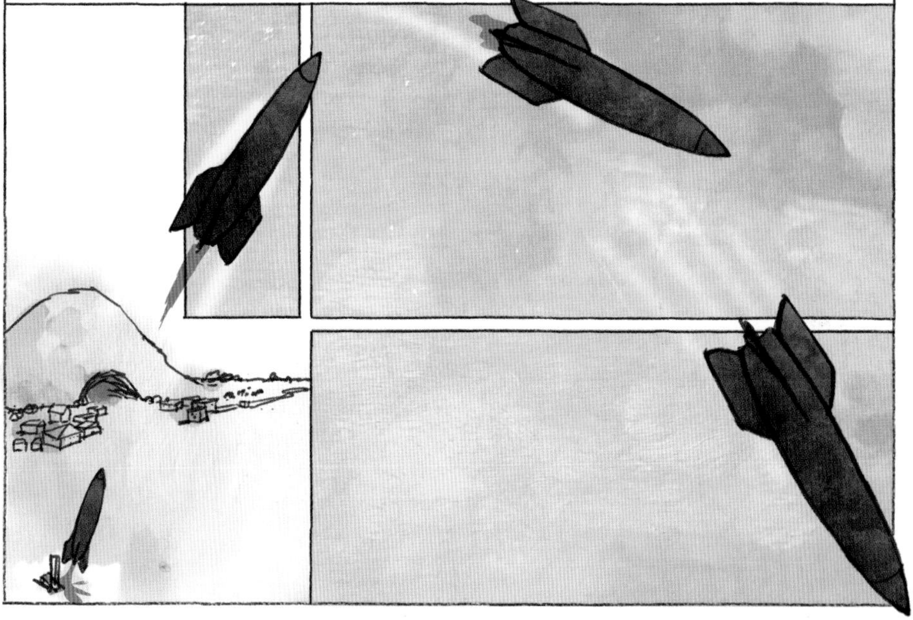

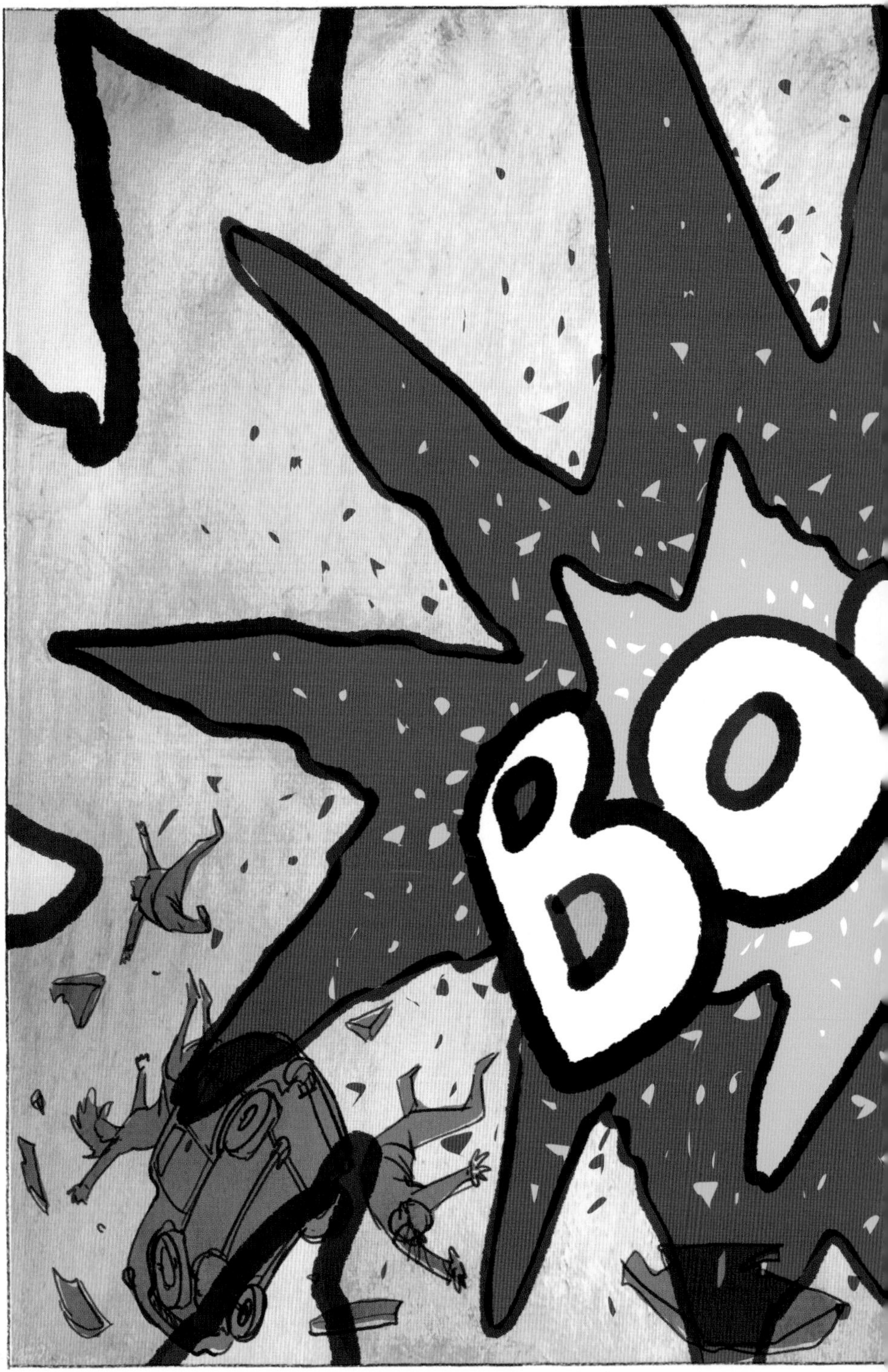
BO

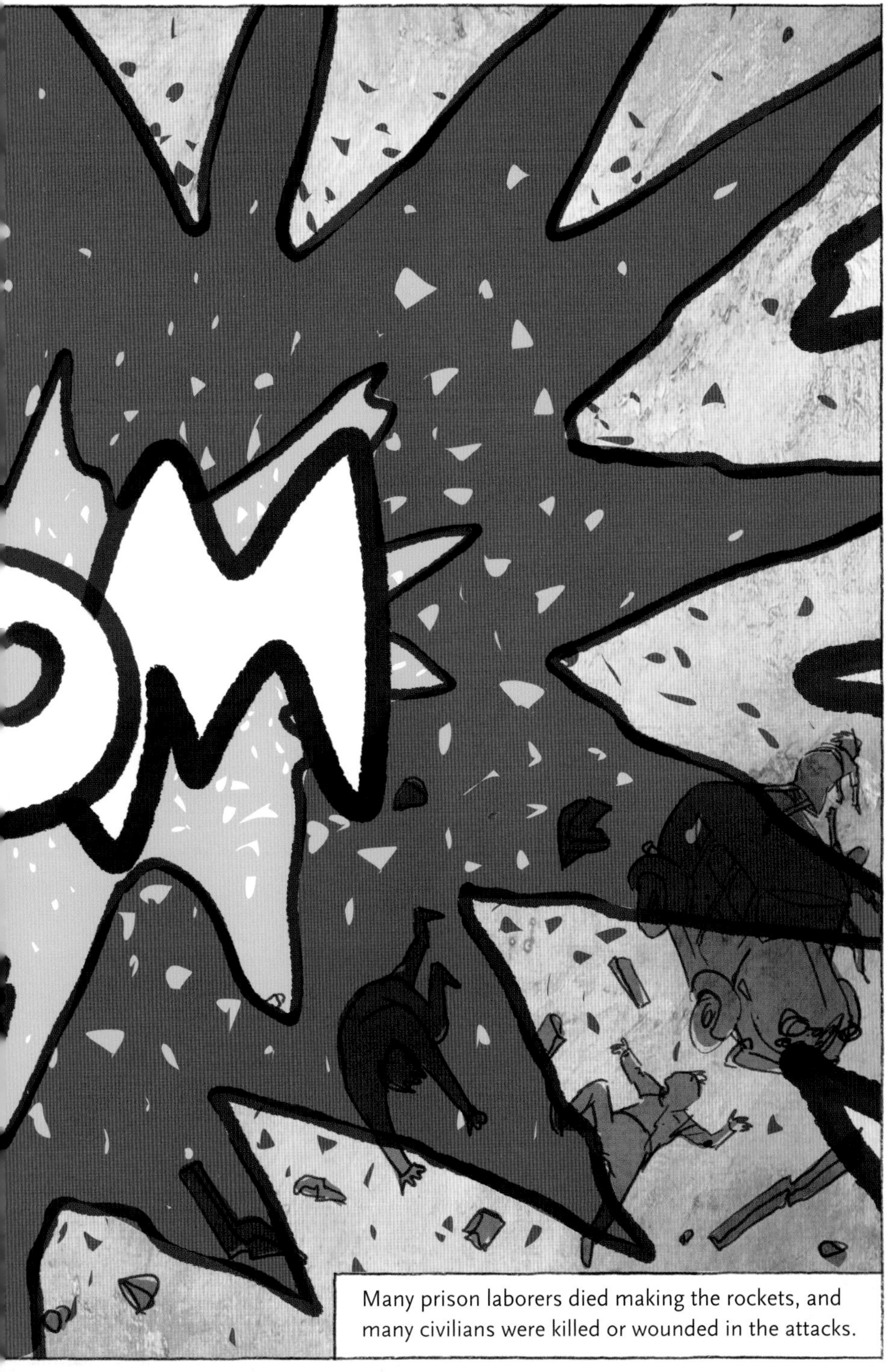
Many prison laborers died making the rockets, and many civilians were killed or wounded in the attacks.

It was awful stuff, but it didn't change the course of the war. By 1945, the Germans were nearly beaten. Von Braun and his team saw the end coming and were certain they'd be captured. They had an idea.

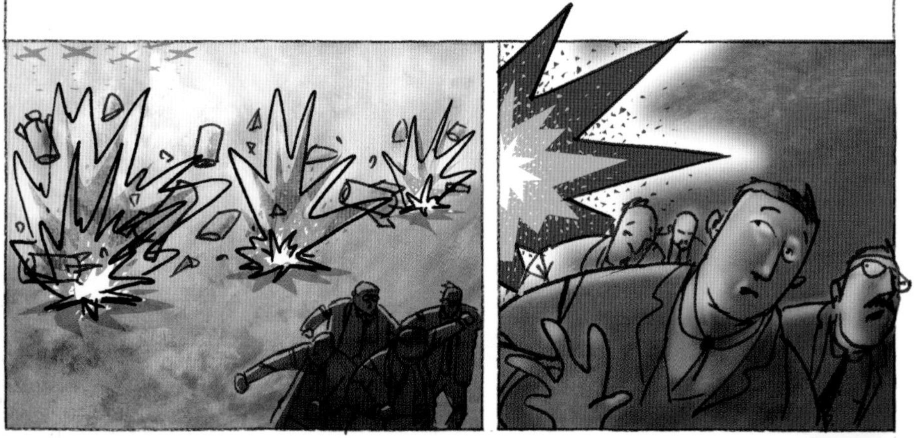

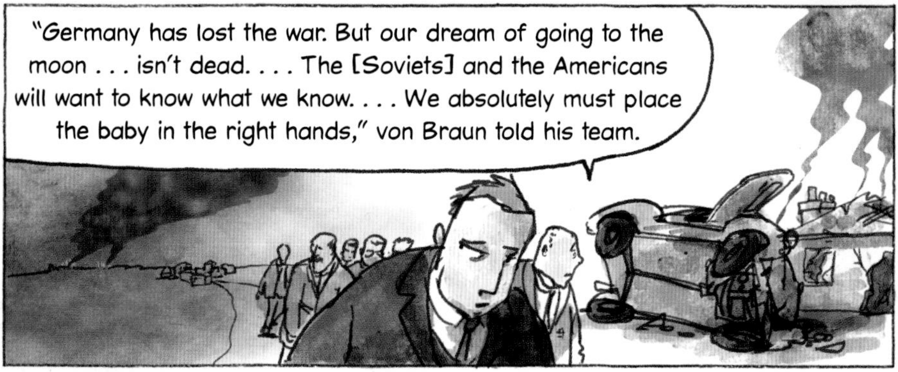
"Germany has lost the war. But our dream of going to the moon . . . isn't dead. . . . The [Soviets] and the Americans will want to know what we know. . . . We absolutely must place the baby in the right hands," von Braun told his team.

They ignored Hitler's order to destroy their research and raced to surrender . . . to the Americans.

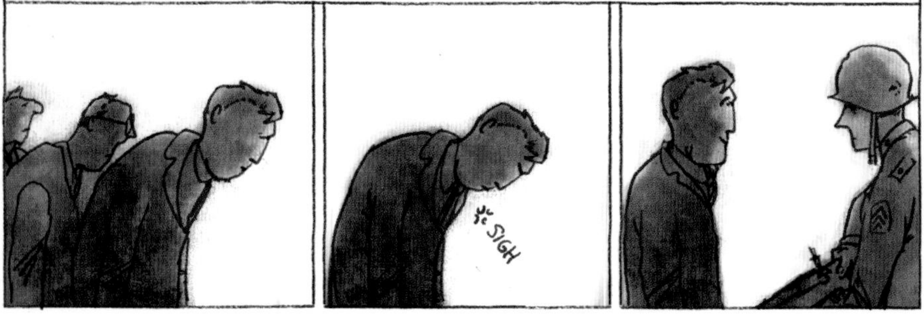
SIGH

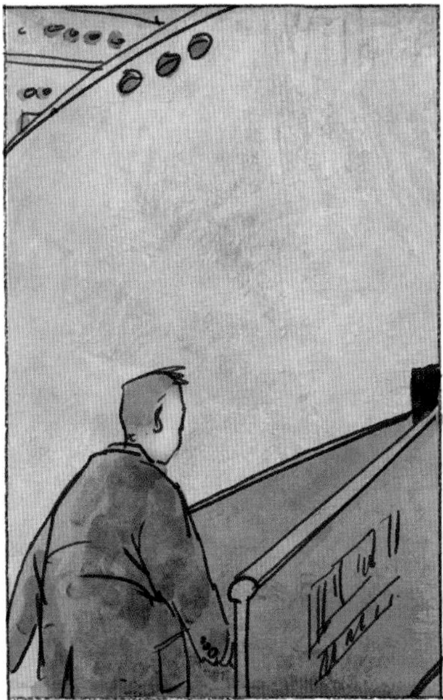

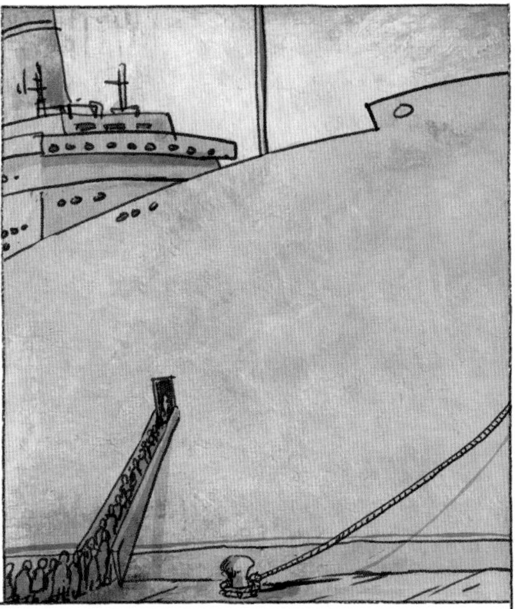

Within months, von Braun and some of his German rocketeers were at White Sands Proving Grounds in New Mexico, working for the US Army. Others of his colleagues were captured by the Soviet Union, officially the Union of Soviet Socialist Republics (USSR).

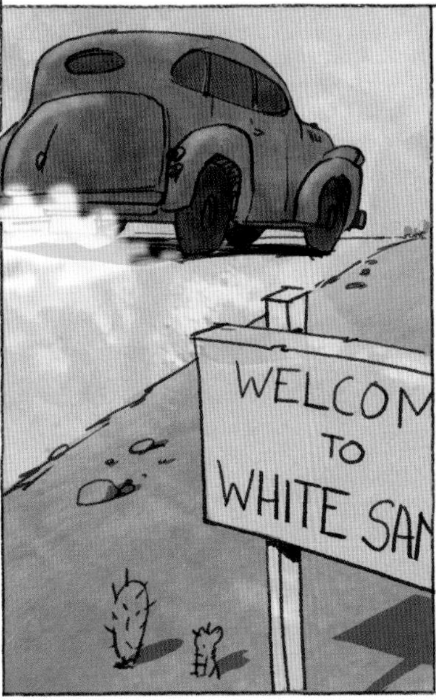
WELCOM
TO
WHITE SAN

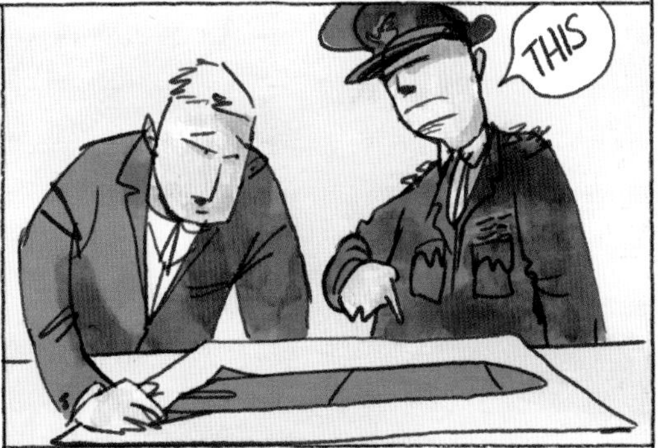
THIS

America wanted to equip rockets with atomic warheads. There was also some talk of employing rockets to lift satellites into orbit. Some people thought satellites might be useful for gathering, sending, and receiving vital information, but they weren't entirely sure.

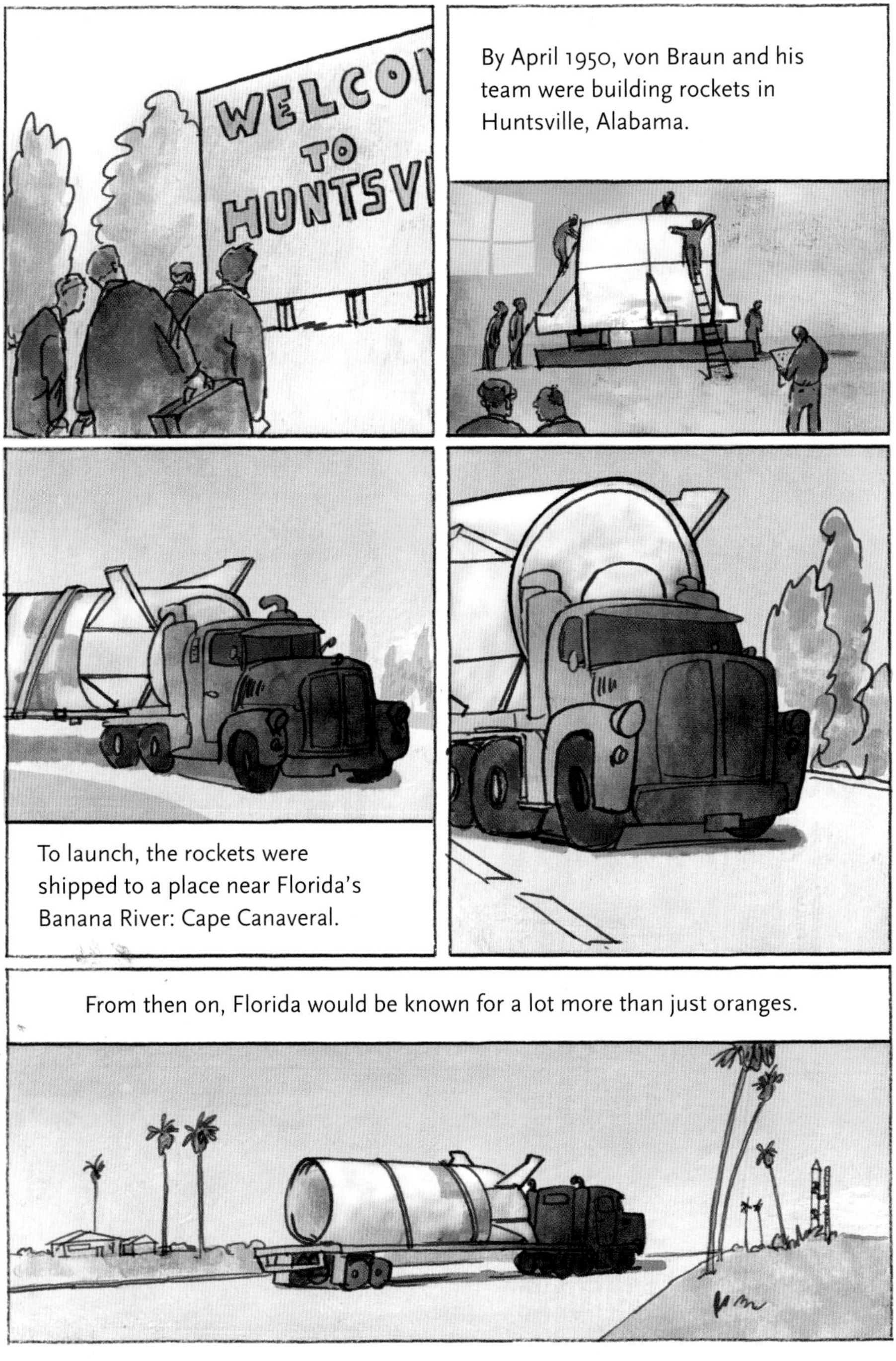
WELCO
TO
HUNTSVI
By April 1950, von Braun and his team were building rockets in Huntsville, Alabama.
To launch, the rockets were shipped to a place near Florida's Banana River: Cape Canaveral.
From then on, Florida would be known for a lot more than just oranges.

Von Braun had improved on his World War II V-2 rocket with a bigger, more powerful one called the Redstone. He planned to use it to launch a 5 lb (2 kg) satellite, an object designed to orbit Earth. Yeah, hurling the first man-made moon would have been great . . .

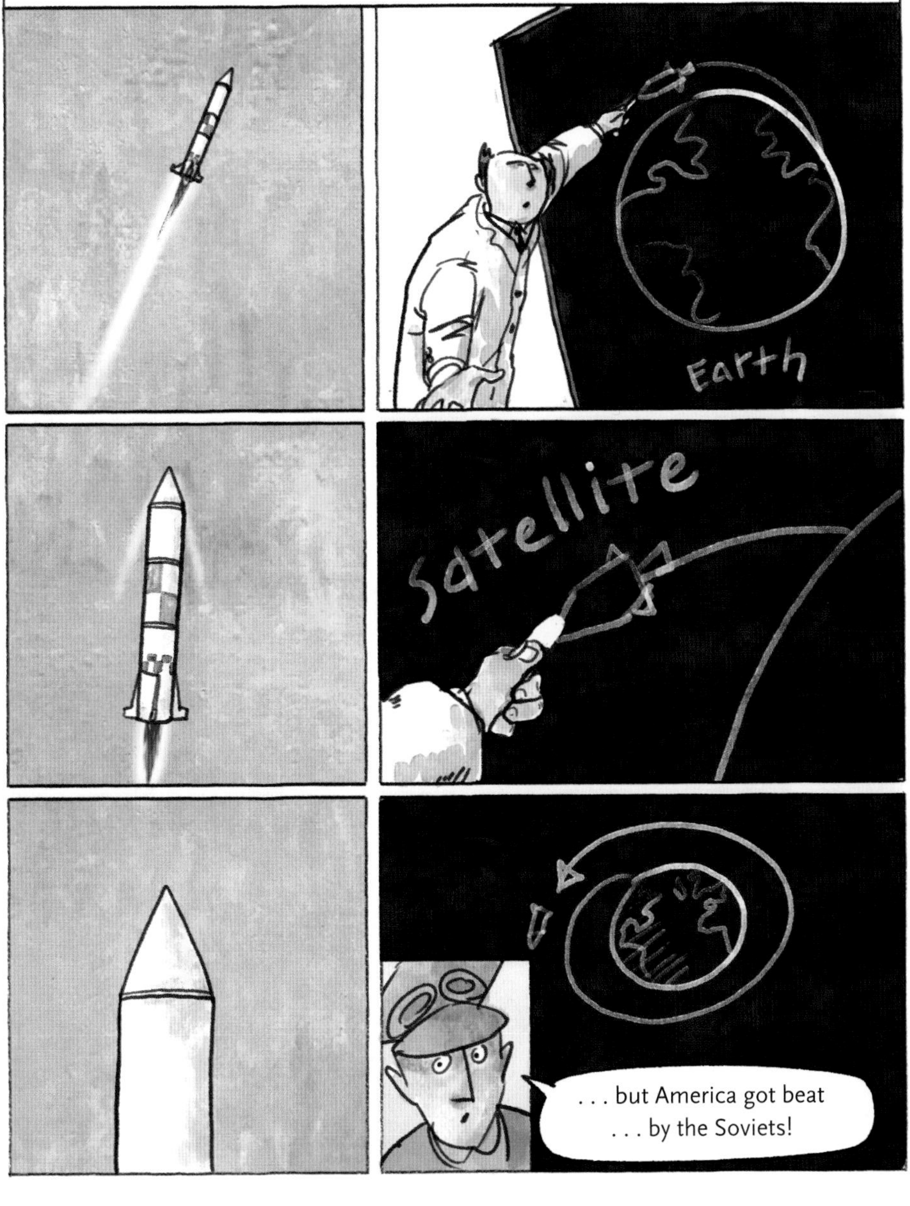
Earth
Satellite
. . . but America got beat . . . by the Soviets!

On October 4, 1957, the Soviets shot a 184 lb (83 kg) beach ball–shaped satellite into orbit. It was the centennial of the birth year of good ol' Konstantin Tsiolkovsky.

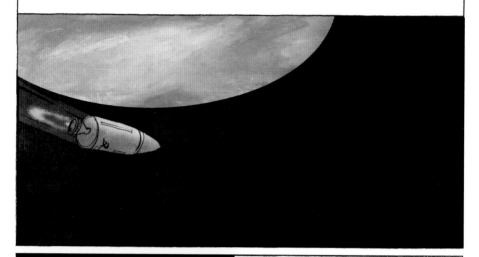

It was called "Sputnik Zemlyi," Russian for "traveling companion of the world." Sputnik for short.

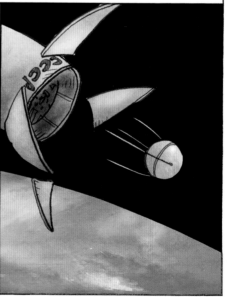

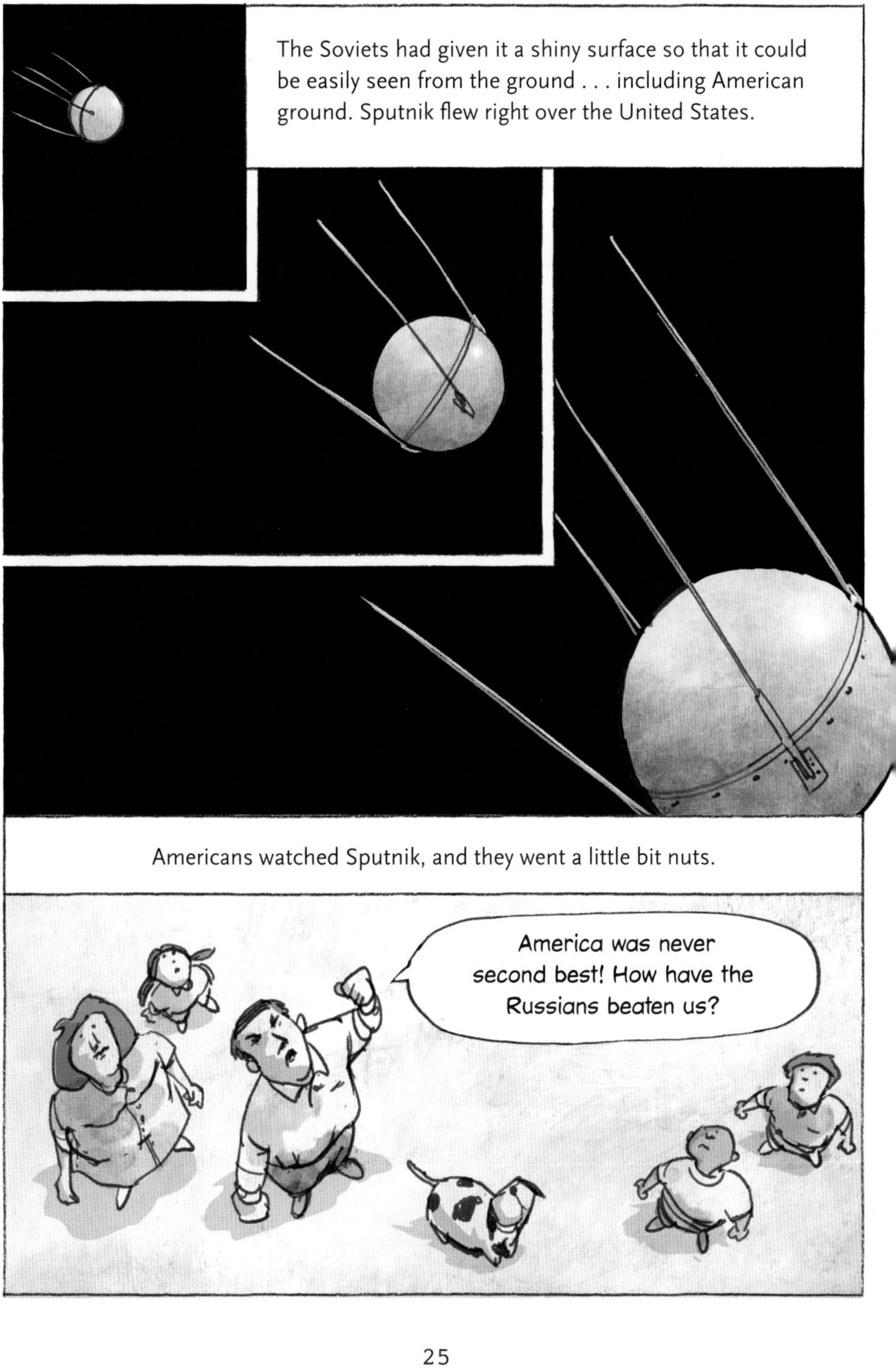
The Soviets had given it a shiny surface so that it could be easily seen from the ground . . . including American ground. Sputnik flew right over the United States.
Americans watched Sputnik, and they went a little bit nuts.
America was never second best! How have the Russians beaten us?

A month later, the Soviets launched Laika the dog into orbit.

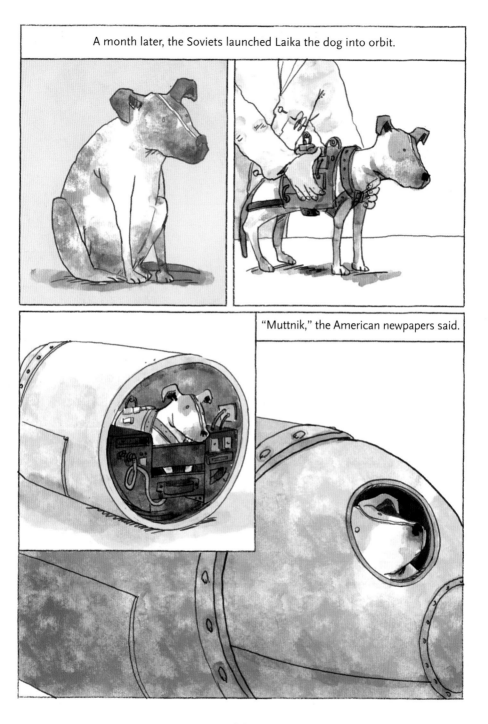

"Muttnik," the American newpapers said.

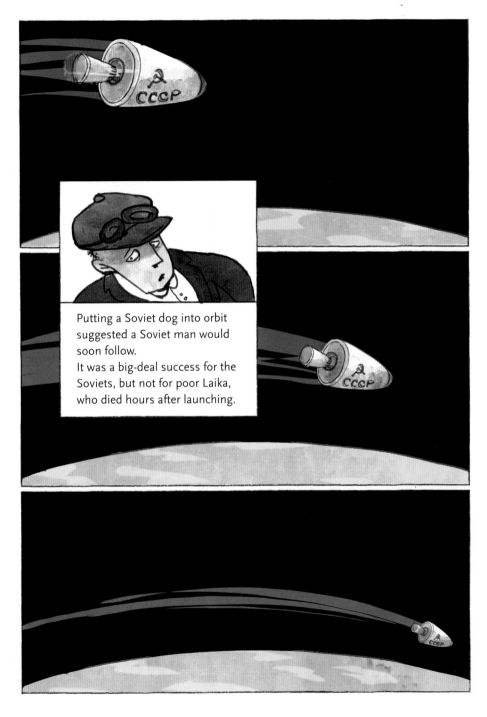

Putting a Soviet dog into orbit suggested a Soviet man would soon follow.
It was a big-deal success for the Soviets, but not for poor Laika, who died hours after launching.

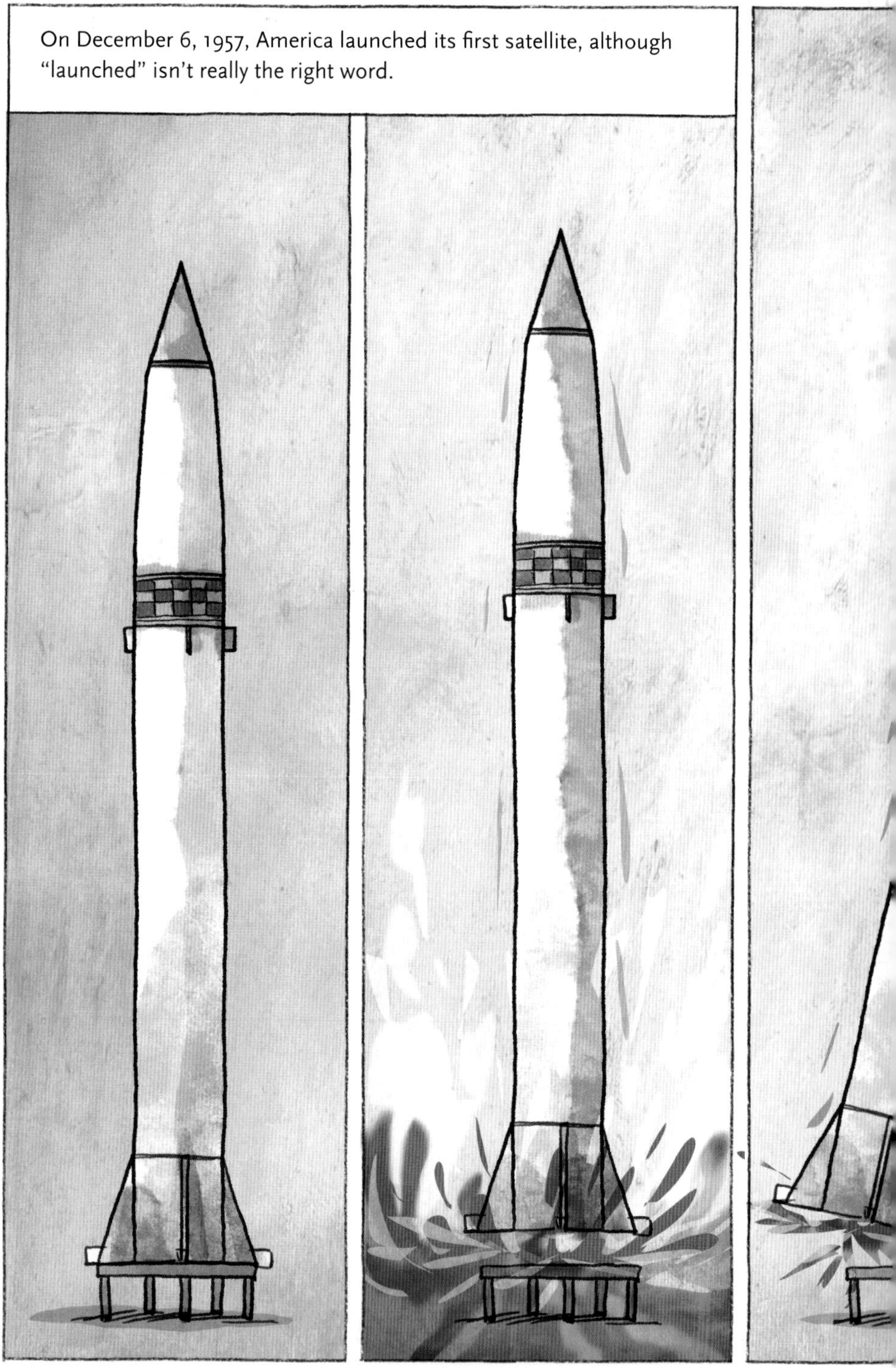
On December 6, 1957, America launched its first satellite, although "launched" isn't really the right word.

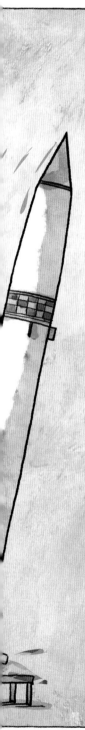

After a 4 ft (1 m) flight—yes, four feet—the rocket carrying it sank down and exploded with a spectacular roar and blast.

That was a big black eye for the American space program!

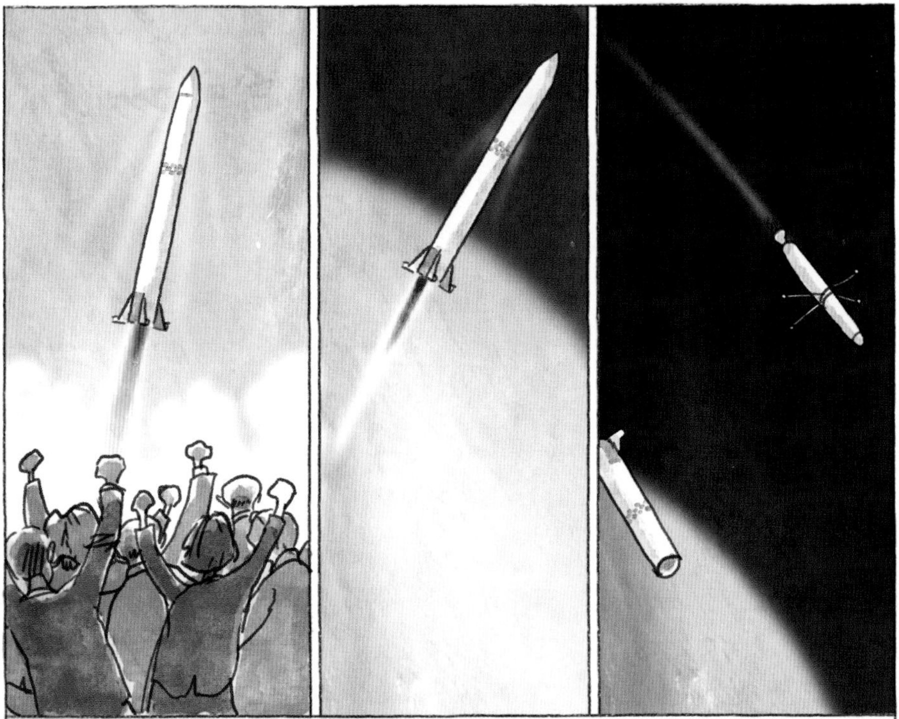

Von Braun managed to launch a satellite into orbit almost two months later.

By now, Americans were talking about the need to win the "space race" with the Soviets. People believed losing it would mean the end of America.

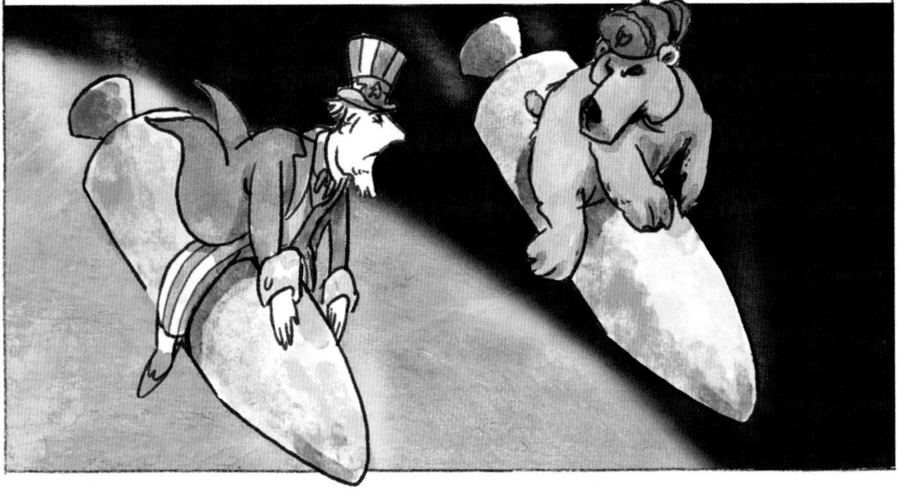

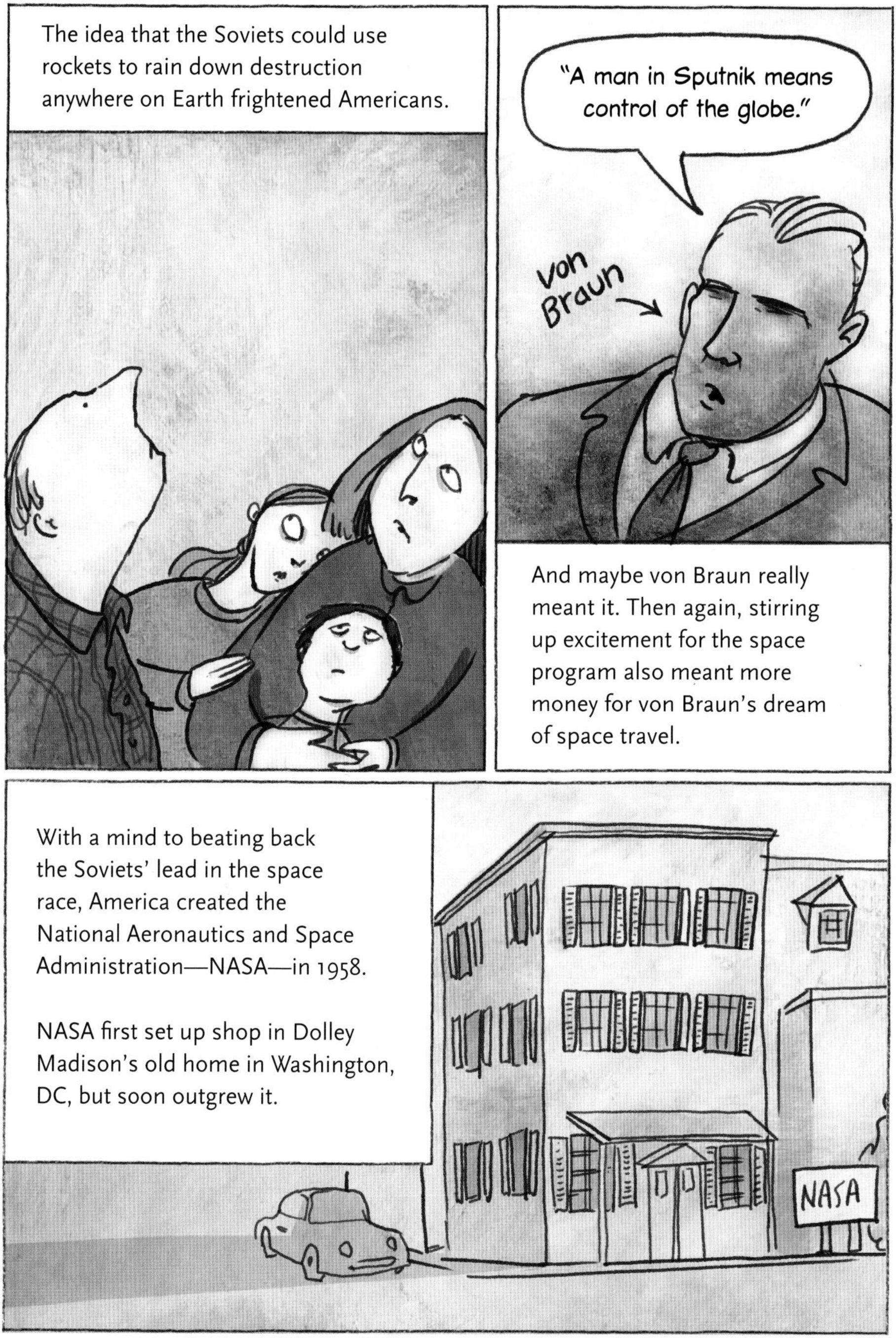
The idea that the Soviets could use rockets to rain down destruction anywhere on Earth frightened Americans.
"A man in Sputnik means control of the globe."
von Braun
And maybe von Braun really meant it. Then again, stirring up excitement for the space program also meant more money for von Braun's dream of space travel.
With a mind to beating back the Soviets' lead in the space race, America created the National Aeronautics and Space Administration—NASA—in 1958.
NASA first set up shop in Dolley Madison's old home in Washington, DC, but soon outgrew it.
NASA

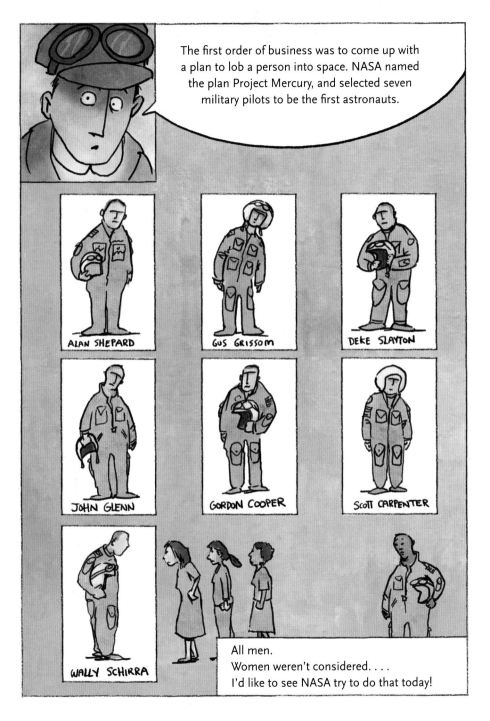

The first order of business was to come up with a plan to lob a person into space. NASA named the plan Project Mercury, and selected seven military pilots to be the first astronauts.

ALAN SHEPARD

GUS GRISSOM

DEKE SLAYTON

JOHN GLENN

GORDON COOPER

SCOTT CARPENTER

WALLY SCHIRRA

All men.
Women weren't considered. . . .
I'd like to see NASA try to do that today!

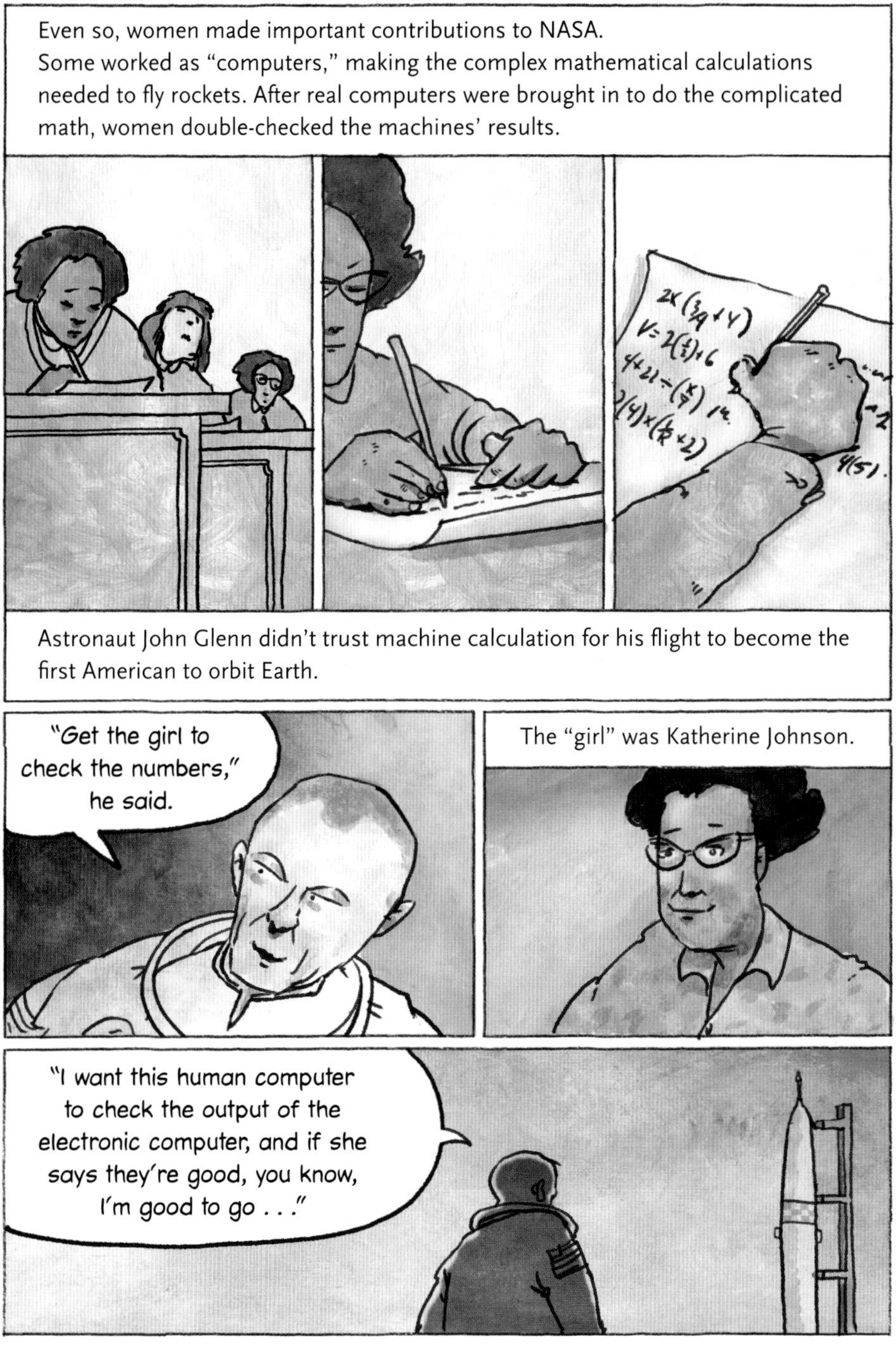
Even so, women made important contributions to NASA.
Some worked as "computers," making the complex mathematical calculations needed to fly rockets. After real computers were brought in to do the complicated math, women double-checked the machines' results.
Astronaut John Glenn didn't trust machine calculation for his flight to become the first American to orbit Earth.
"Get the girl to check the numbers," he said.
The "girl" was Katherine Johnson.
"I want this human computer to check the output of the electronic computer, and if she says they're good, you know, I'm good to go . . ."

The NASA team didn't give up. They were sure they could get an astronaut into space, but they weren't exactly sure what would happen to him when he got there. To help solve the mystery, they launched mice, chimpanzees, and small monkeys.

The animals were shot into space so that scientists could gather data on their experience, and then they fell back to Earth.

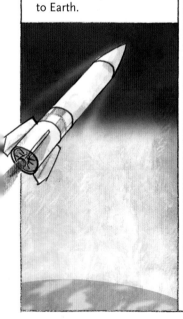

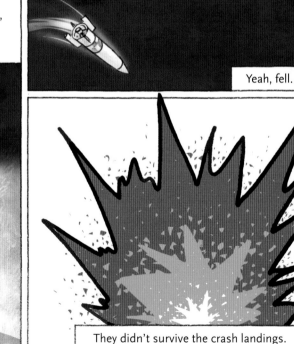

Yeah, fell.

They didn't survive the crash landings.

In 1952, Patricia and Mike, a couple of Philippine monkeys, made a 2,000 mph (3,219 kmh) trip to an altitude of 36 mi (58 km). No primate had ever reached that height. On this flight, a parachute made for a safe return.

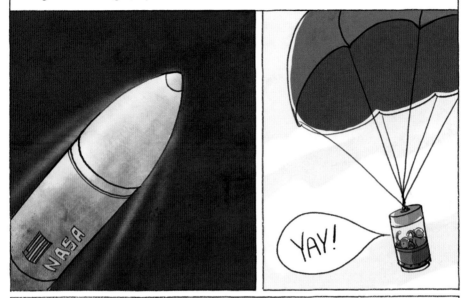

Chimpanzee astronaut "Ham" survived an early Project Mercury trip, but barely. His capsule flew crazily and almost sank after its ocean landing. When Ham was removed from it, he tried to bite anyone who got close.

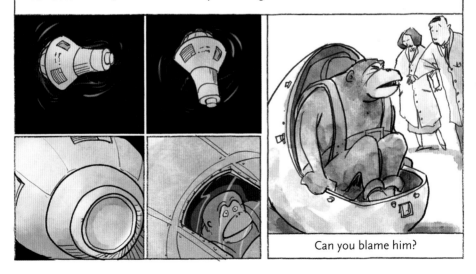

Can you blame him?

The grand space plan got off to a rough start.
In 1960, an unmanned NASA test flight blew up after soaring for just a minute.

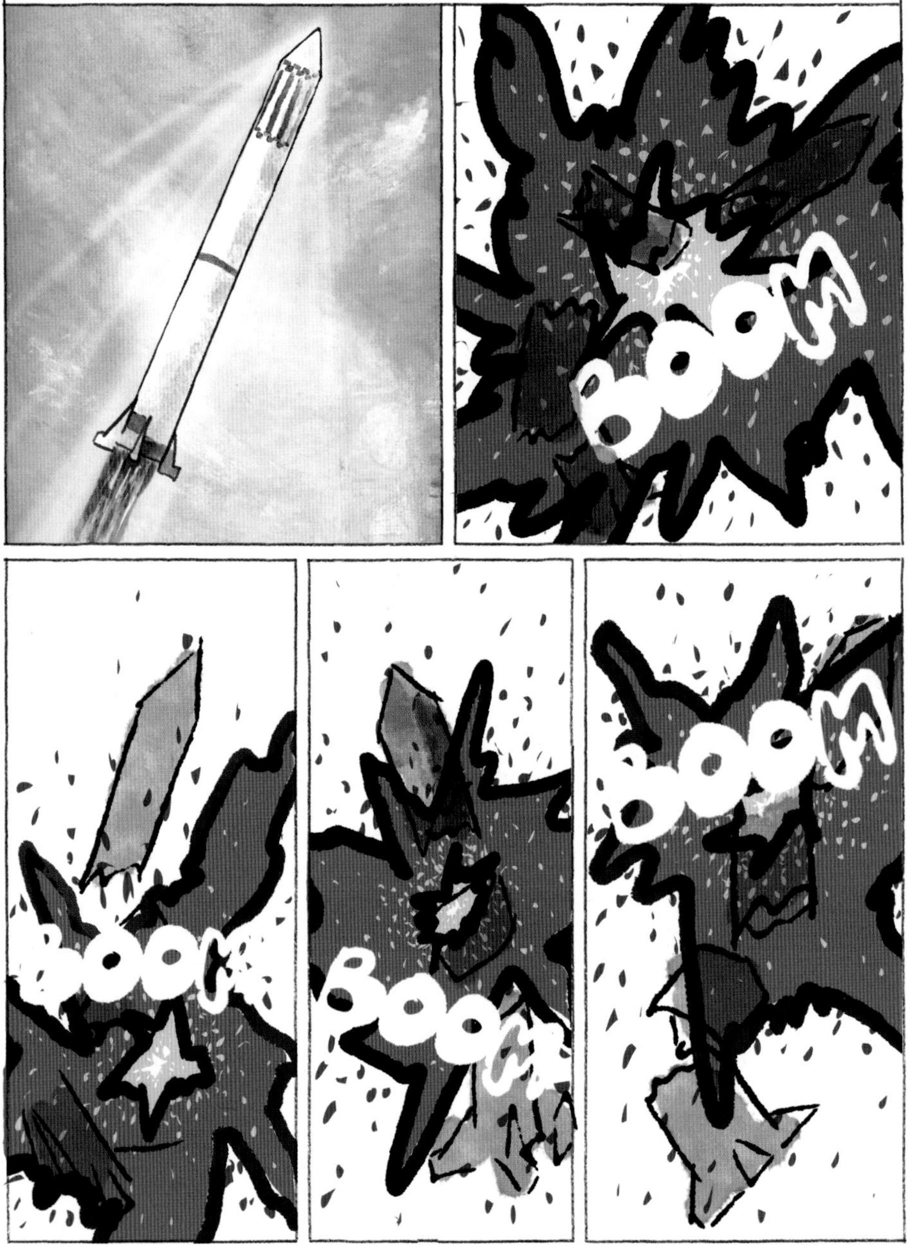
BOOM
BOOM
BOOM
BOOM

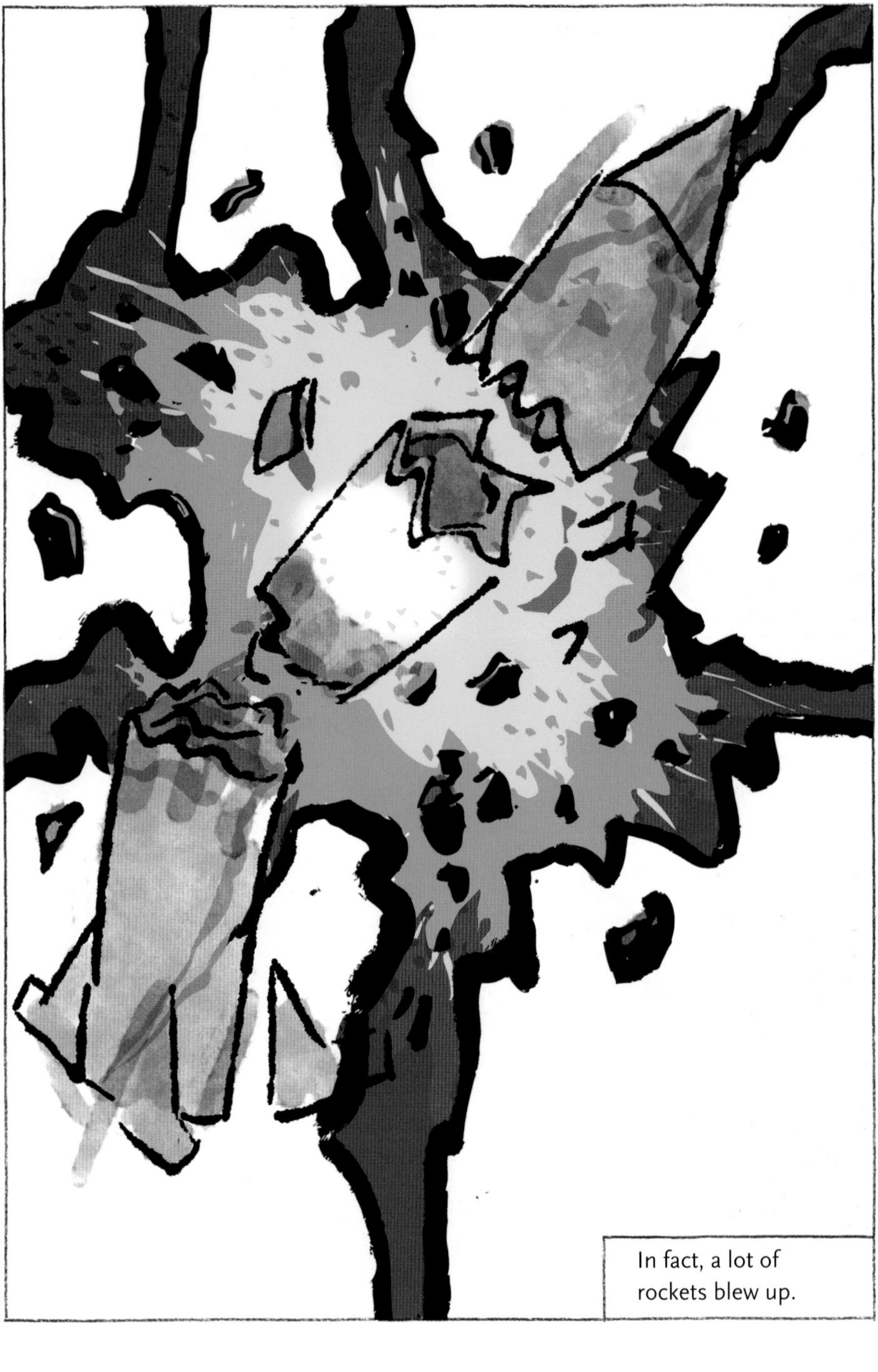
In fact, a lot of
rockets blew up.

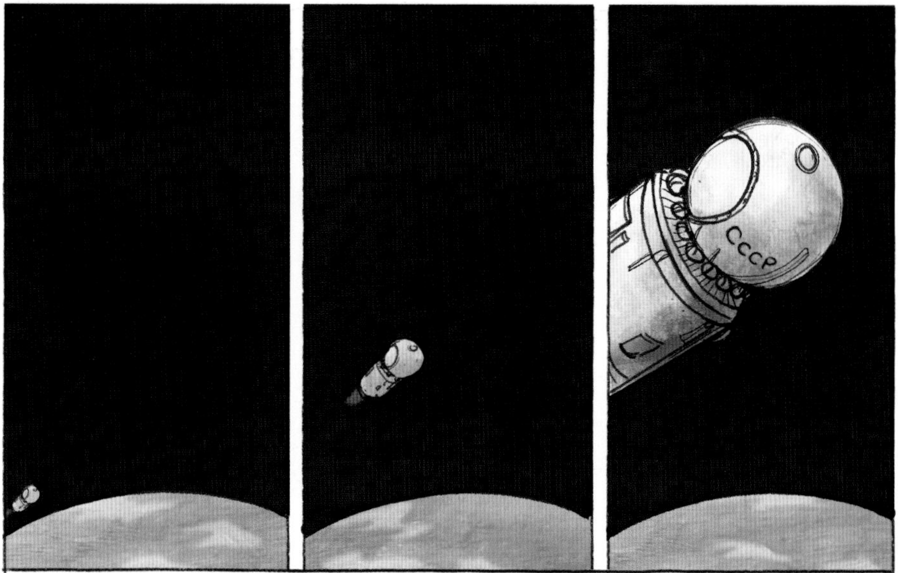
CCCP

Of course, right about here the Soviets managed to twist the noses of the American rocketeers again when they launched the very first person into space on April 12, 1961.

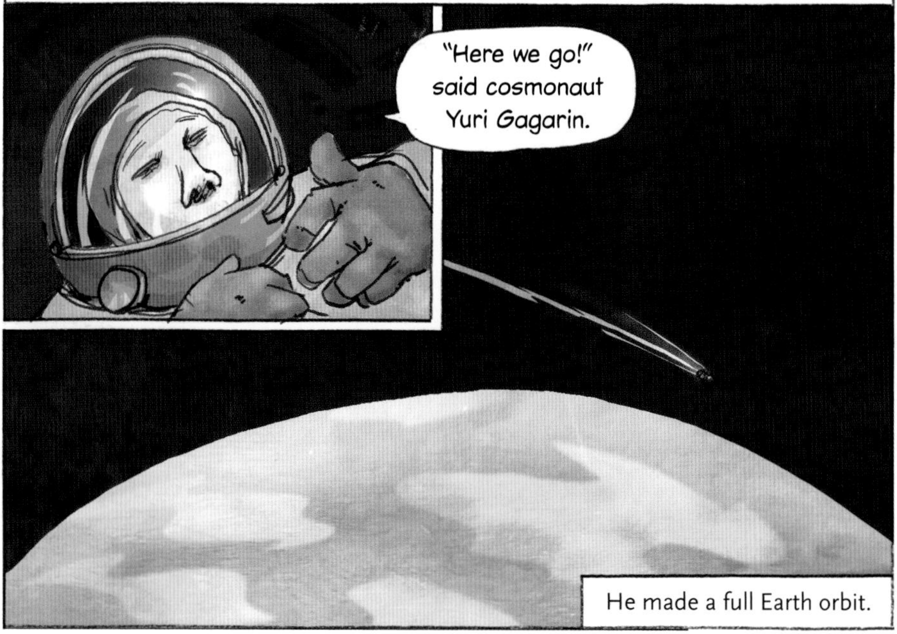
"Here we go!" said cosmonaut Yuri Gagarin.
He made a full Earth orbit.

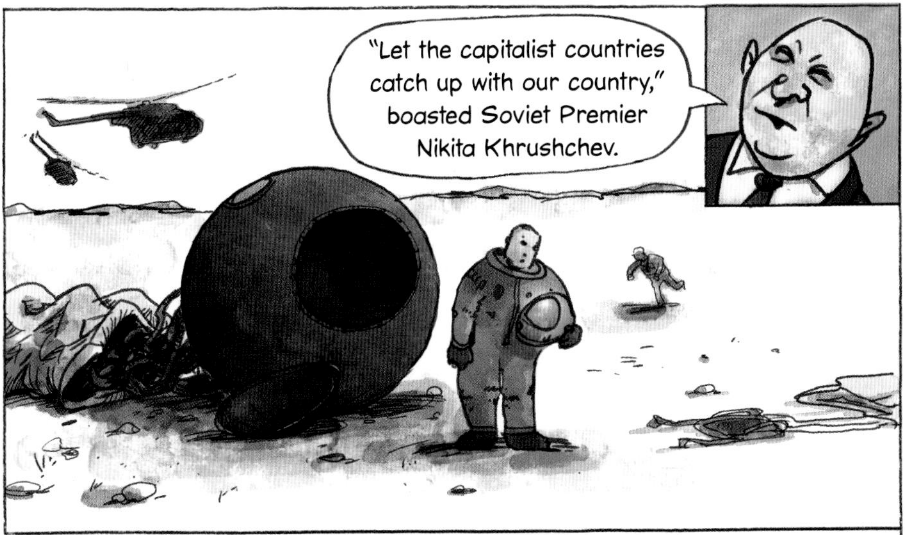
"Let the capitalist countries catch up with our country," boasted Soviet Premier Nikita Khrushchev.

Things looked dim for the Americans. People wondered whether the Soviets were going to be the first to fly two people into space, then the first to fly three. They were likely to be the first to launch a space station.

No way was President Kennedy going to let the Soviets beat America at the space game.

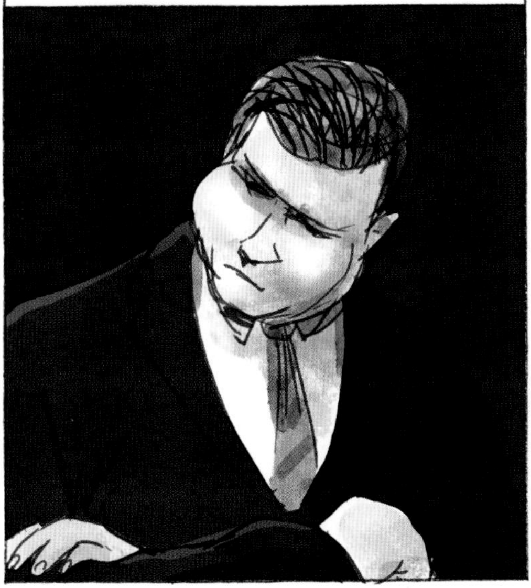

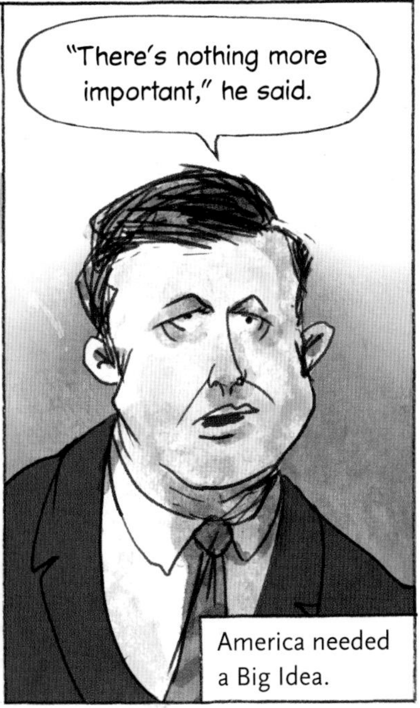
"There's nothing more important," he said.
America needed a Big Idea.

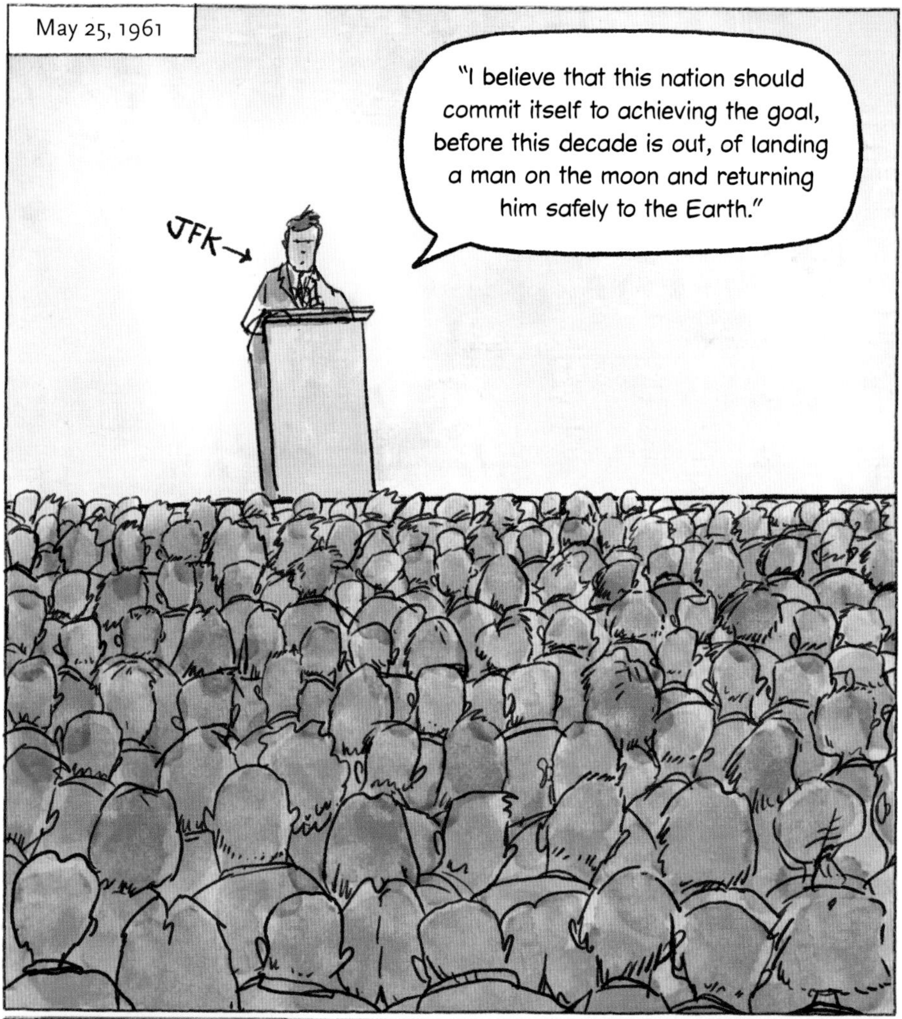
May 25, 1961
"I believe that this nation should commit itself to achieving the goal, before this decade is out, of landing a man on the moon and returning him safely to the Earth."
JFK→

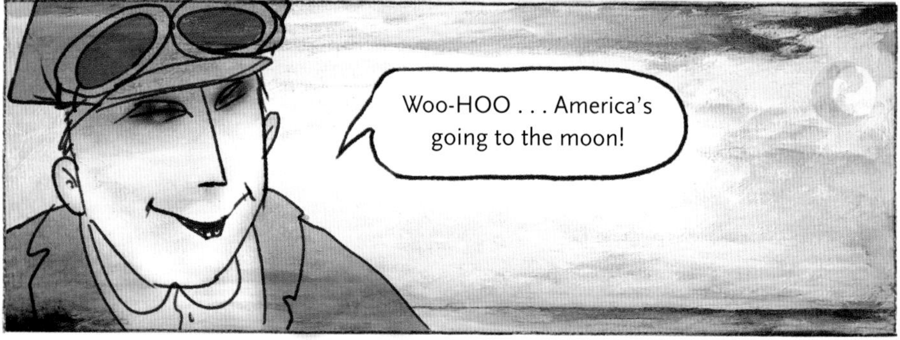
Woo-HOO . . . America's going to the moon!

It wasn't going to be cheap, expected to cost somewhere between $20 billion and $40 billion . . . at a time when running the whole federal government for a year was only $97 billion.

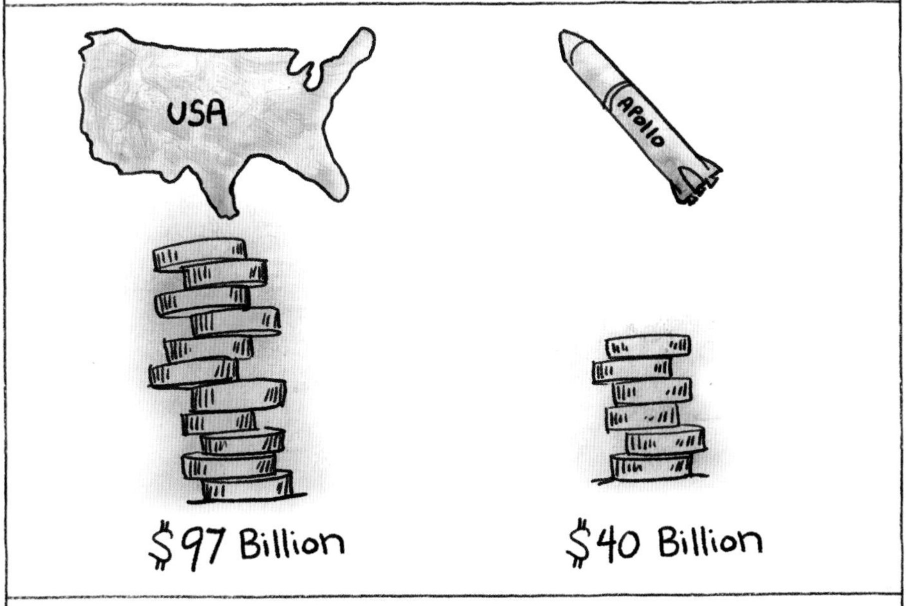
USA
APOLLO
$97 Billion
$40 Billion

Expensive and risky. A NASA study pointed to only a 10 percent chance of successfully meeting the end-of-the-decade deadline. The findings were so dismal that they were destroyed before the public got wind of them.

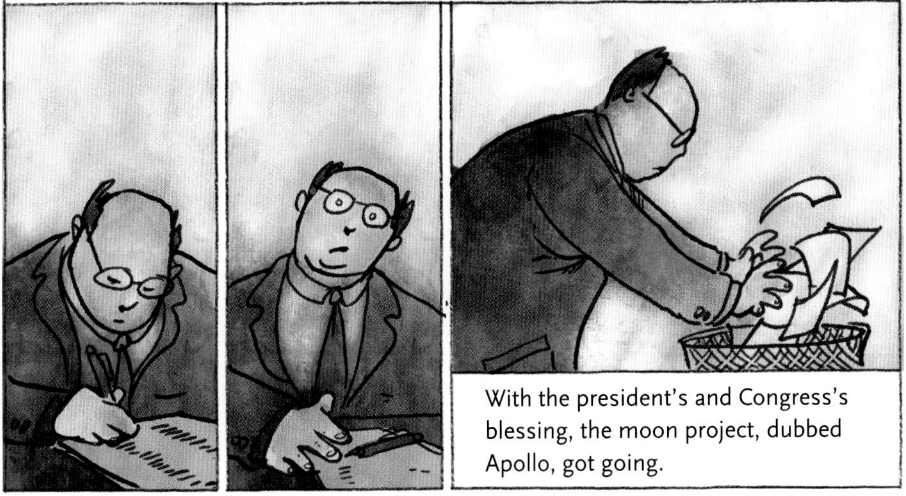

With the president's and Congress's blessing, the moon project, dubbed Apollo, got going.

Right off, the basic Earth-to-the-moon plan had to be settled upon. The rocket, the crew capsule, the training, the budget, and the schedule depended on it. Rocket scientists had several ideas.

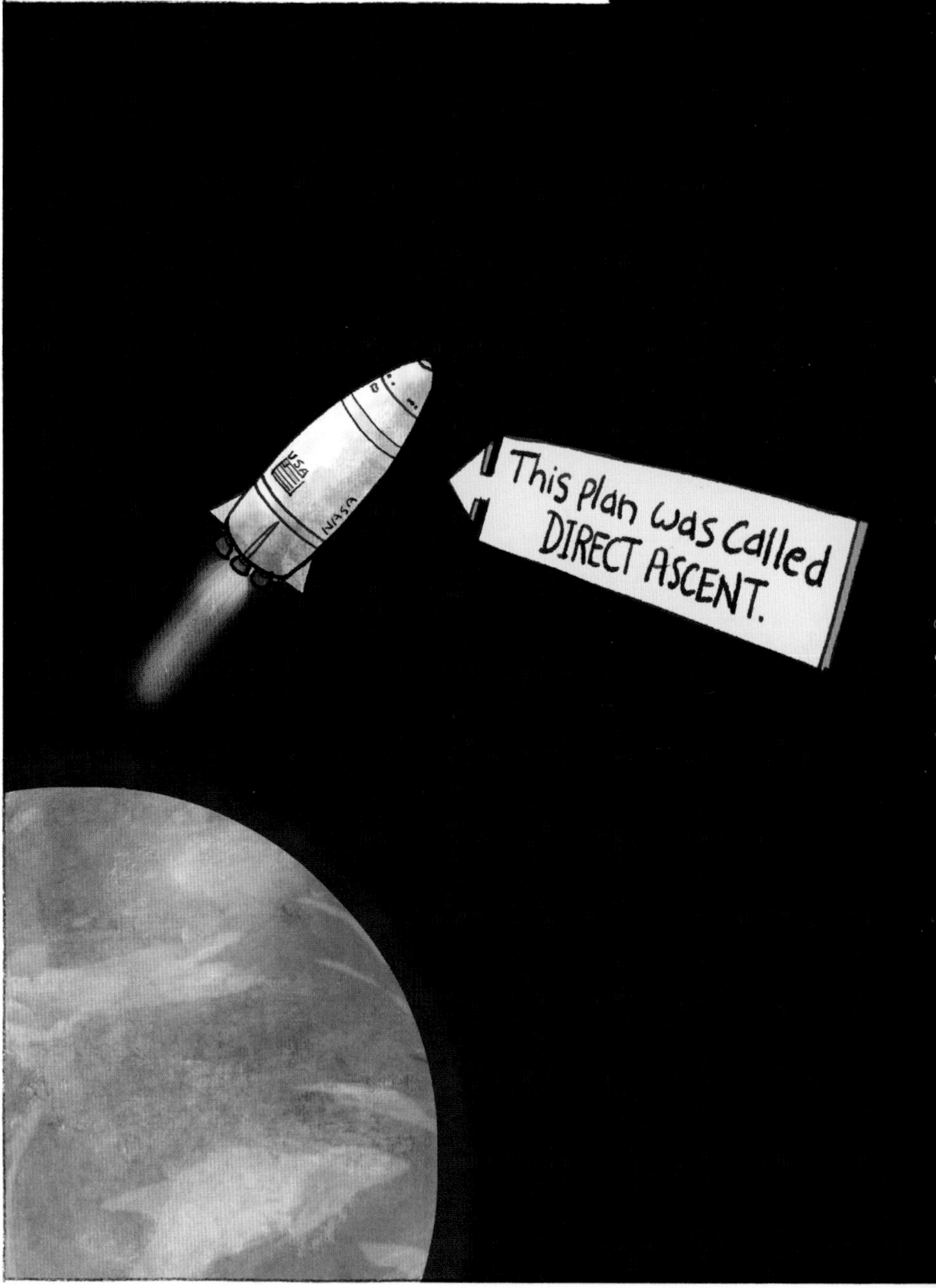
USA
NASA
This plan was called DIRECT ASCENT.

The simplest way would be to shoot a single rocket to the moon, land, and then fly home. But it would require a massive rocket, one loaded with enough fuel to make the return trip . . . and nearly enough fuel to destroy Cape Canaveral if it exploded on liftoff!

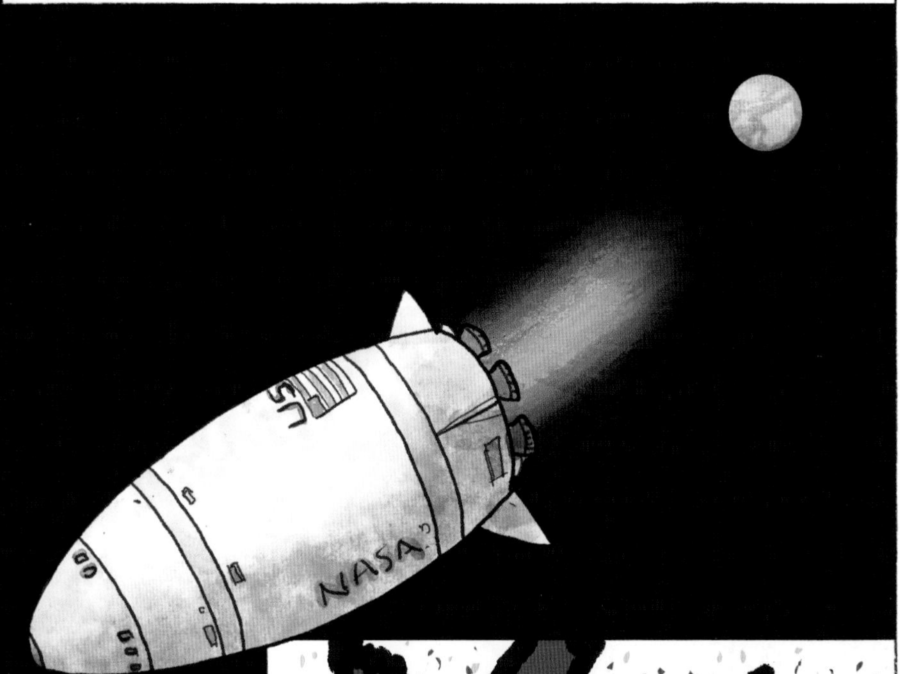
US
NASA

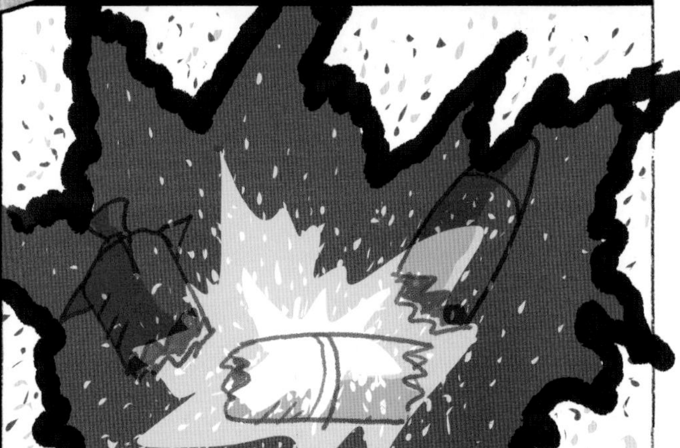

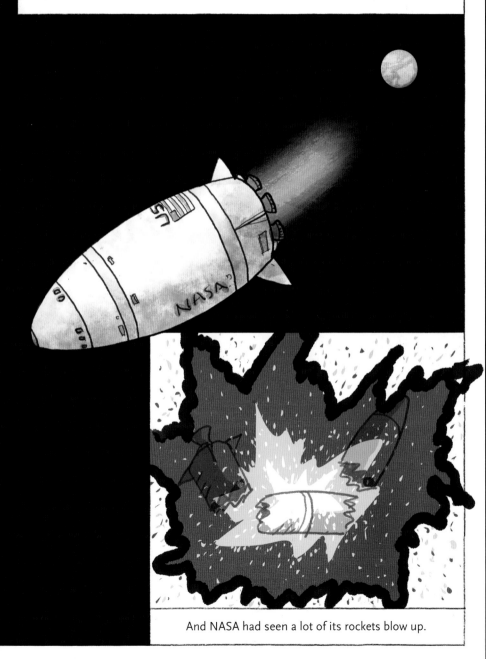

And NASA had seen a lot of its rockets blow up.

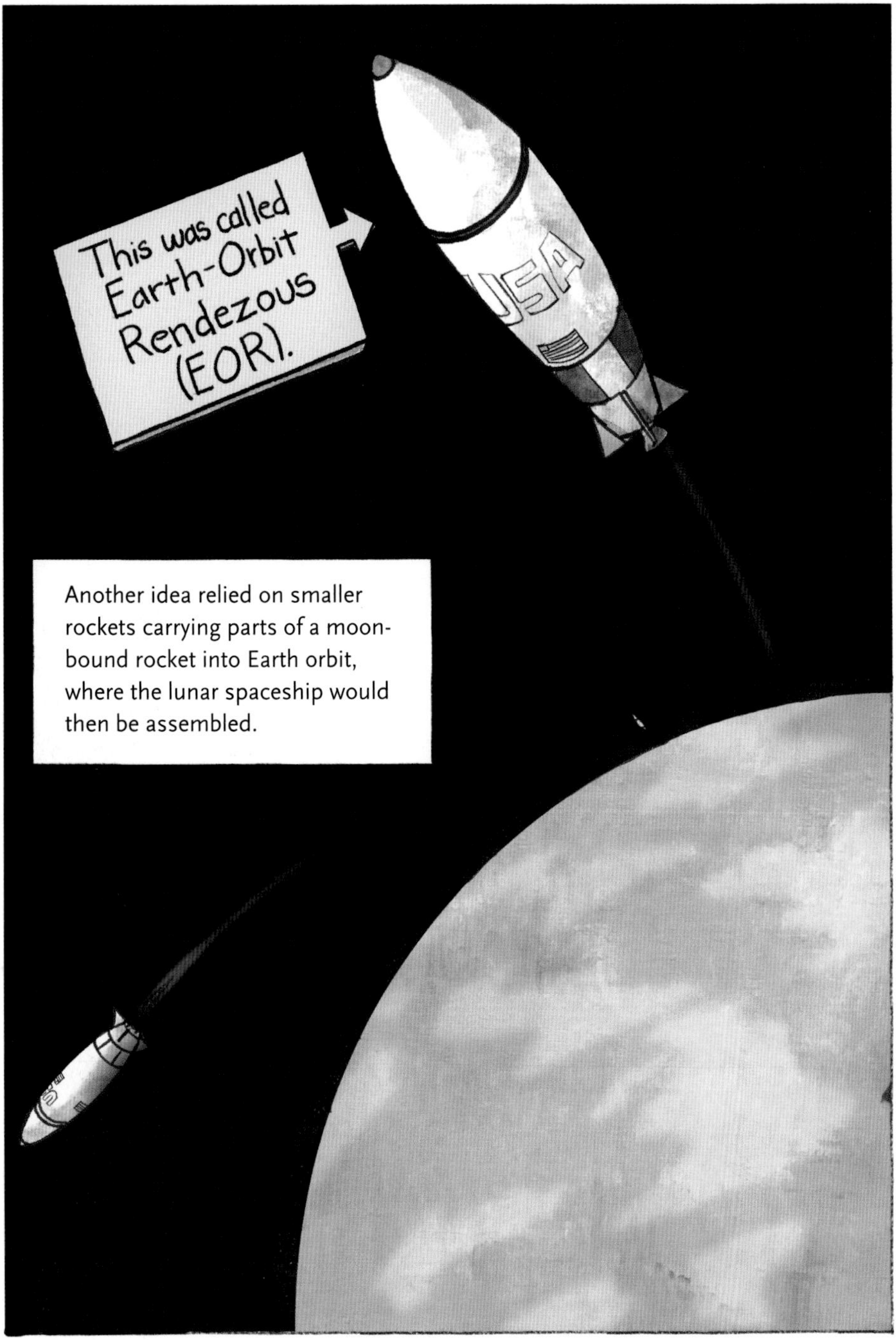
This was called Earth-Orbit Rendezous (EOR).
Another idea relied on smaller rockets carrying parts of a moon-bound rocket into Earth orbit, where the lunar spaceship would then be assembled.
USA

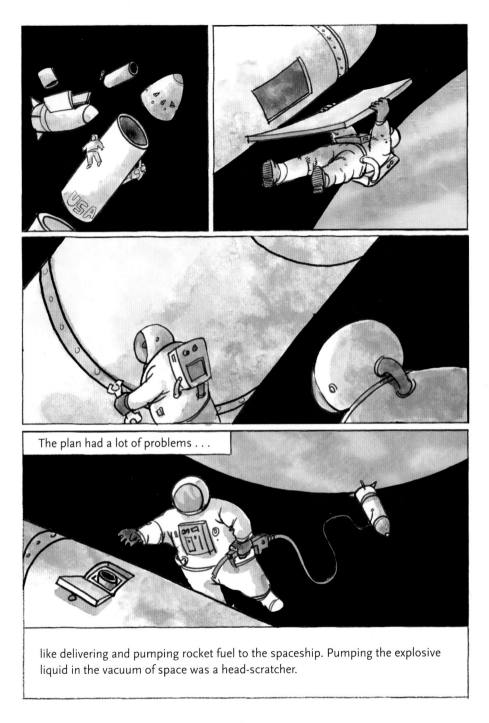

The plan had a lot of problems . . .

like delivering and pumping rocket fuel to the spaceship. Pumping the explosive liquid in the vacuum of space was a head-scratcher.

And though the rocket didn't have to be massive, it did have to be large enough to carry crew quarters, life-support equipment, and fuel to get to the moon with enough left over to escape the moon's gravity and fly back home. It also needed a heavy heat shield to protect it when it reentered Earth's atmosphere. In other words, the rocket had to be pretty big.

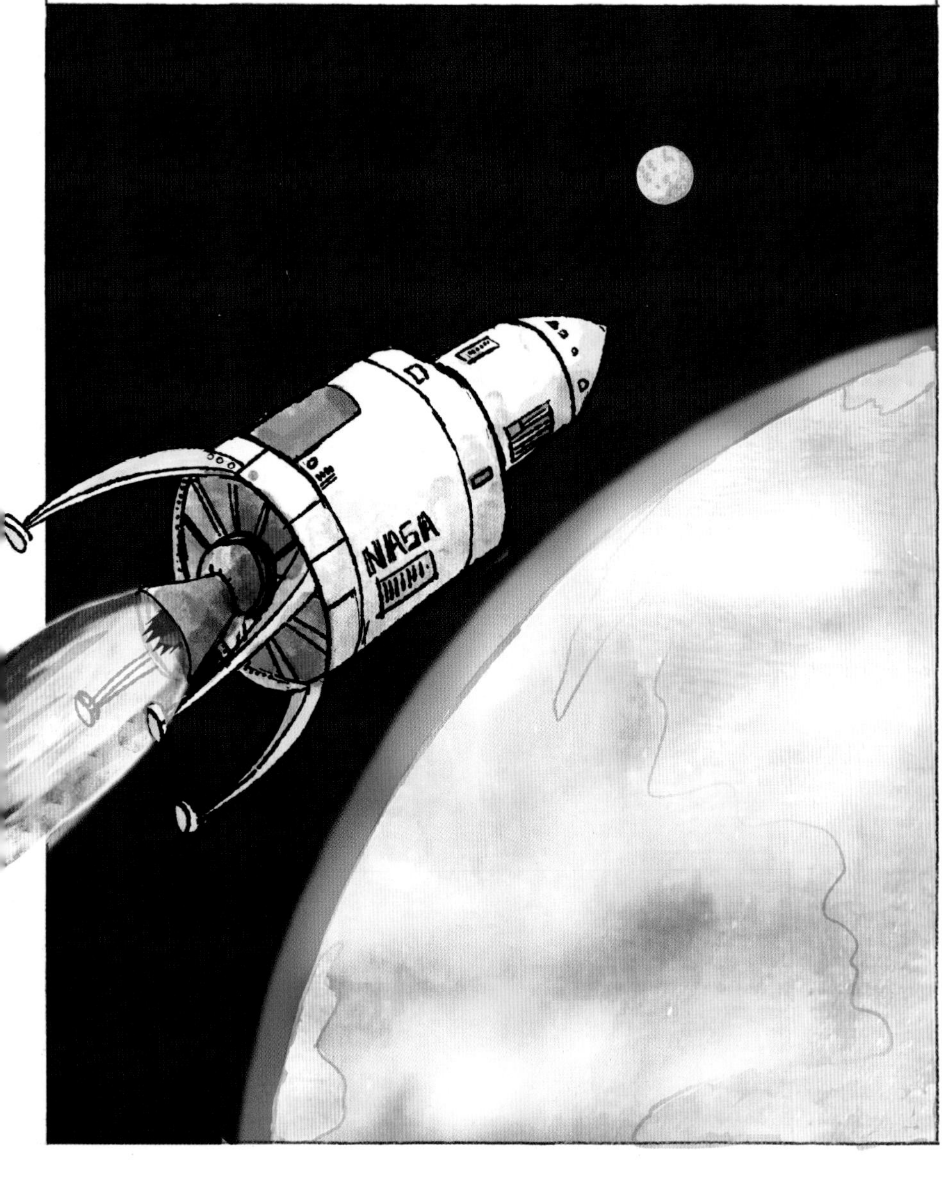
NASA

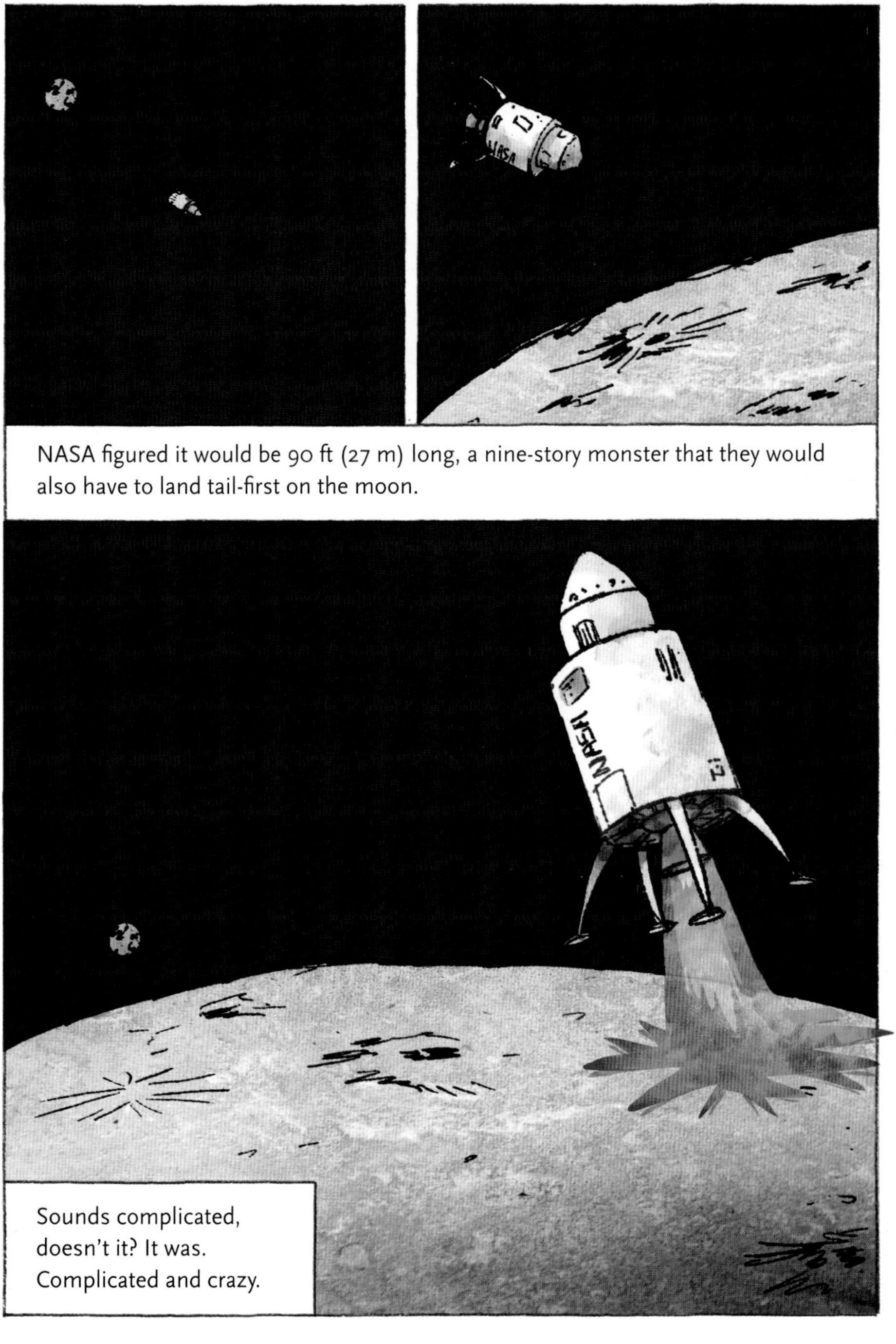
NASA figured it would be 90 ft (27 m) long, a nine-story monster that they would also have to land tail-first on the moon.
Sounds complicated, doesn't it? It was. Complicated and crazy.

In the end, they decided on an even more complicated and crazy idea.
This was called LUNAR-ORBIT RENDEZVOUS (LOR).
A smaller rocket would fly to the moon, bringing with it a special lunar lander, sometimes referred to as the "bug."
NASA
As the rocket circled the moon, the bug—piloted by a couple of astronauts—would make its way to the moon's surface.

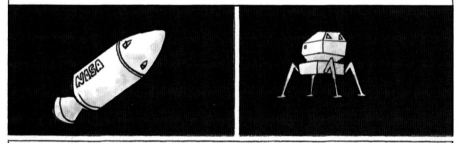

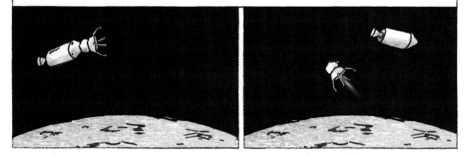

Later, the astronauts would disengage and launch part of the bug and rendezvous with the orbiting rocket. The astronauts would then fly home, discarding the bug on the moon to save weight and fuel.

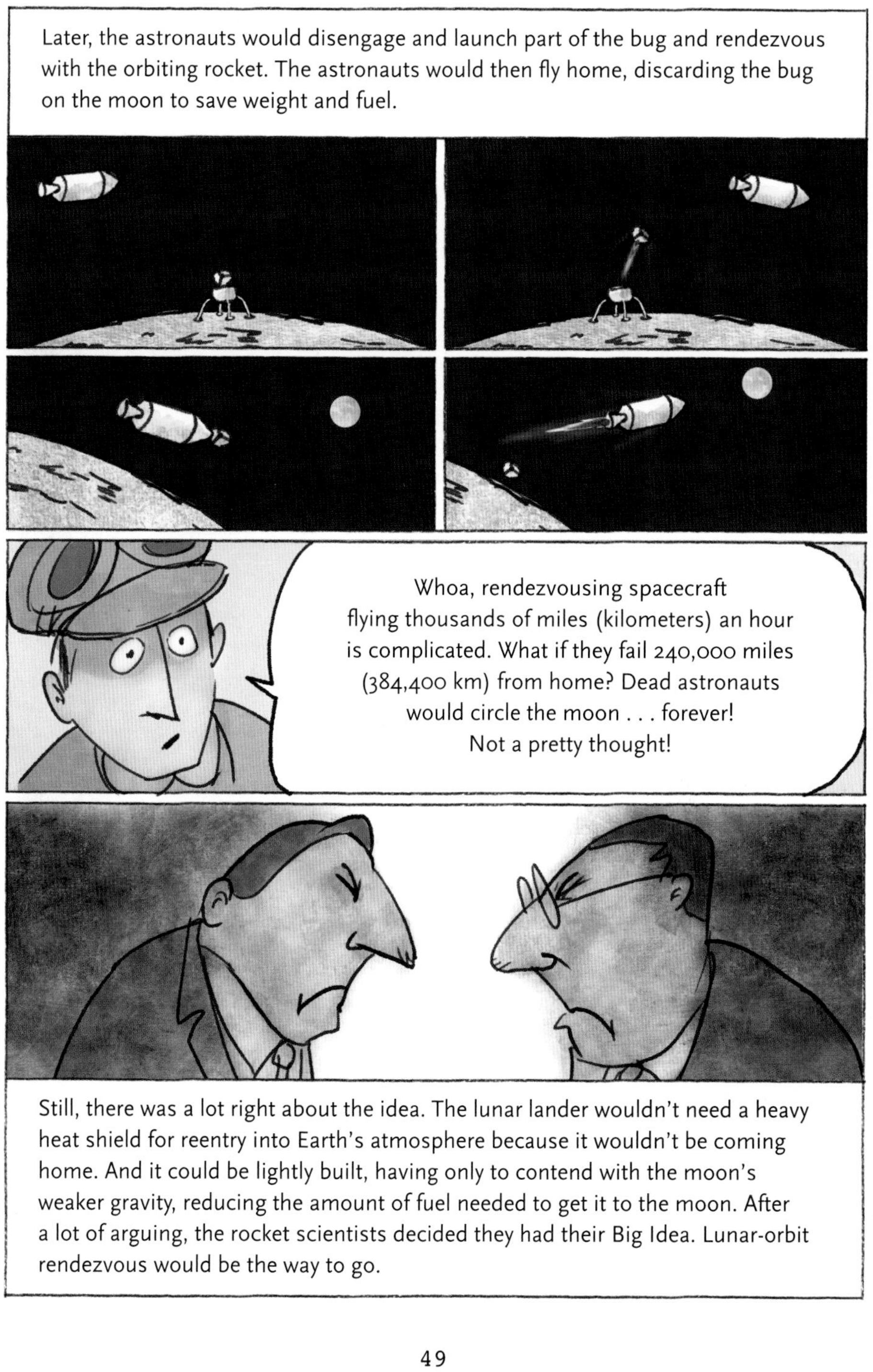
Whoa, rendezvousing spacecraft flying thousands of miles (kilometers) an hour is complicated. What if they fail 240,000 miles (384,400 km) from home? Dead astronauts would circle the moon . . . forever! Not a pretty thought!

Still, there was a lot right about the idea. The lunar lander wouldn't need a heavy heat shield for reentry into Earth's atmosphere because it wouldn't be coming home. And it could be lightly built, having only to contend with the moon's weaker gravity, reducing the amount of fuel needed to get it to the moon. After a lot of arguing, the rocket scientists decided they had their Big Idea. Lunar-orbit rendezvous would be the way to go.

Meanwhile, the Project Mercury astronauts were being shot into space and were returning safely.

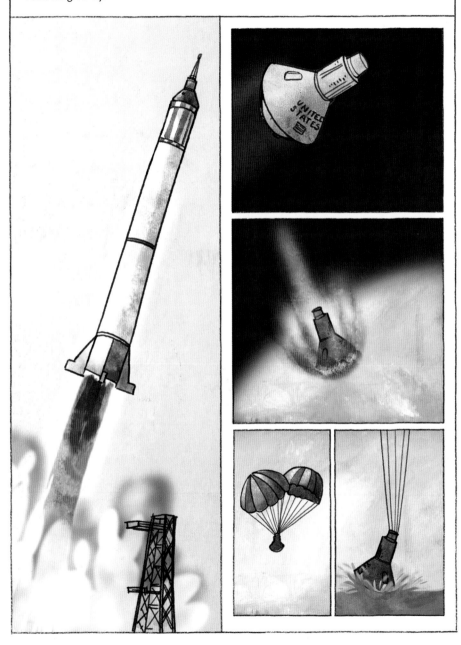

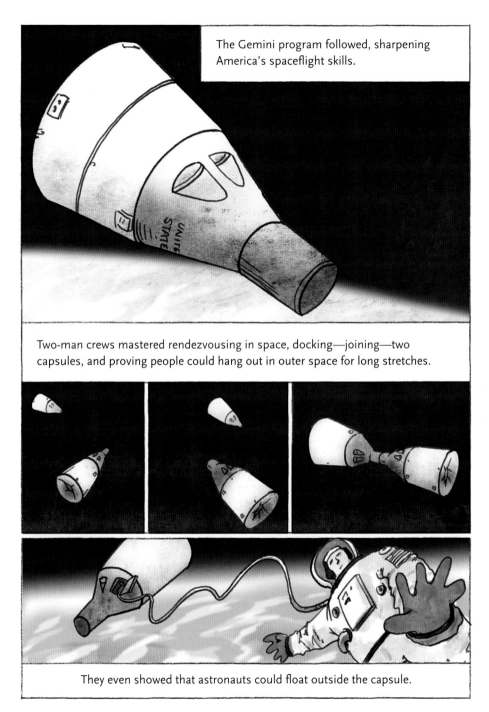

The Gemini program followed, sharpening America's spaceflight skills.

Two-man crews mastered rendezvousing in space, docking—joining—two capsules, and proving people could hang out in outer space for long stretches.

They even showed that astronauts could float outside the capsule.

Soon, the Apollo capsule was built. It was the spaceship that the astronauts would ride to the moon. Apollo would be hurtled into space by a giant rocket engine called Saturn V. All eyes were on the prize . . . and then tragedy struck.

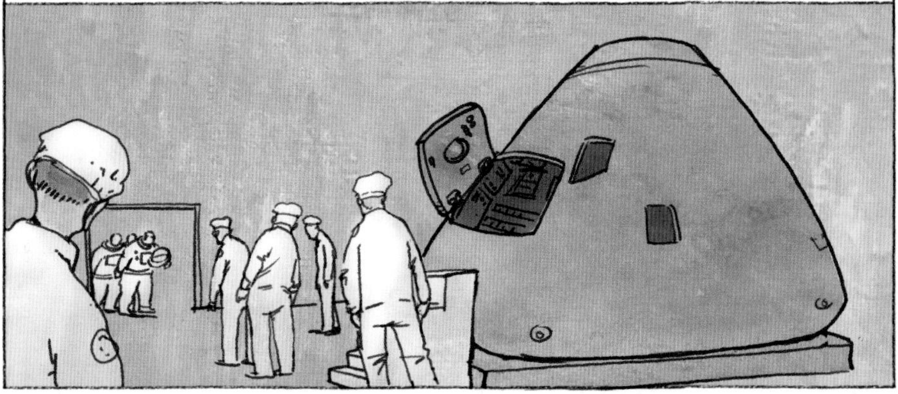

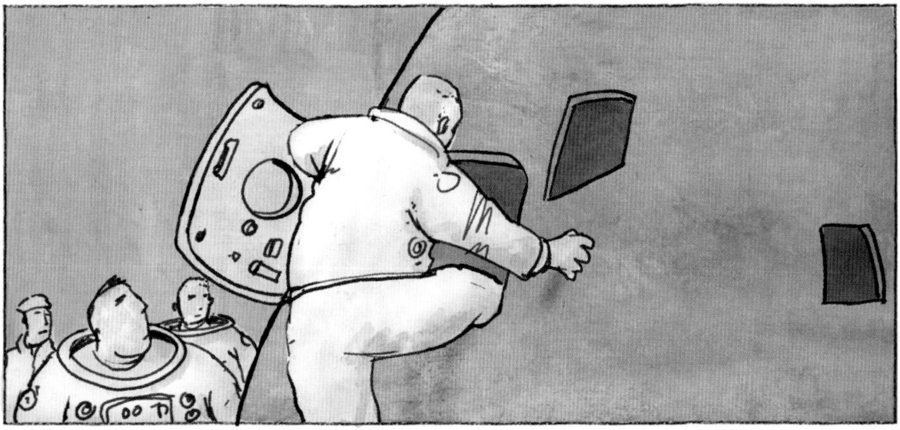

Apollo 1 was set to make a two-week-long Earth-orbit test flight. On January 27, 1967, three astronauts—Gus Grissom, Ed White, and Roger Chaffee—climbed into the capsule for an elaborate practice run of Apollo 1.

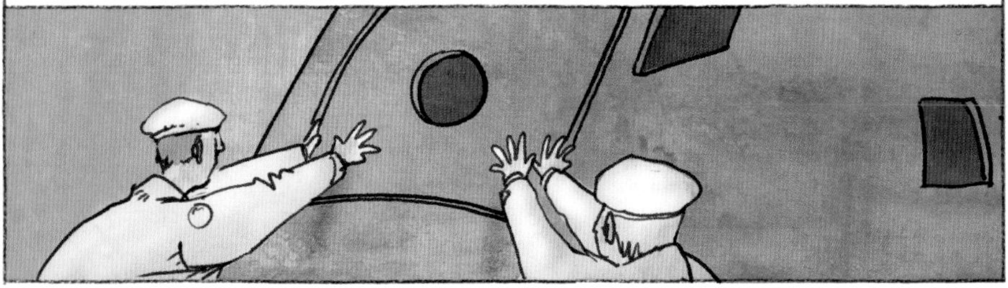

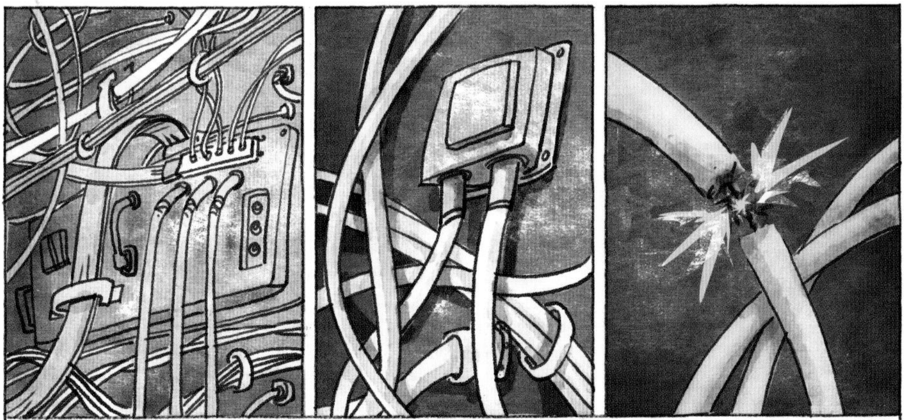
A spark ignited somewhere in the 30 mi (48 km) of wiring within the spacecraft. Flames filled the capsule.

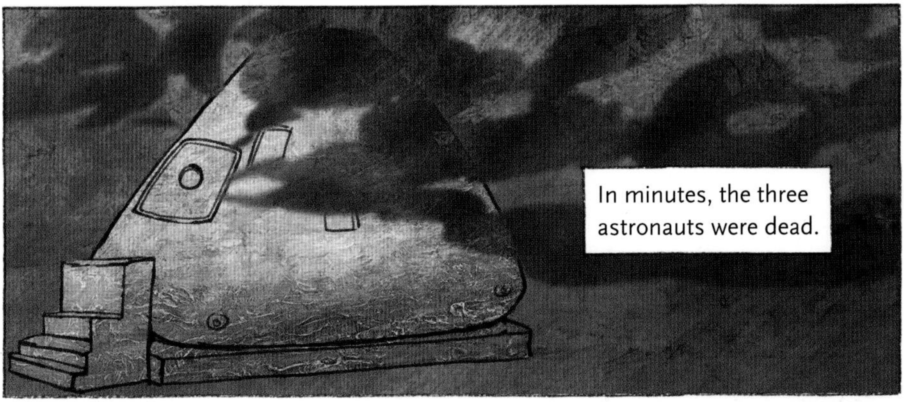
In minutes, the three astronauts were dead.

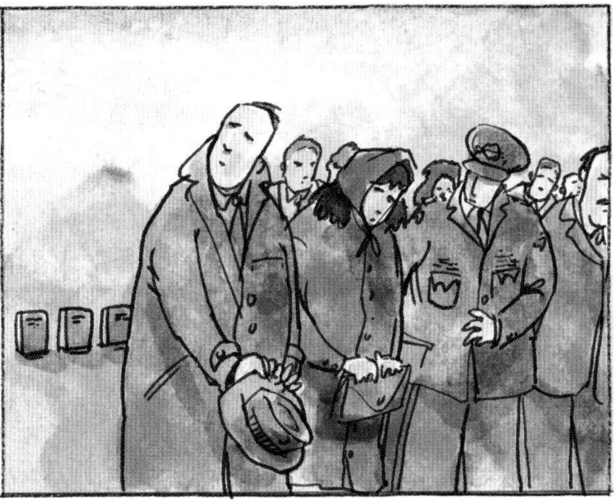
It was a brutal reminder: "You lose crew. Pilots die flying experimental aircraft." America grieved. And America started having second thoughts about the moon race. A poll showed that 46 percent of Americans opposed the aim of landing a man on the moon.

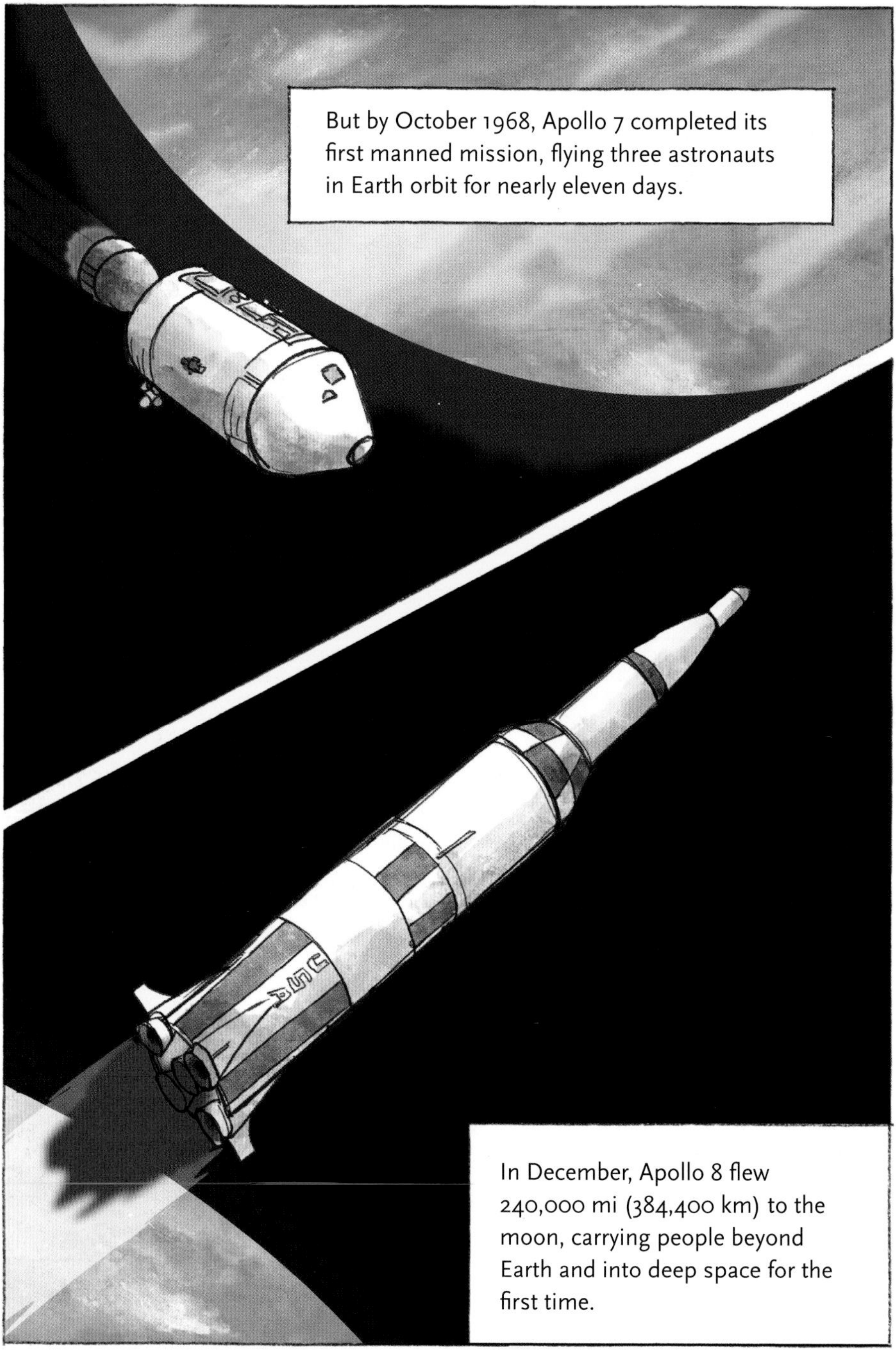
But by October 1968, Apollo 7 completed its first manned mission, flying three astronauts in Earth orbit for nearly eleven days.
In December, Apollo 8 flew 240,000 mi (384,400 km) to the moon, carrying people beyond Earth and into deep space for the first time.

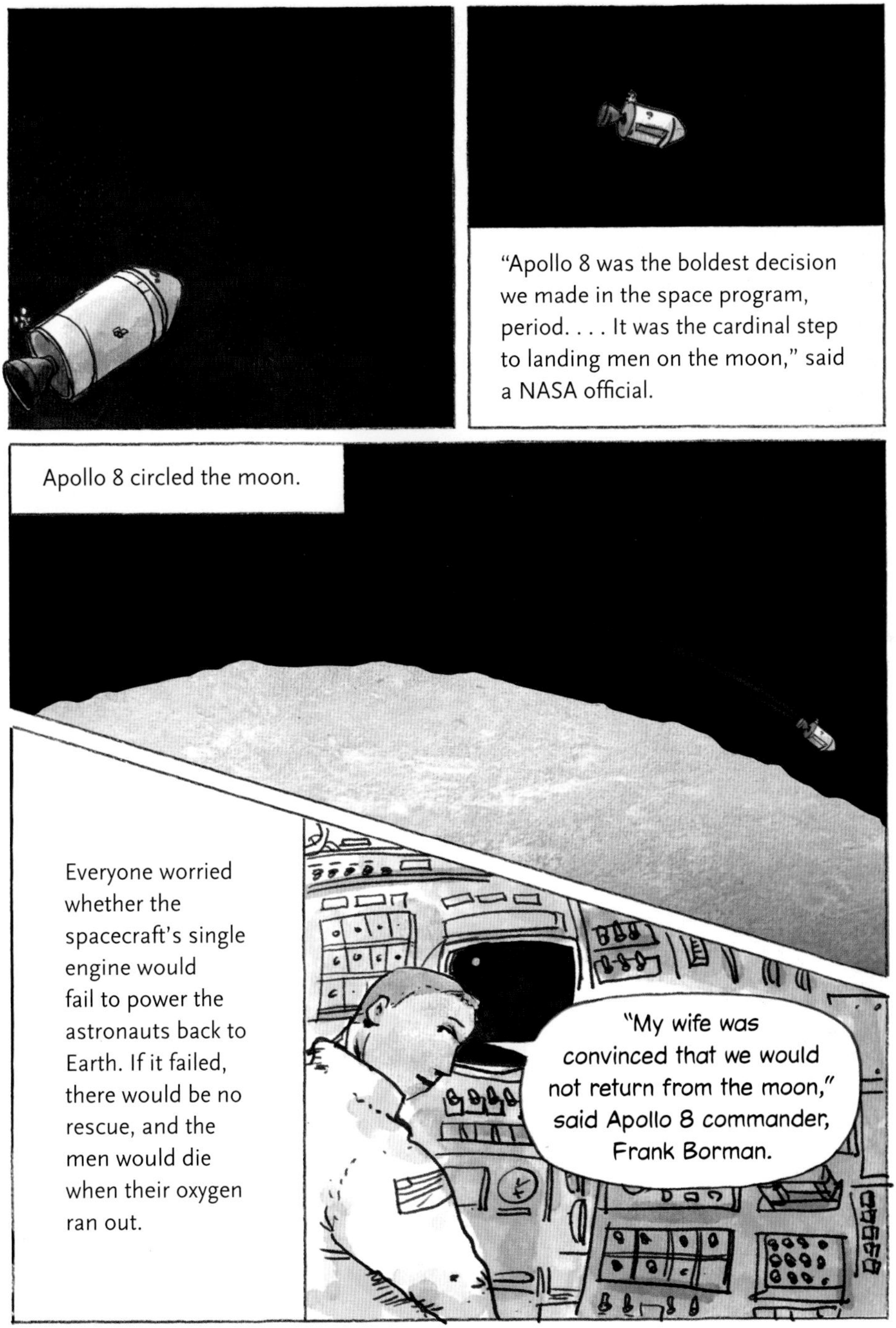
"Apollo 8 was the boldest decision we made in the space program, period. . . . It was the cardinal step to landing men on the moon," said a NASA official.
Apollo 8 circled the moon.
Everyone worried whether the spacecraft's single engine would fail to power the astronauts back to Earth. If it failed, there would be no rescue, and the men would die when their oxygen ran out.
"My wife was convinced that we would not return from the moon," said Apollo 8 commander, Frank Borman.

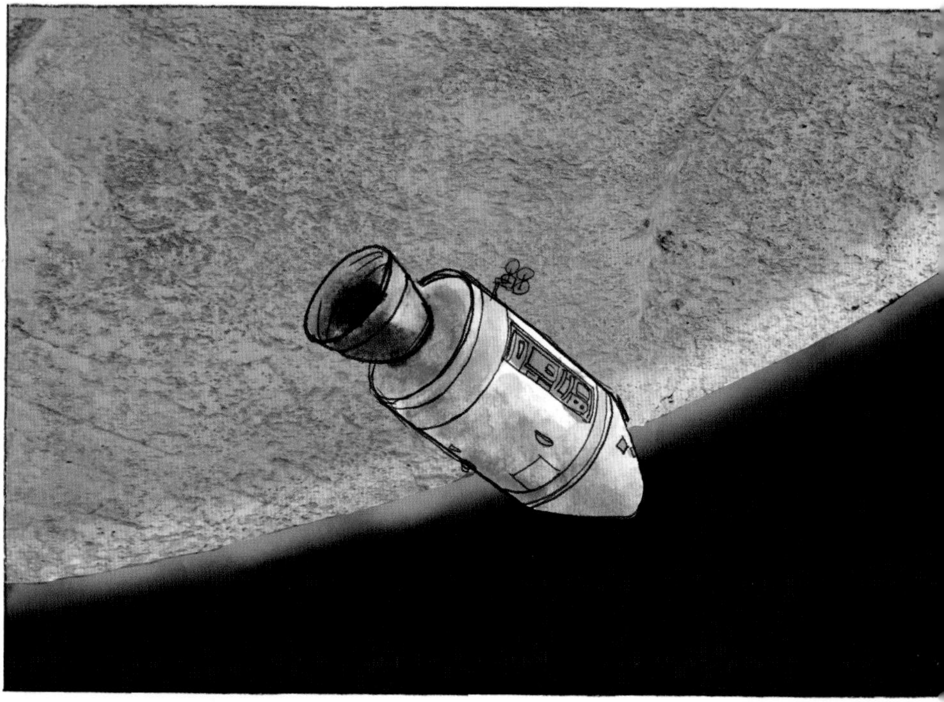

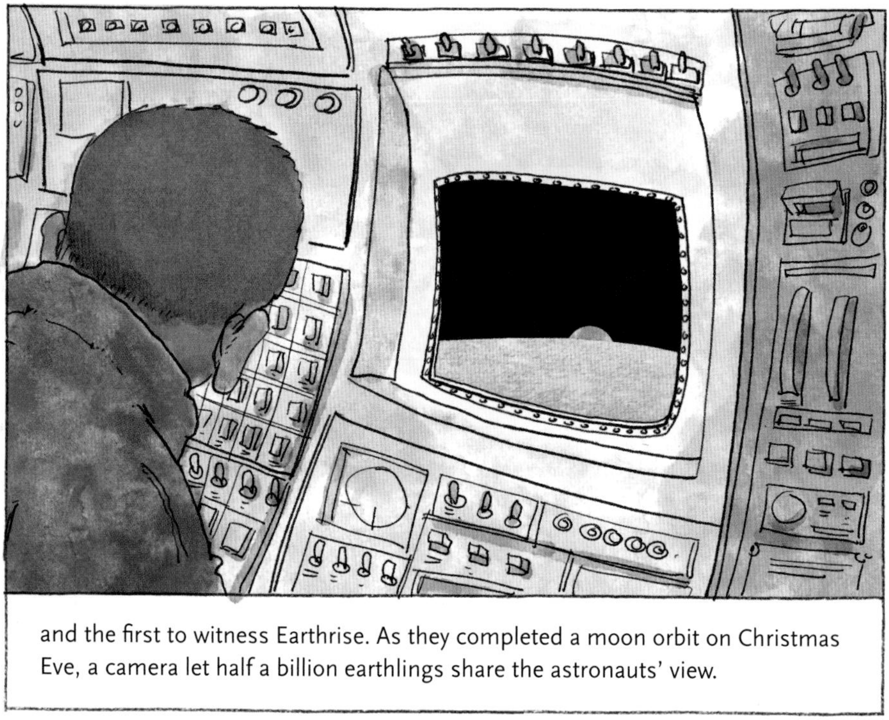

and the first to witness Earthrise. As they completed a moon orbit on Christmas Eve, a camera let half a billion earthlings share the astronauts' view.

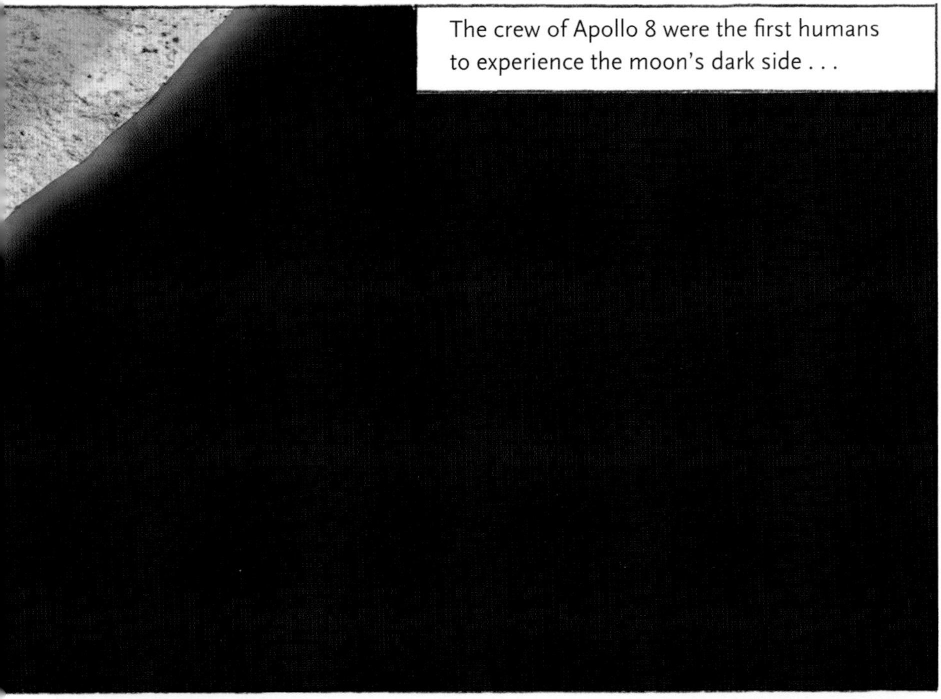
The crew of Apollo 8 were the first humans to experience the moon's dark side . . .

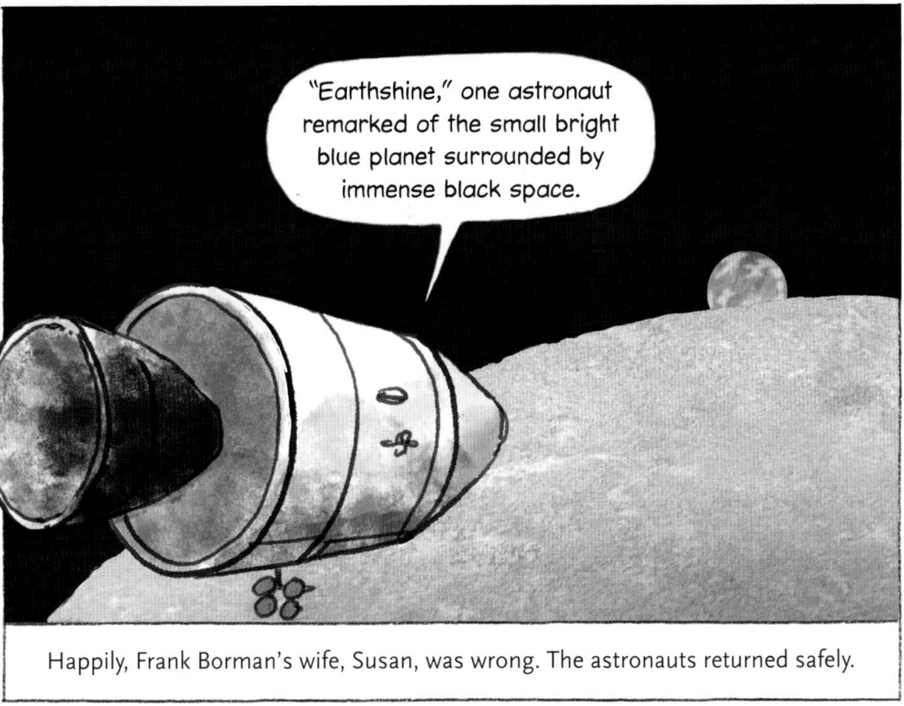
"Earthshine," one astronaut remarked of the small bright blue planet surrounded by immense black space.
Happily, Frank Borman's wife, Susan, was wrong. The astronauts returned safely.

Afterward, Apollos 9 and 10 repeated the trip, this time bringing along the bug—the lunar module—the craft that would touch down on the moon's surface.

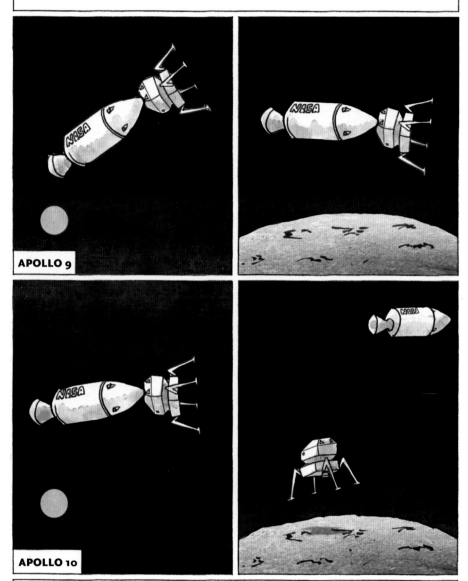

APOLLO 9

APOLLO 10

Each crew practiced the skills needed for a successful moon landing. Apollo 10 completed all the steps short of landing.

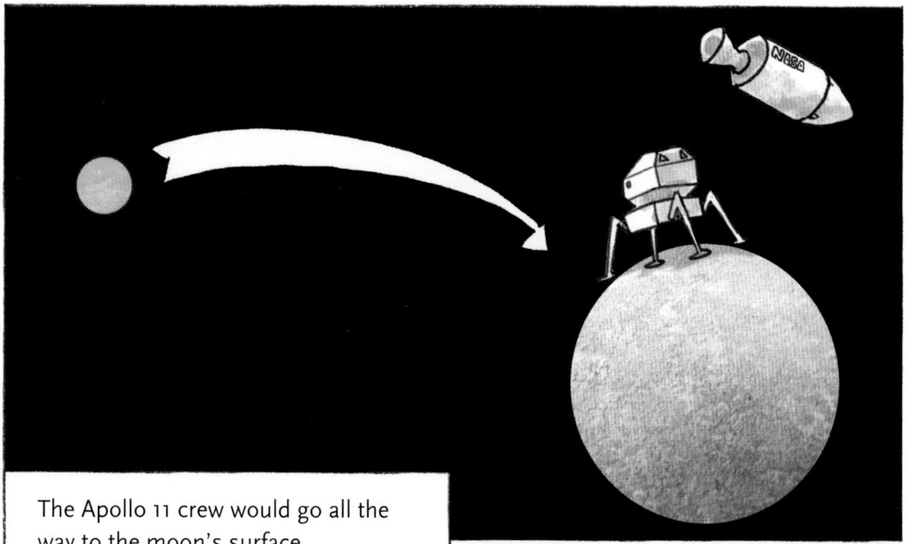
NASA

The Apollo 11 crew would go all the way to the moon's surface.
Neil Armstrong would command.

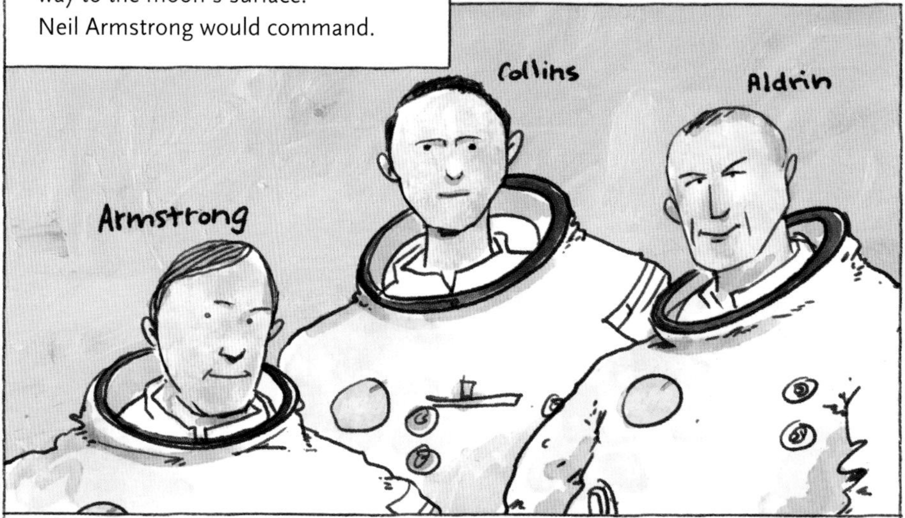
Collins
Aldrin
Armstrong

I would have bet that Armstrong was really something extra special to be chosen to be the first man on the moon, but I would have been wrong. Oh, he was a terrific astronaut, but all the astronauts were terrific. It came down to astronaut rotation. Simply put: It was his turn.
Buzz Aldrin and Michael Collins rounded out the crew. Collins was talkative and friendly, Aldrin less so, and Armstrong was intensely private and once was described as "extraordinarily remote."

On May 20, 1969, Saturn—the giant rocket that would lift the astronauts to the moon—rolled out of the Vehicle Assembly Building (VAB).

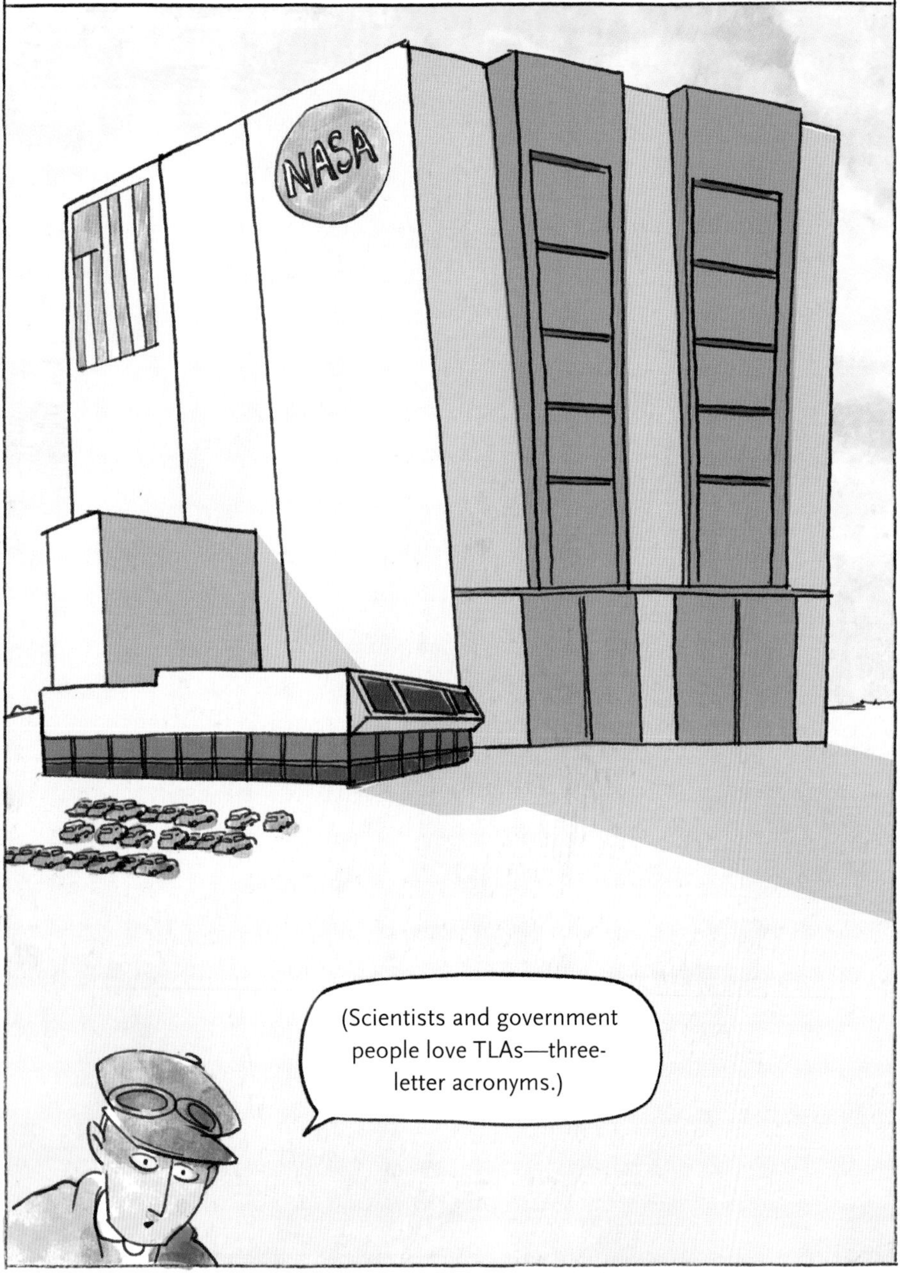
NASA
(Scientists and government people love TLAs—three-letter acronyms.)

The VAB was one of the largest enclosed spaces in the world, tall enough to accommodate the 363 ft (111 m) Saturn and the cranes needed to assemble it, and roomy enough to build four Saturns at a time. More than 4,000 pilings were used to keep the 525 ft (160 m) high shed from flying away in a Florida hurricane.

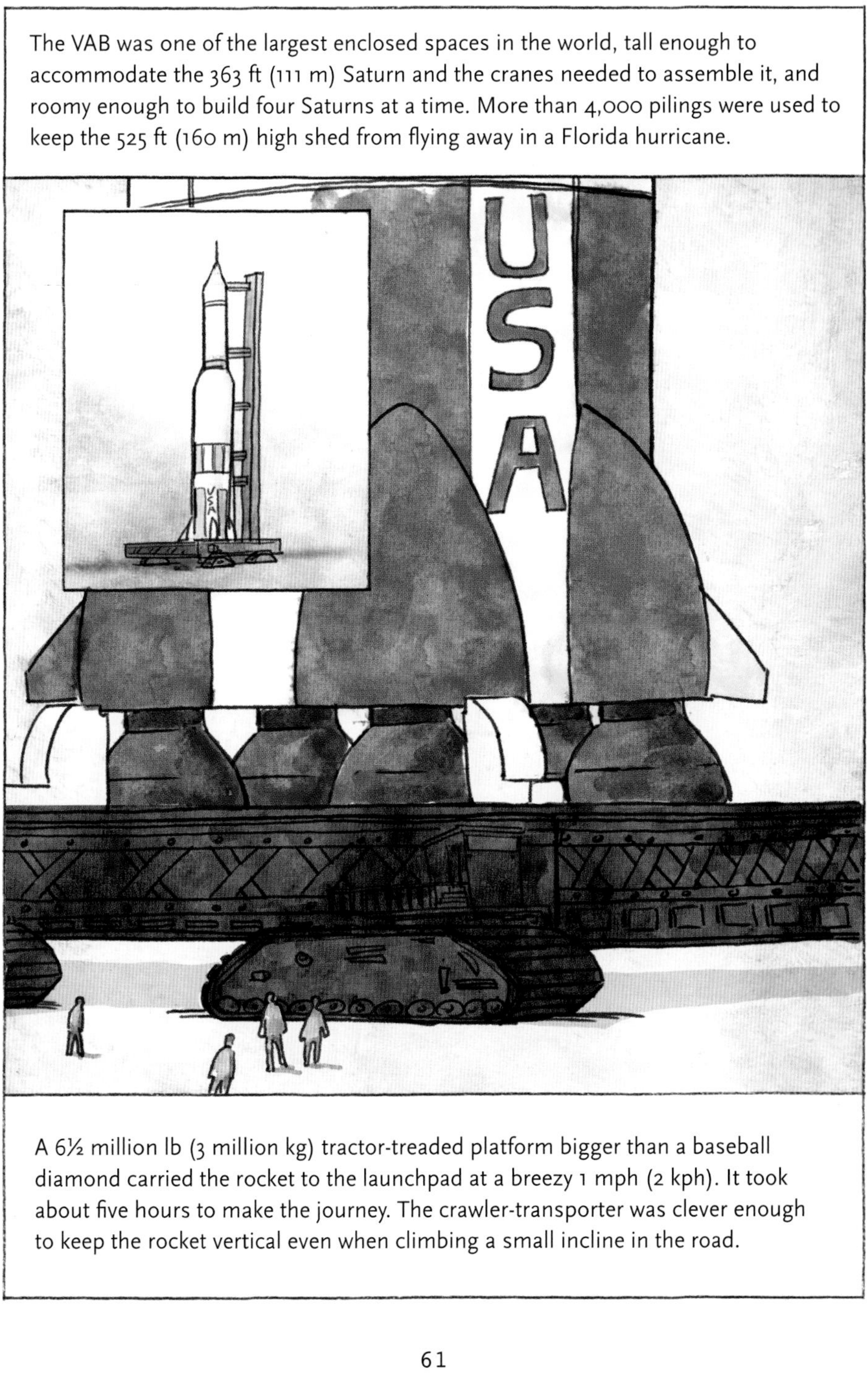
USA

A 6½ million lb (3 million kg) tractor-treaded platform bigger than a baseball diamond carried the rocket to the launchpad at a breezy 1 mph (2 kph). It took about five hours to make the journey. The crawler-transporter was clever enough to keep the rocket vertical even when climbing a small incline in the road.

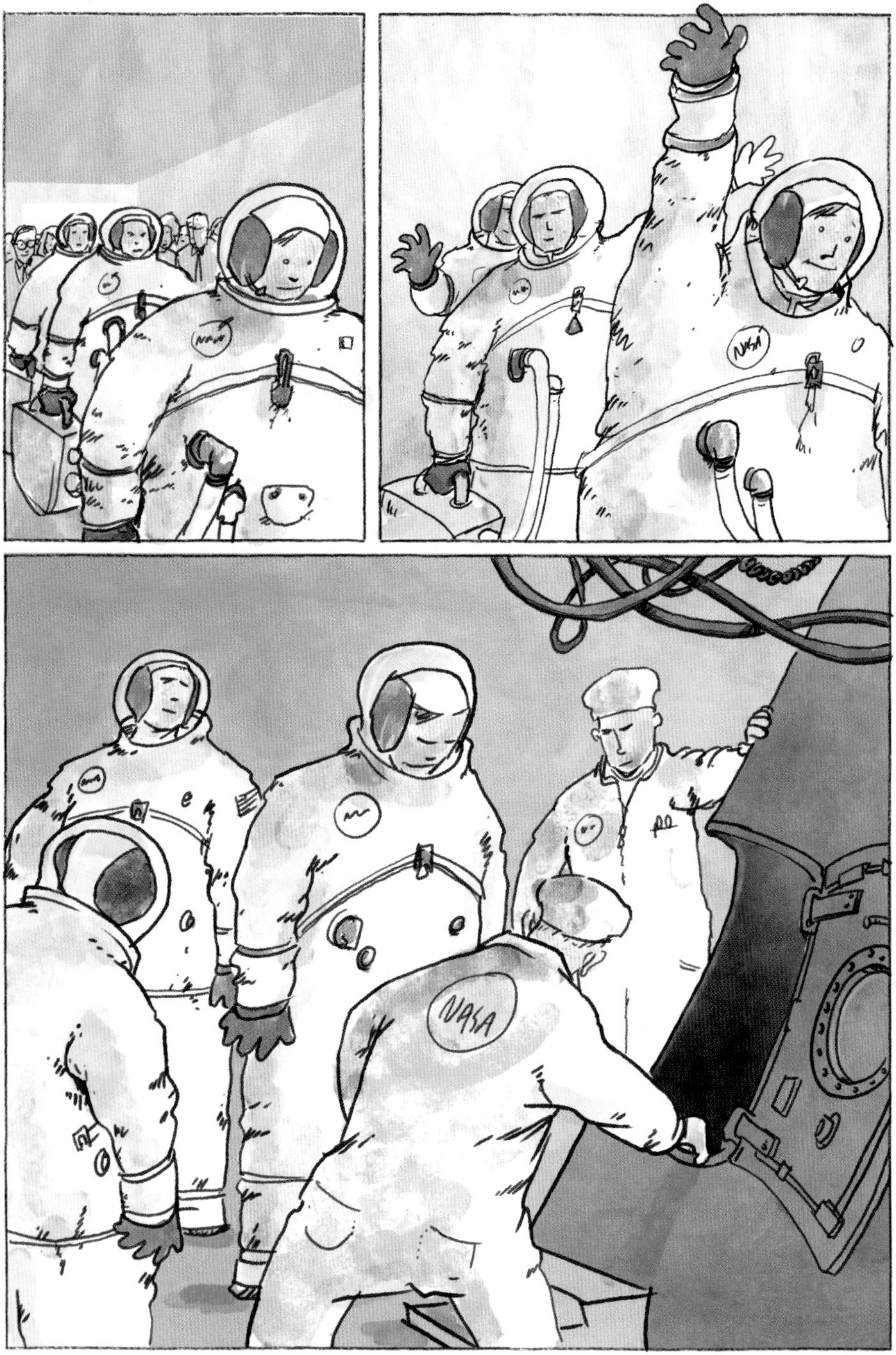
NASA

On July 16, 1969, Armstrong, Aldrin, and Collins were strapped into their seats inside the cone-shaped command module of Apollo 11 that sat atop Saturn.

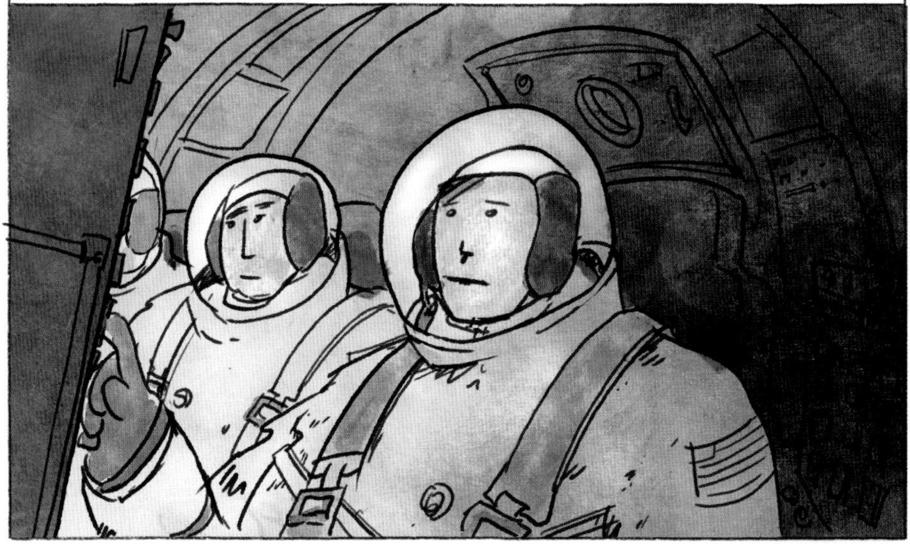

An hour before launch, support crews were gone, and the astronauts were alone in the nose of the rocket.

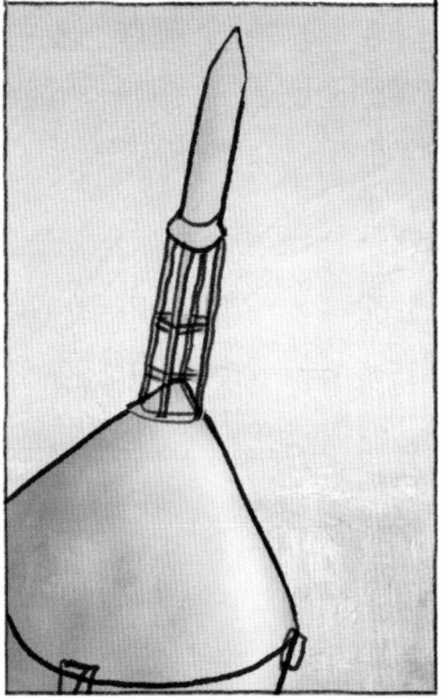

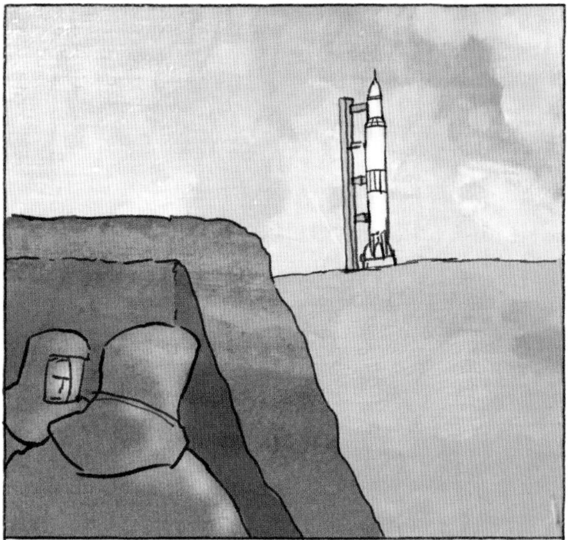

NASA didn't forget about their exploding rockets: A half mile (0.8 km) away, a fourteen-person rescue team clad in protective gear waited in a sand bunker . . . just in case.

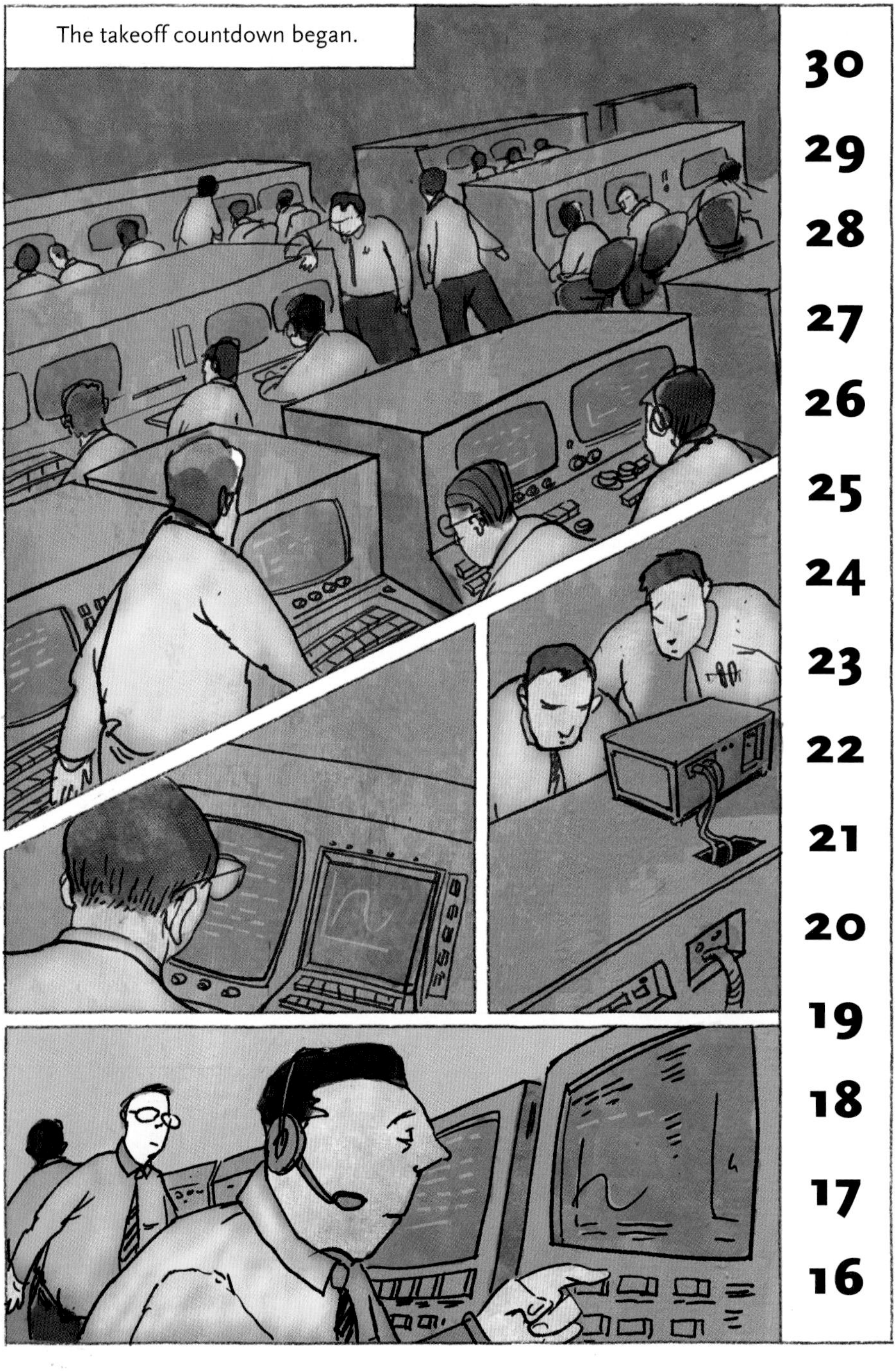

The takeoff countdown began.
30
29
28
27
26
25
24
23
22
21
20
19
18
17
16

At 8.9 seconds, Saturn's five main engines ignited.
Four massive hold-down arms pinned the rocket to the pad until the engines reached nearly full power, and then released within milliseconds of one another. Failing to do so would have toppled the rocket.

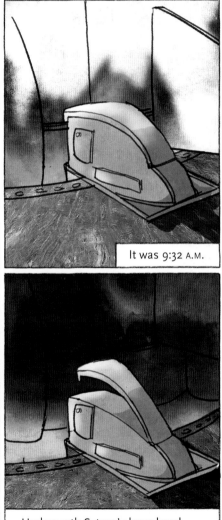

It was 9:32 A.M.

Underneath Saturn's launchpad, deflectors streamed the rocket's flames away, keeping them from destroying the rocket.

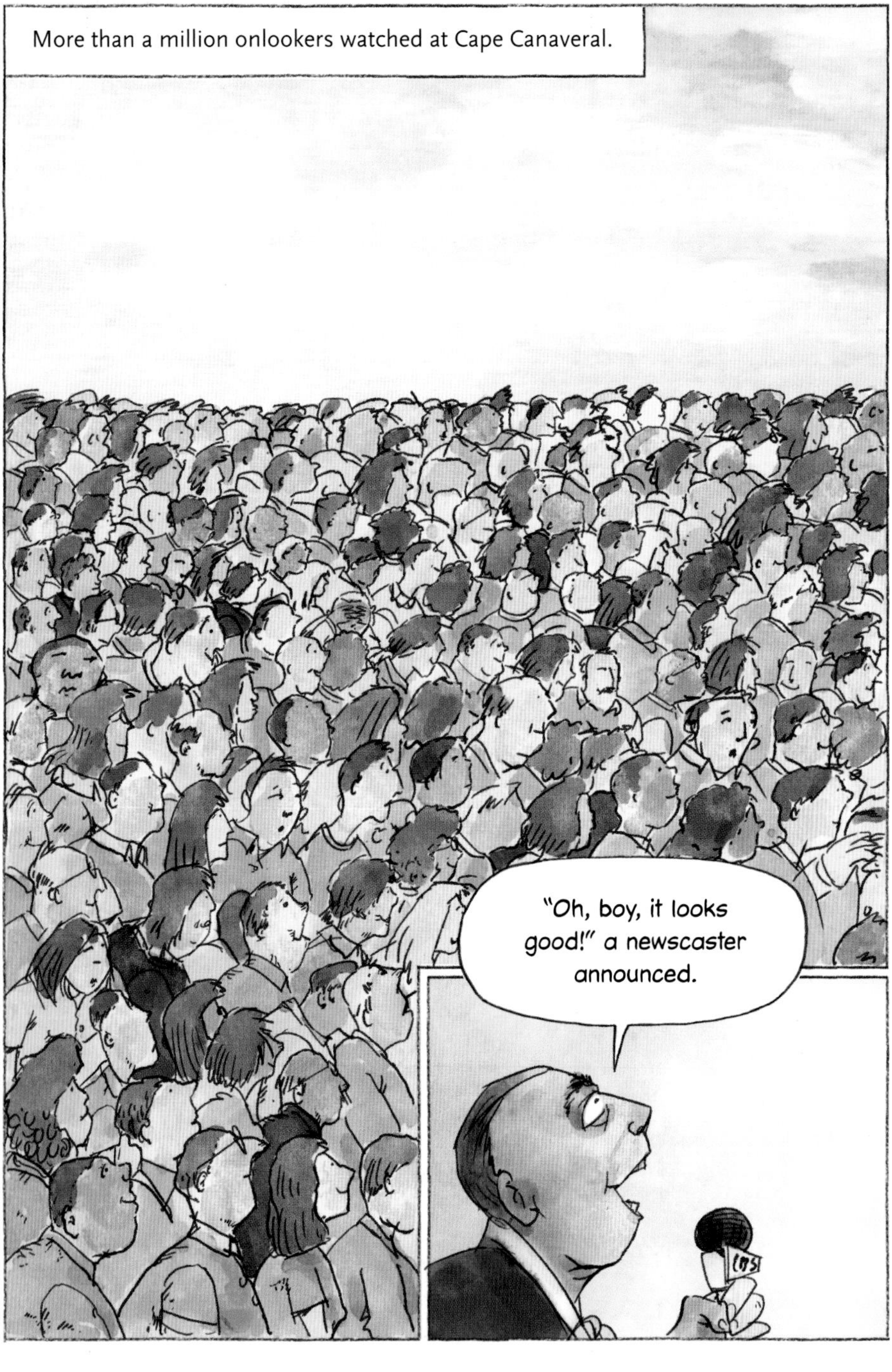
More than a million onlookers watched at Cape Canaveral.
"Oh, boy, it looks good!" a newscaster announced.
CBS

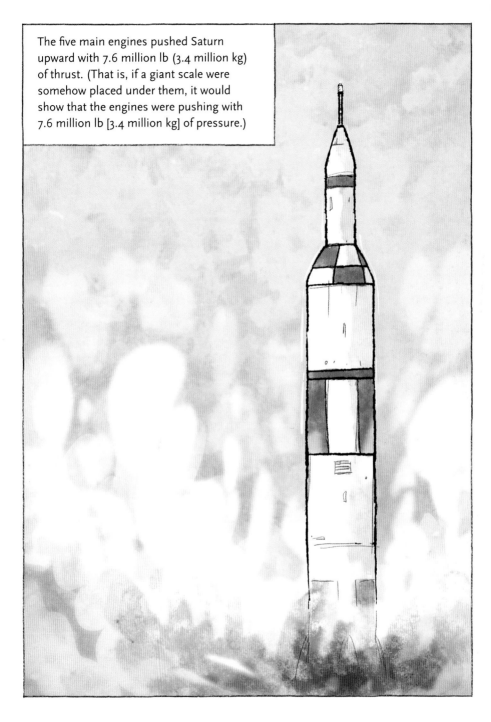

The five main engines pushed Saturn upward with 7.6 million lb (3.4 million kg) of thrust. (That is, if a giant scale were somehow placed under them, it would show that the engines were pushing with 7.6 million lb [3.4 million kg] of pressure.)

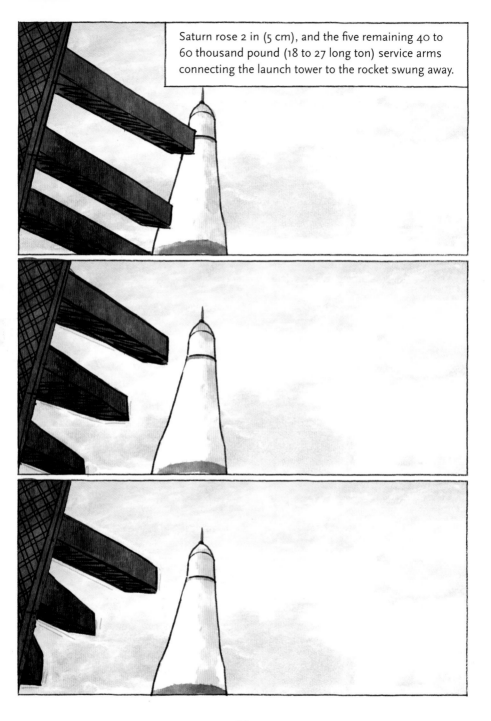

Saturn rose 2 in (5 cm), and the five remaining 40 to 60 thousand pound (18 to 27 long ton) service arms connecting the launch tower to the rocket swung away.

Barely off the ground, the monster rocket tilted slightly, allowing Saturn to clear the launch tower.

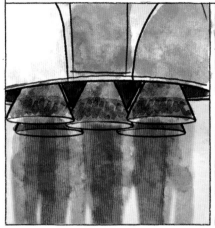

Hundreds of feet (meters) in the air, Saturn's flames still reached back to Earth.

It lurched this way and that to maintain its proper path.

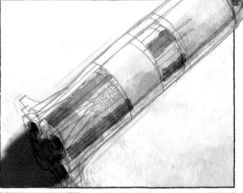

Michael Collins described the rocket's bouncing around as "steering like crazy."

Saturn carried about 950,000 gal (3.6 million L) of liquid propellant. (You could say it was really just a collection of enormous fuel tanks wrapped in thin metal. In some places, its "skin" was just a quarter inch [6 mm] thick, and in others one twenty-fifth of an inch [1 mm]!)

Two and a half minutes later—two and a half minutes!—Saturn burned 500,000 gal (1.9 million L) of kerosene and liquid oxygen fuel, making the rocket 4.5 million lb (2 million kg) lighter.

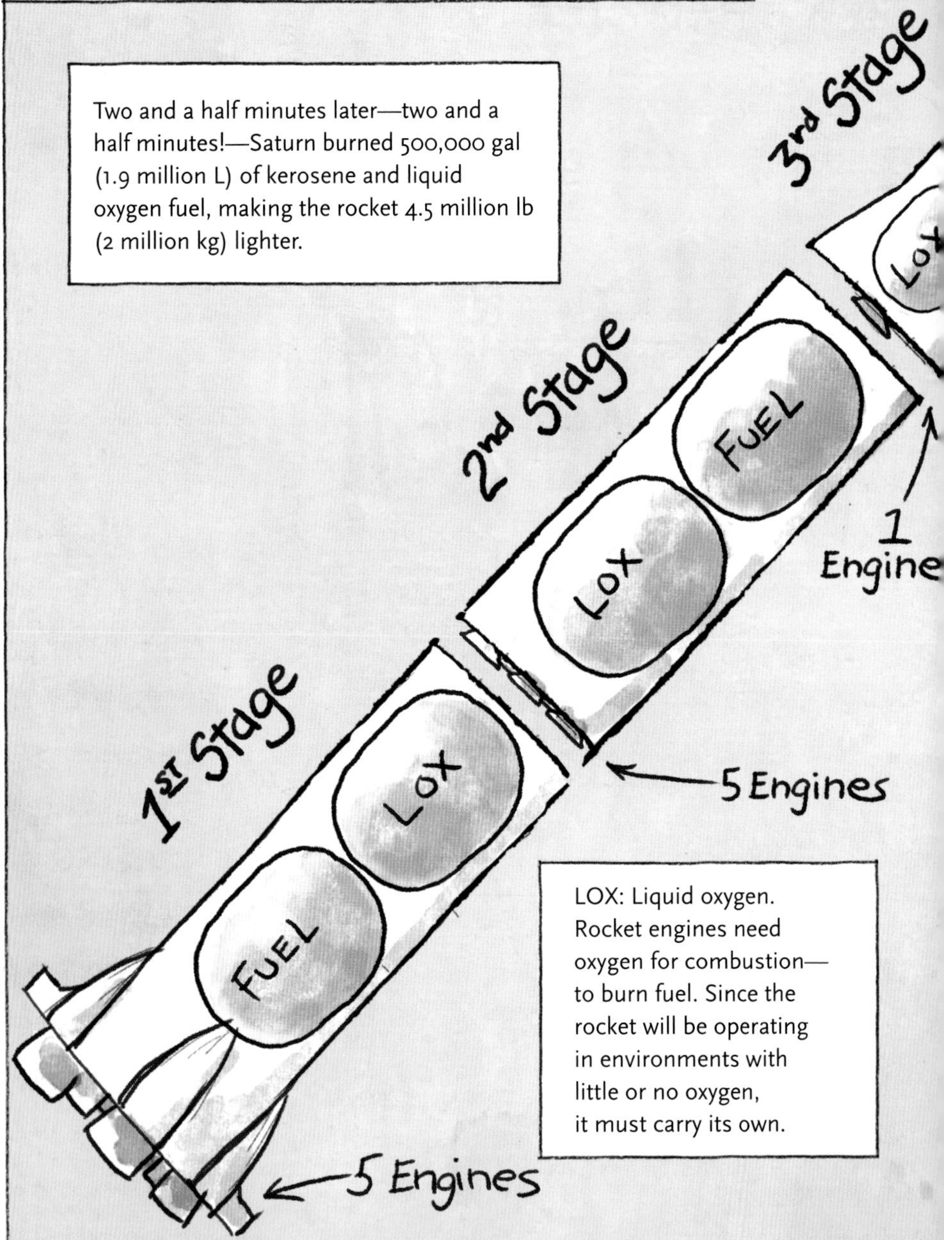

3rd Stage
2nd Stage
FUEL
LOX
1
Engine
1st Stage
LOX
FUEL
5 Engines
5 Engines

LOX: Liquid oxygen. Rocket engines need oxygen for combustion—to burn fuel. Since the rocket will be operating in environments with little or no oxygen, it must carry its own.

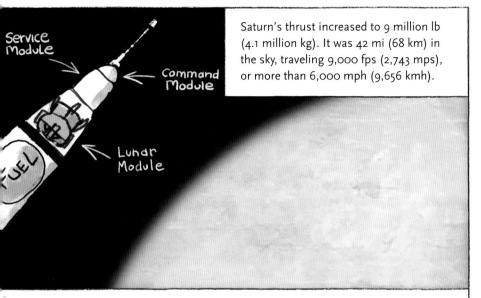

Service Module

Command Module

Lunar Module

Saturn's thrust increased to 9 million lb (4.1 million kg). It was 42 mi (68 km) in the sky, traveling 9,000 fps (2,743 mps), or more than 6,000 mph (9,656 kmh).

The first stage's job was complete, and its engines shut down. It separated and fell away as the second stage's five engines took over and hurtled the astronauts at 4½ mi (7 km) a second!

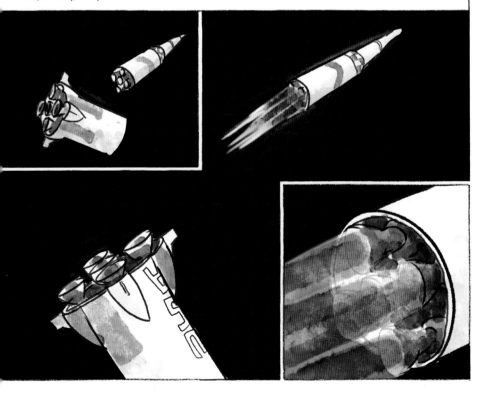

At the tip of Saturn, a small emergency rocket, designed to carry the men and the capsule away from Saturn in case of trouble, was no longer needed. It fired and flew off, taking with it a cap that had covered the nose of the capsule to protect it from small objects during takeoff.

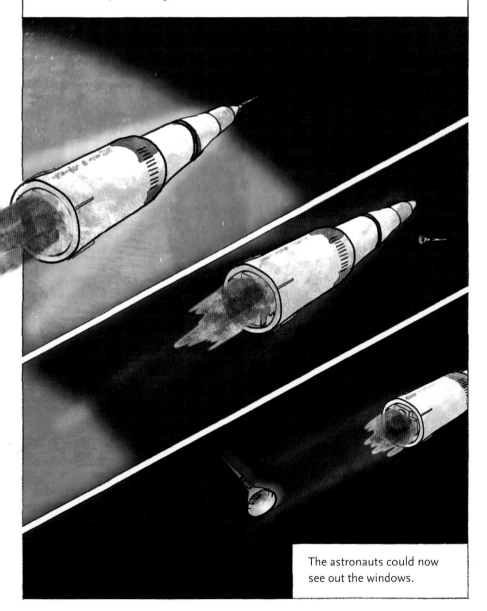

The astronauts could now see out the windows.

Eight and a half minutes after starting, the second stage was spent. It separated and dropped away. The single engine of the third stage fired for about another three minutes, slinging Apollo 11 at 17,500 mph (28,163 kmh) into Earth orbit. Apollo 11 whirled around Earth one and a half times.

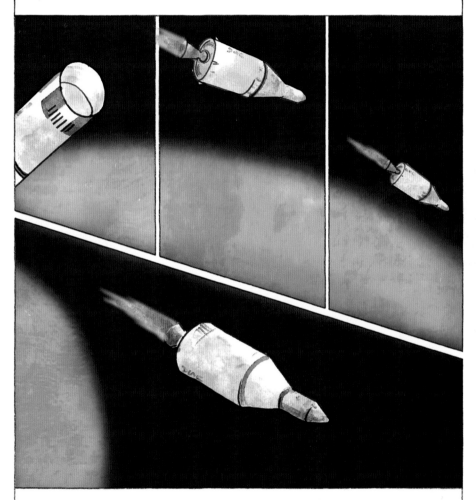

Then the NASA command center, located in Houston, Texas, gave the OK to fire the third-stage rocket again, racing the spacecraft to 24,500 mph (39,429 kmh)— the magic speed needed to escape Earth's gravity and head toward the moon. TLI, they called it: translunar injection. The engine burned for five and a half minutes, giving Apollo 11 its top speed of nearly 25,000 mph (40,234 kmh).

Inside Apollo 11, the three astronauts tried to keep their heads still. People depend on the liquid in their inner ear for balance, and if the liquid sloshes around, they can feel very nauseated. No one wanted retch floating around the cabin!

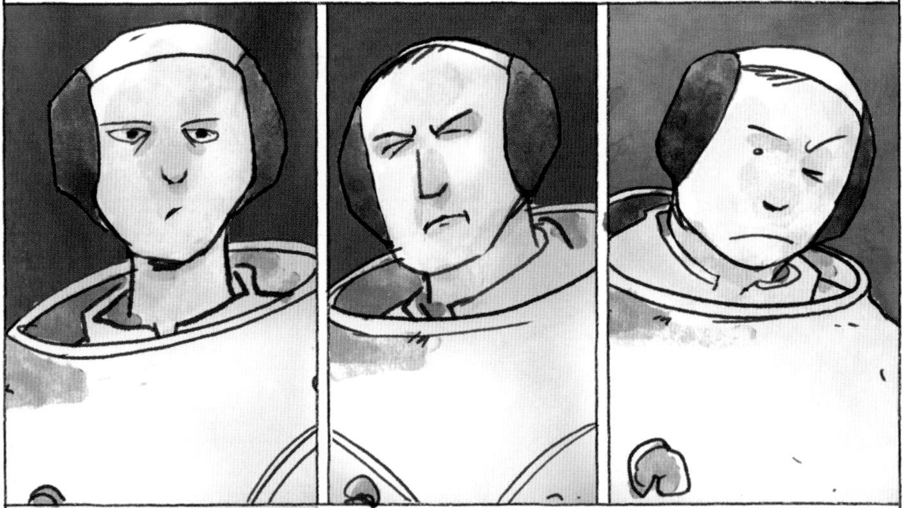

Now it was time to get the bug—lunar module—that was stowed behind Apollo 11.

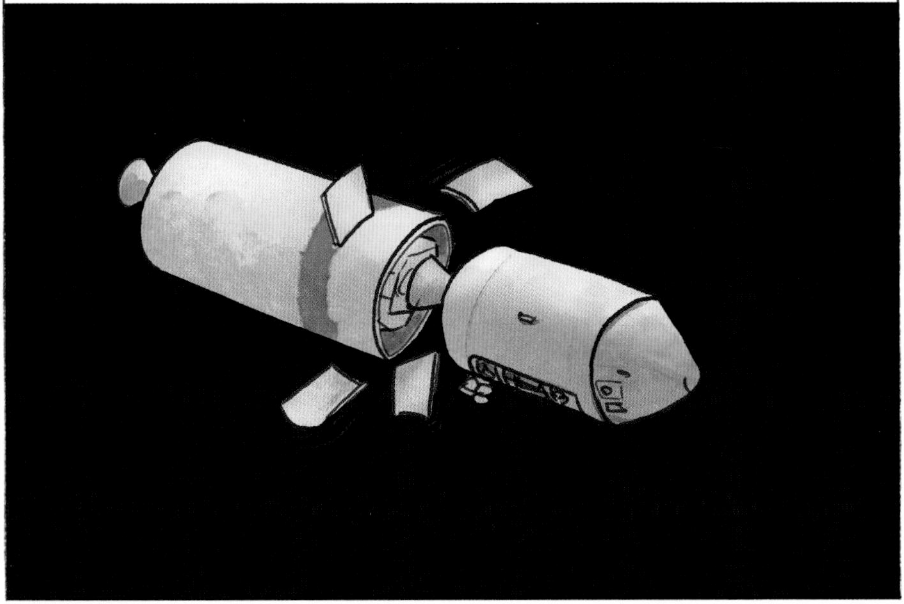

Collins took control of the command capsule, separating it from the third stage and rotating it until it faced the lunar module resting within Saturn. He gingerly docked the two together. A crash here could end the mission and their lives!

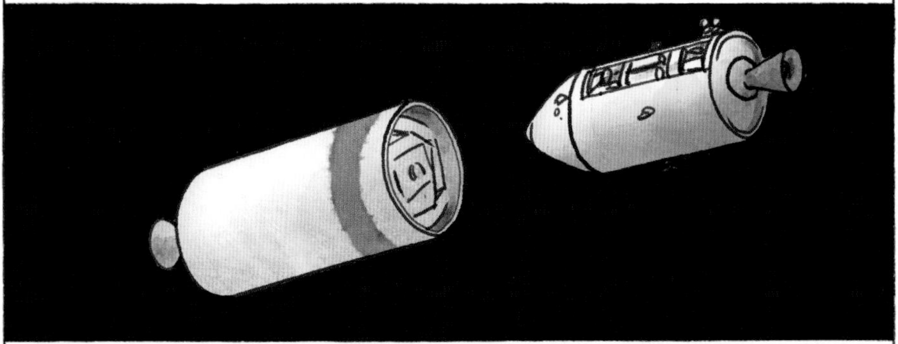

Then he eased the pair away from Saturn's third stage, leaving it behind. Of course, there was a TLA for Collins's trick: LME. Lunar module extraction.

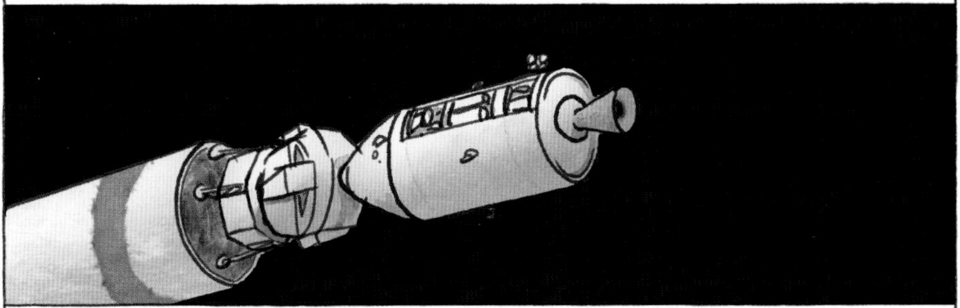

The crew had nicknamed Apollo 11 Columbia, after the fictional spacecraft Columbiad from good ol' Jules Verne's book *From the Earth to the Moon*. The lunar module's nickname was Eagle. Once Columbia and Eagle were joined, the crew could move between them through a hatch.

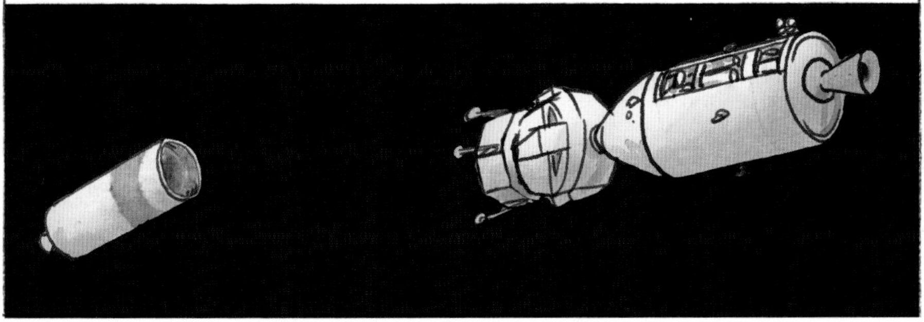

Three hours after launch, Armstrong, Aldrin, and Collins were about 1,200 mi (1,900 km) from Earth. The spacecraft slowly rolled broadside to the sun, preventing the sunny side from becoming dangerously hot and the shaded side from becoming dangerously cold. The maneuver was something like cooking a hot dog on a grill and was appropriately called the "barbecue roll."

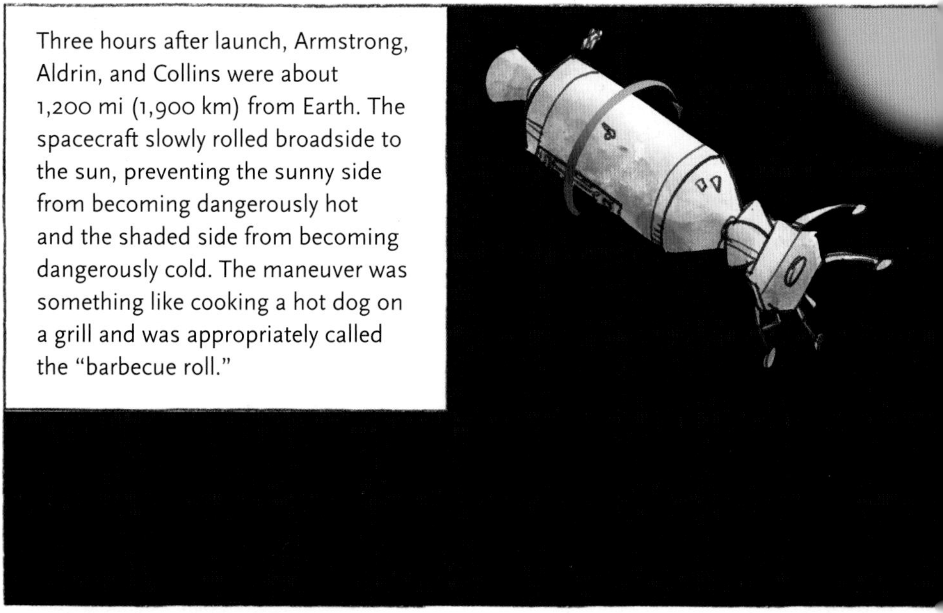

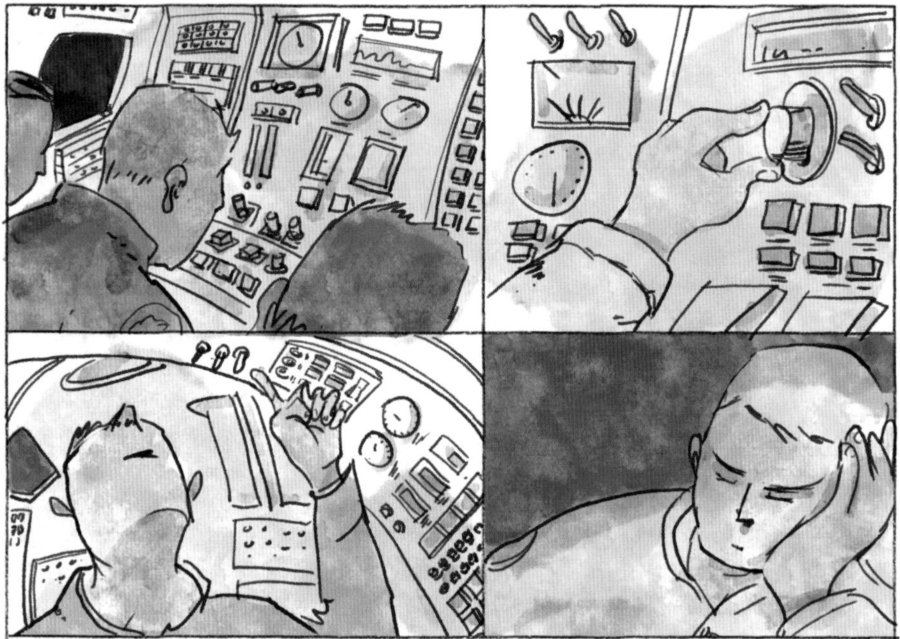

The three men no longer needed the helmets and space suits they'd worn as precautions against possible malfunction of the spacecraft during takeoff. They monitored gauges and unpacked equipment they'd need later. Fourteen hours after liftoff, they slept, dozing to the hums, creaks, and clicks of Apollo 11's equipment.

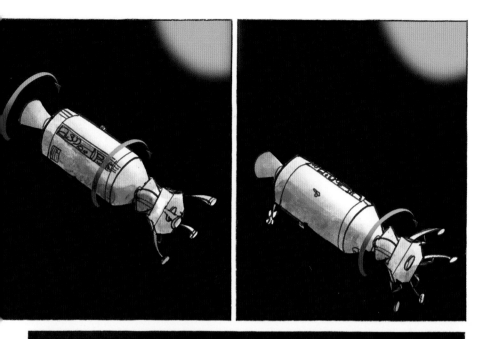

Every moment took Apollo 11 farther into space, but Earth's gravity still tugged, slowing it to a fraction of its top speed. This situation would be reversed on the third afternoon, when the moon would be closer and its gravity would pull the spacecraft toward it at increasingly higher speeds.

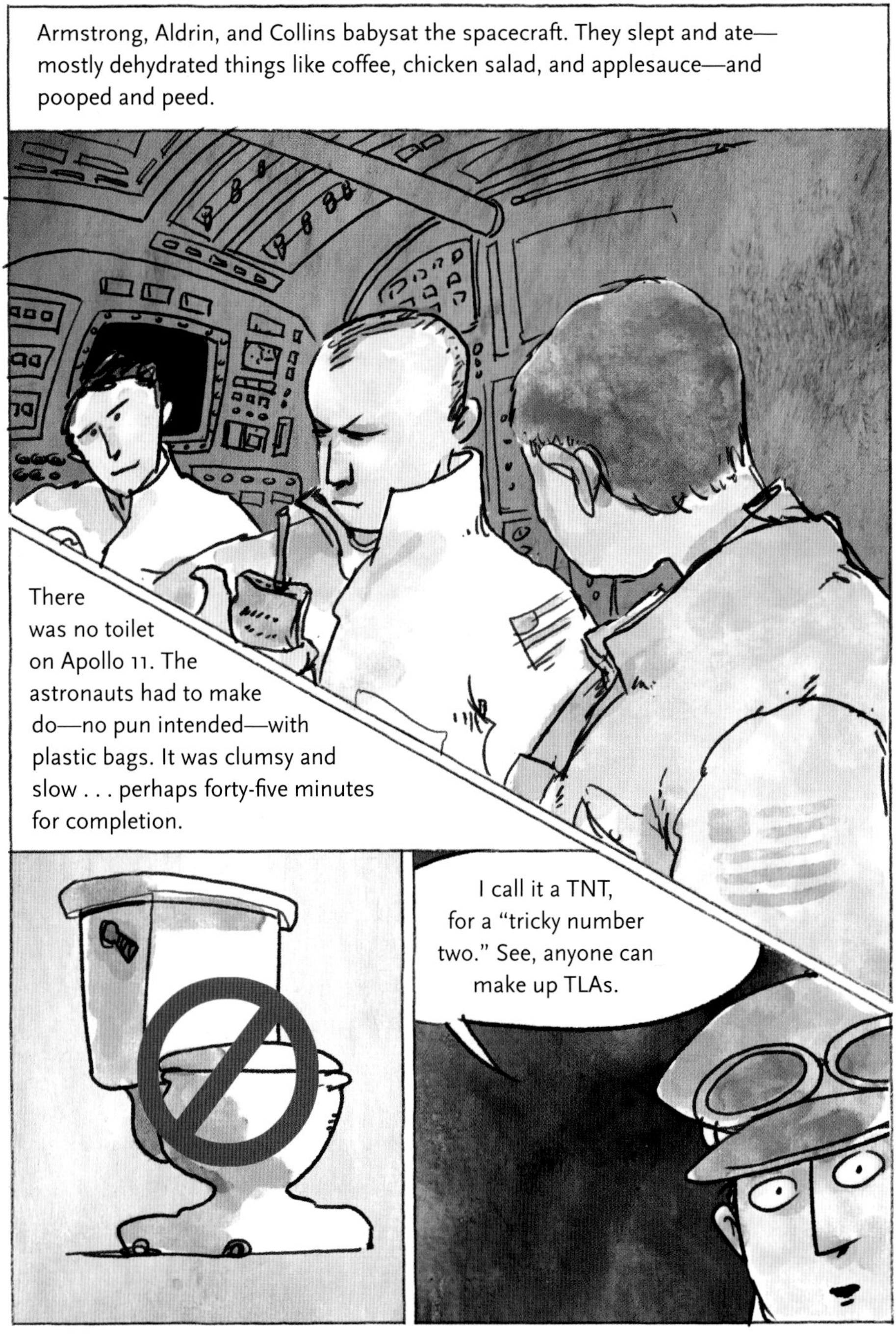
Armstrong, Aldrin, and Collins babysat the spacecraft. They slept and ate—mostly dehydrated things like coffee, chicken salad, and applesauce—and pooped and peed.
There was no toilet on Apollo 11. The astronauts had to make do—no pun intended—with plastic bags. It was clumsy and slow . . . perhaps forty-five minutes for completion.
I call it a TNT, for a "tricky number two." See, anyone can make up TLAs.

TNT could easily go wrong. On Apollo 10, something escaped from a bag, prompting an uncomfortable conversation among the three astronauts:

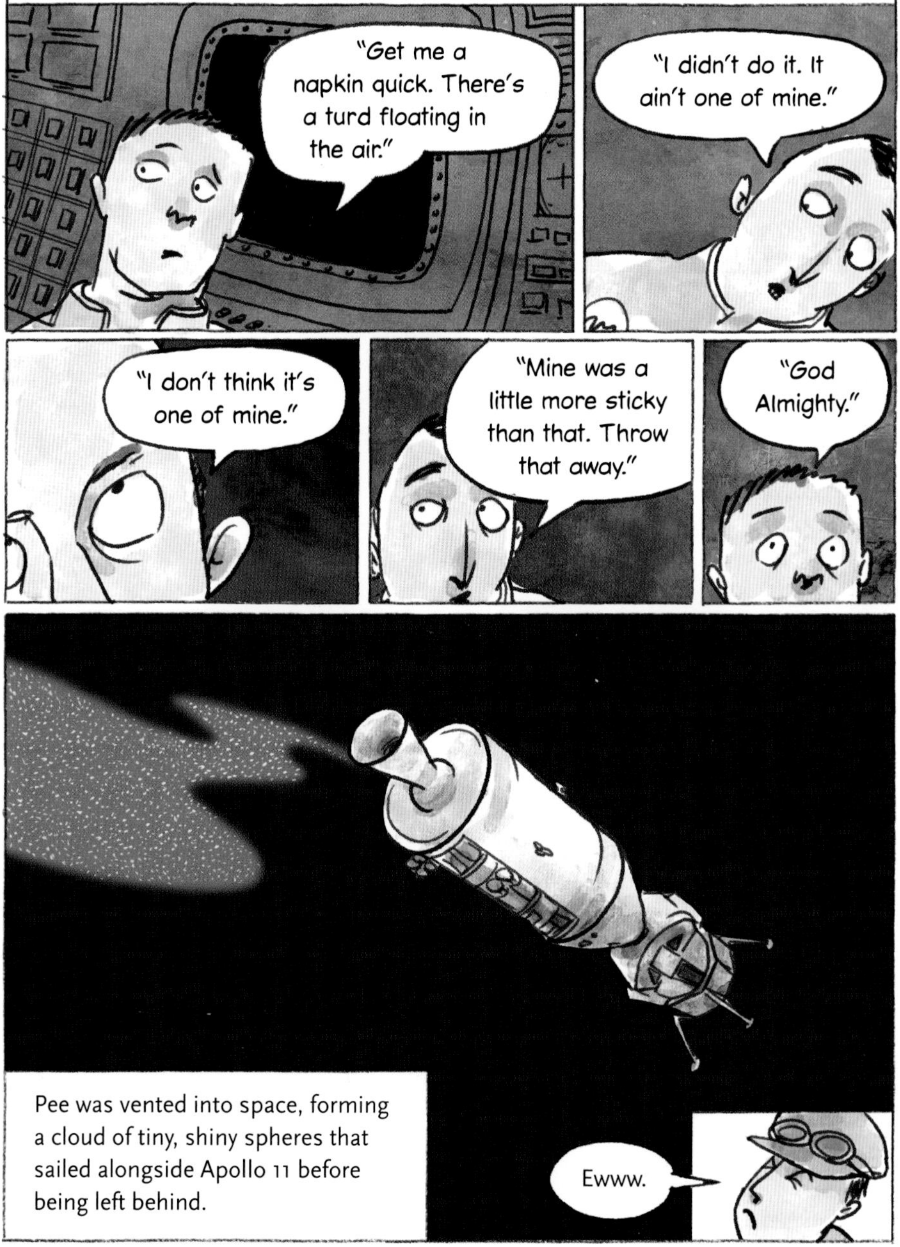
"Get me a napkin quick. There's a turd floating in the air."
"I didn't do it. It ain't one of mine."
"I don't think it's one of mine."
"Mine was a little more sticky than that. Throw that away."
"God Almighty."
Pee was vented into space, forming a cloud of tiny, shiny spheres that sailed alongside Apollo 11 before being left behind.
Ewww.

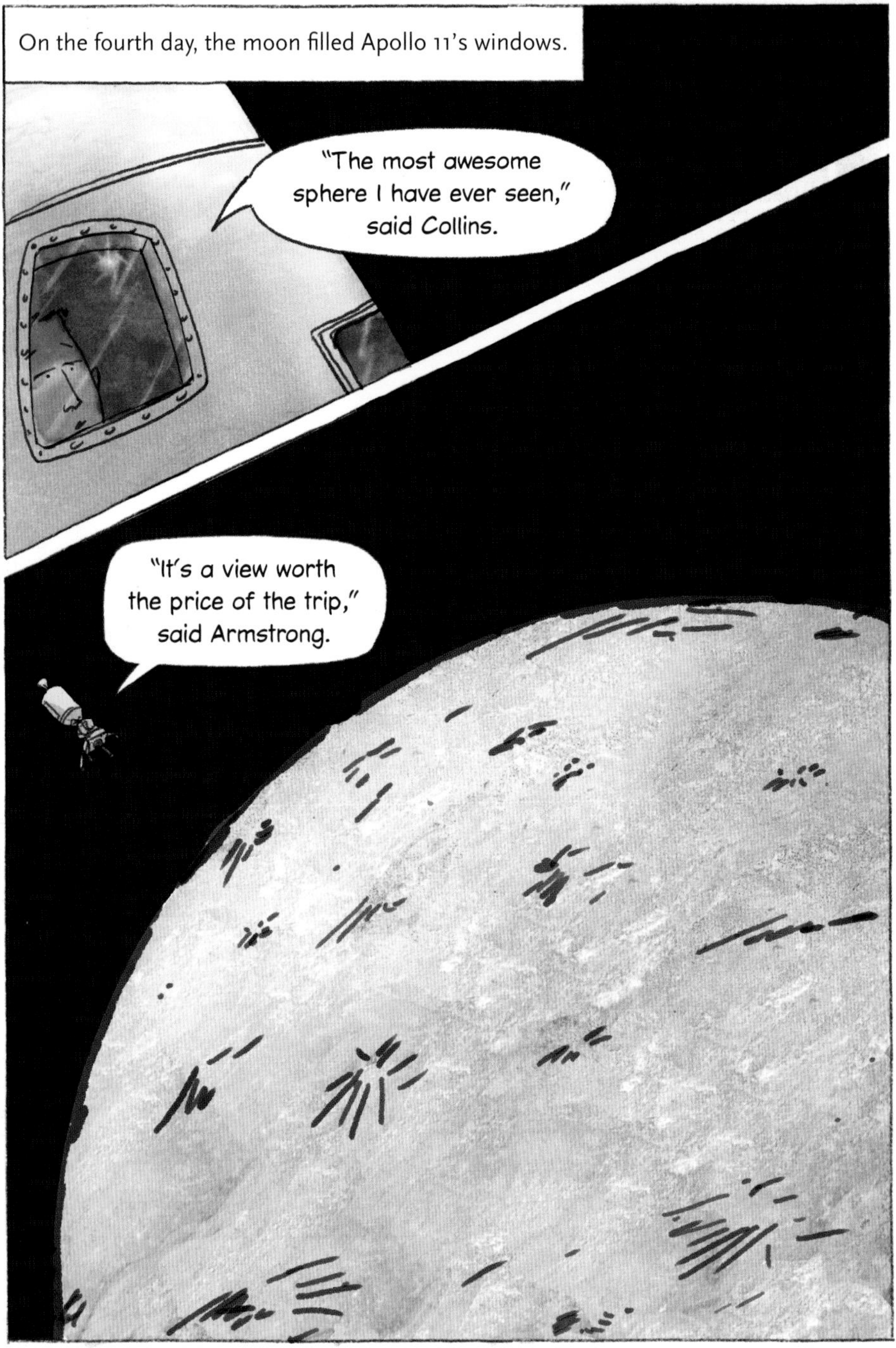
On the fourth day, the moon filled Apollo 11's windows.
"The most awesome sphere I have ever seen," said Collins.
"It's a view worth the price of the trip," said Armstrong.

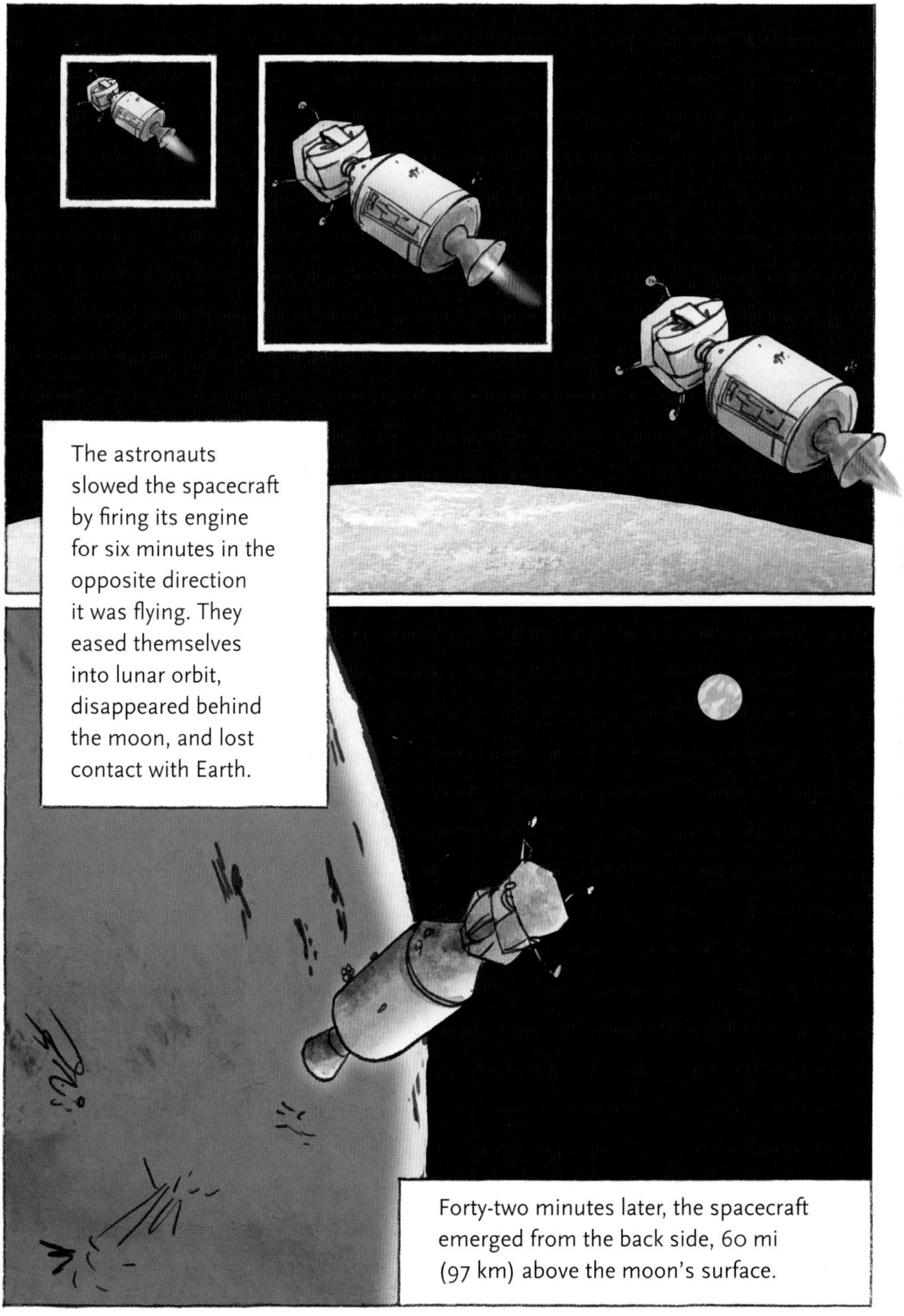
The astronauts slowed the spacecraft by firing its engine for six minutes in the opposite direction it was flying. They eased themselves into lunar orbit, disappeared behind the moon, and lost contact with Earth.
Forty-two minutes later, the spacecraft emerged from the back side, 60 mi (97 km) above the moon's surface.

As Apollo 11 orbited the moon, Armstrong and Aldrin floated from the command module into the lunar module.

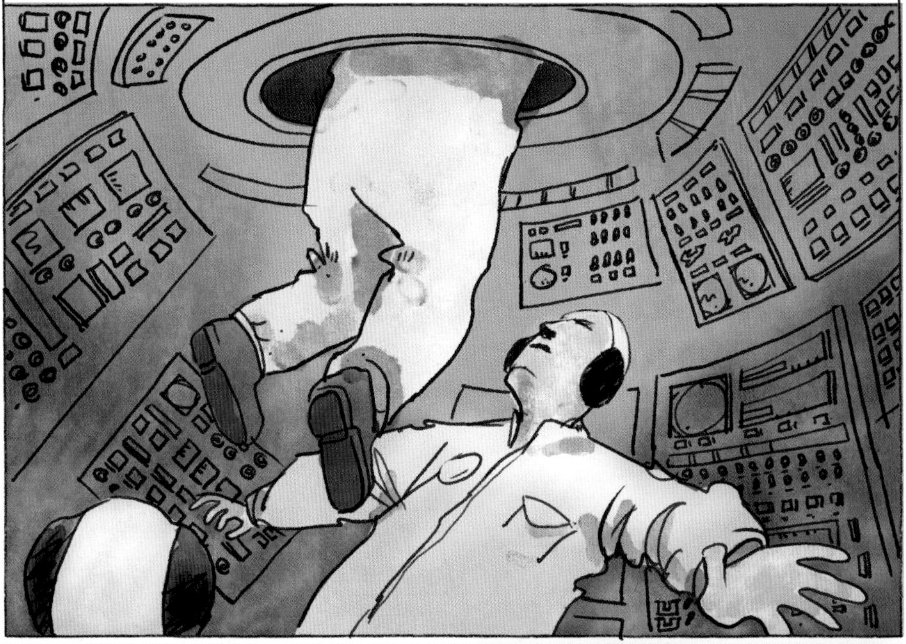

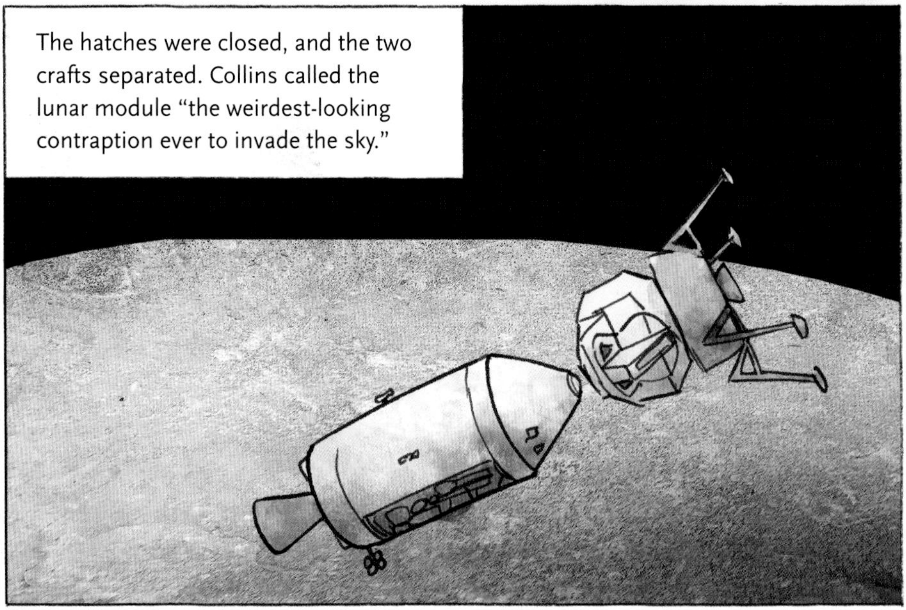
The hatches were closed, and the two crafts separated. Collins called the lunar module "the weirdest-looking contraption ever to invade the sky."

Eagle was designed to land like a stork. Four long legs stuck out of a clumsy body blistered with antennae and radar dishes, rocket engines, thrusters, floodlights, a docking target, and two triangular pilots' windows, each with 2 sq ft (0.2 sq m) of viewing area. Much of the lunar module was wrapped in colorful, insulating foil to combat the heat of the sun.

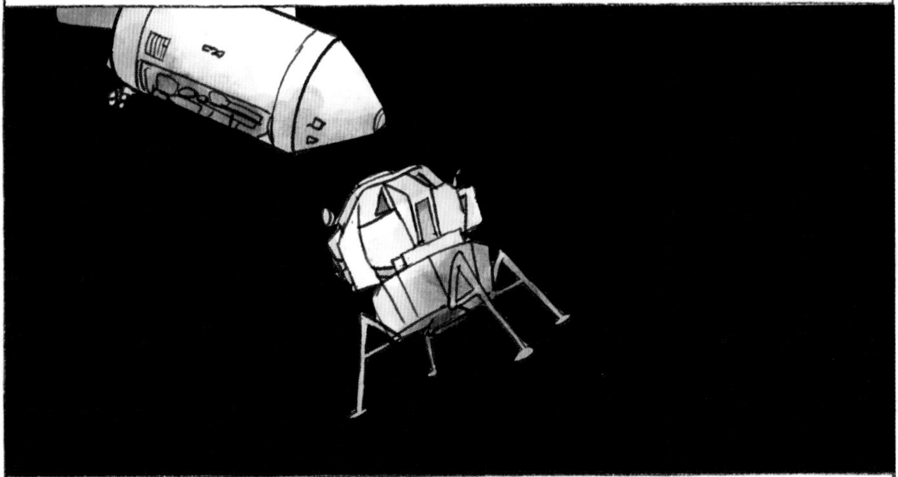

There was nothing aerodynamic about it, because it was never designed to fly through air. Space lacks friction-making air or atmosphere, so nothing on Eagle had to be streamlined.

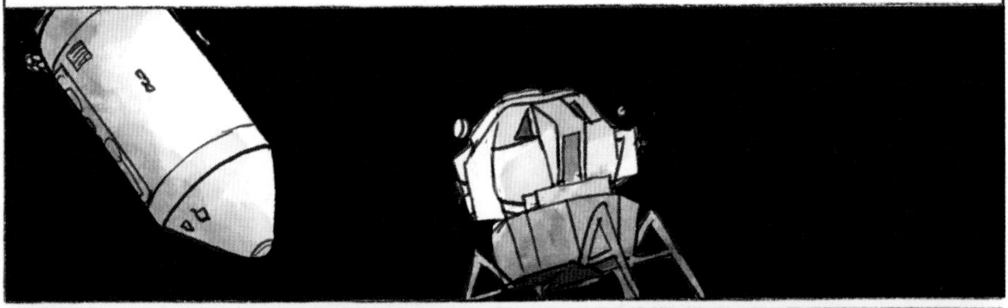

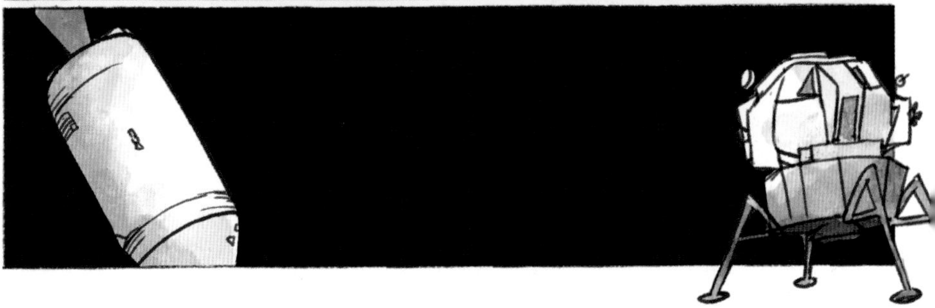

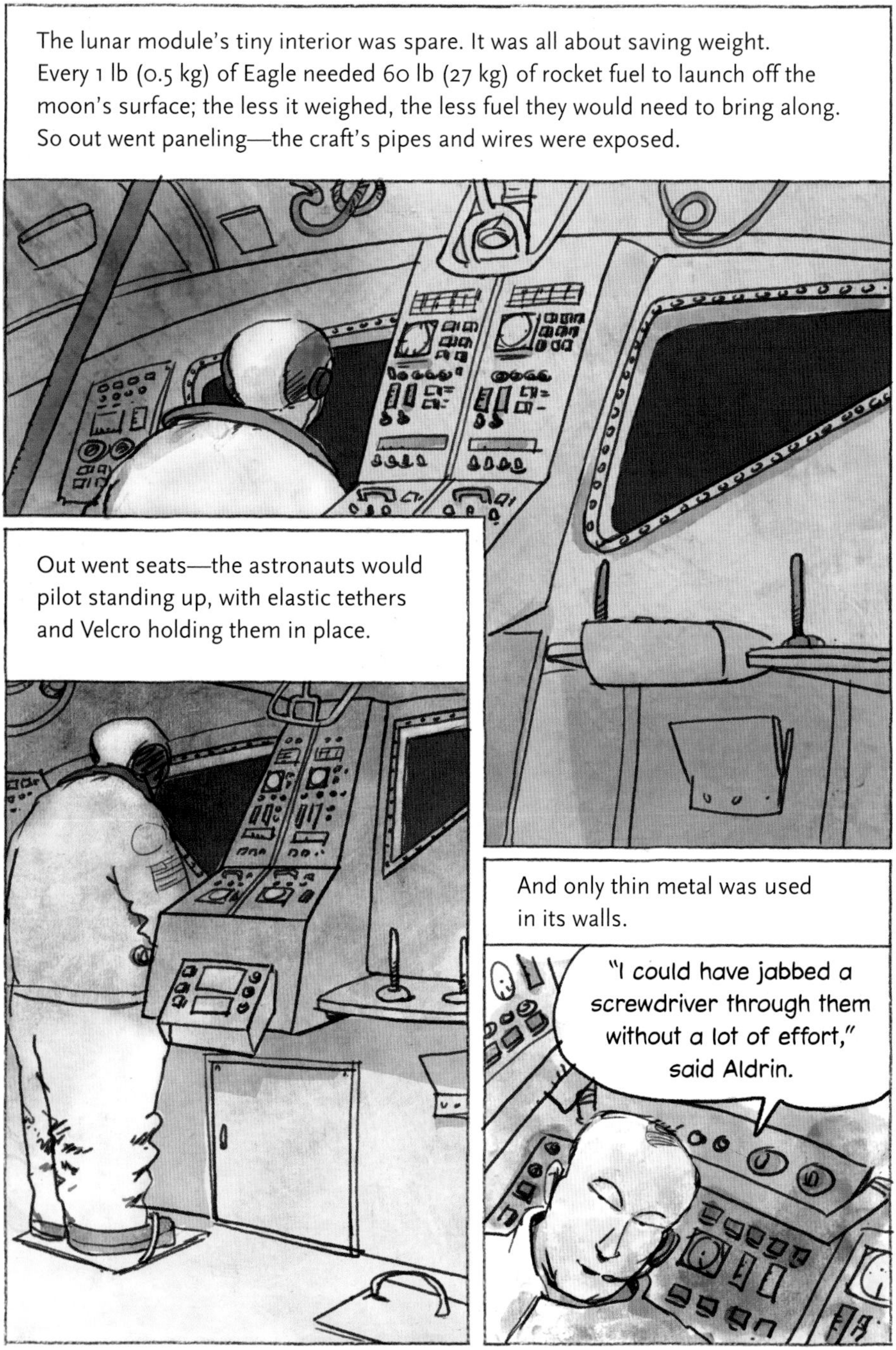
The lunar module's tiny interior was spare. It was all about saving weight. Every 1 lb (0.5 kg) of Eagle needed 60 lb (27 kg) of rocket fuel to launch off the moon's surface; the less it weighed, the less fuel they would need to bring along. So out went paneling—the craft's pipes and wires were exposed.
Out went seats—the astronauts would pilot standing up, with elastic tethers and Velcro holding them in place.
And only thin metal was used in its walls.
"I could have jabbed a screwdriver through them without a lot of effort," said Aldrin.

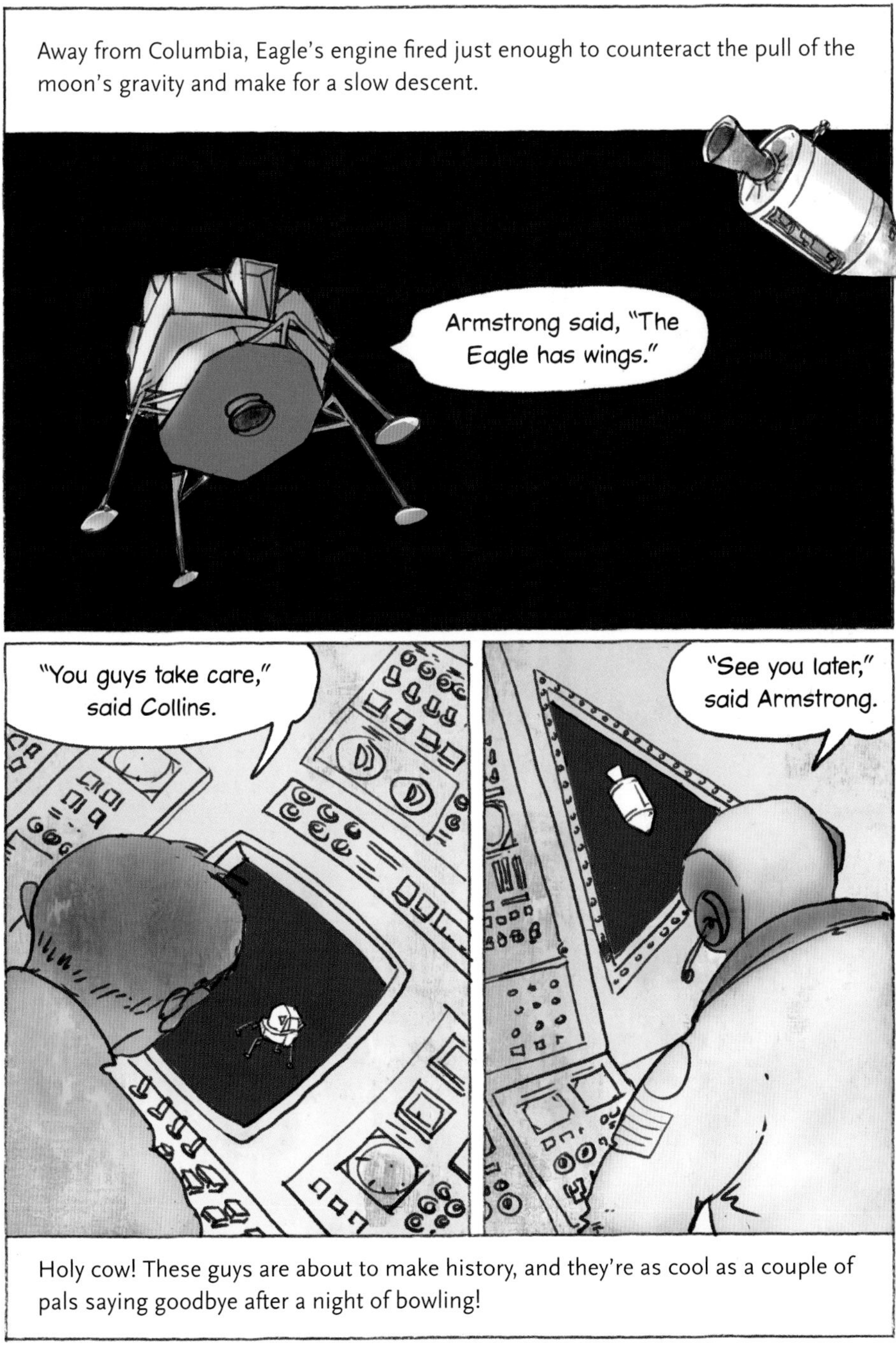
Away from Columbia, Eagle's engine fired just enough to counteract the pull of the moon's gravity and make for a slow descent.
Armstrong said, "The Eagle has wings."
"You guys take care," said Collins.
"See you later," said Armstrong.
Holy cow! These guys are about to make history, and they're as cool as a couple of pals saying goodbye after a night of bowling!

Eagle flew backward, with its two cabin windows parallel to the moon, staring up at Earth. As the lunar module descended, Armstrong slowly turned its legs toward the moon's surface.

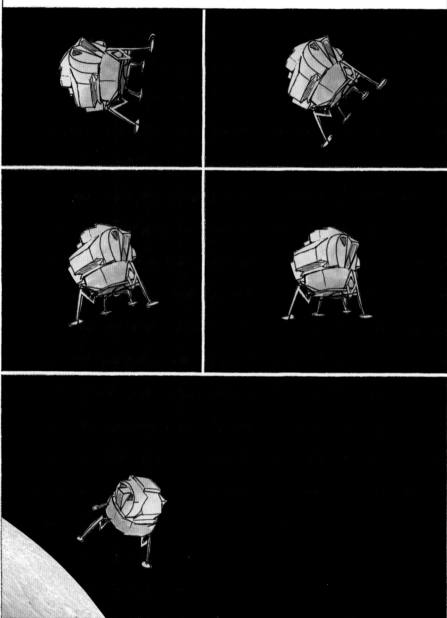

The astronauts could see bleached gray craters. At about 8 mi (13 km) from the moon's surface, the astronauts and the mission engineers back on Earth had to decide if the plan was working. The decision to land on the moon or return to Columbia would be final, because there wasn't enough fuel for a second chance.

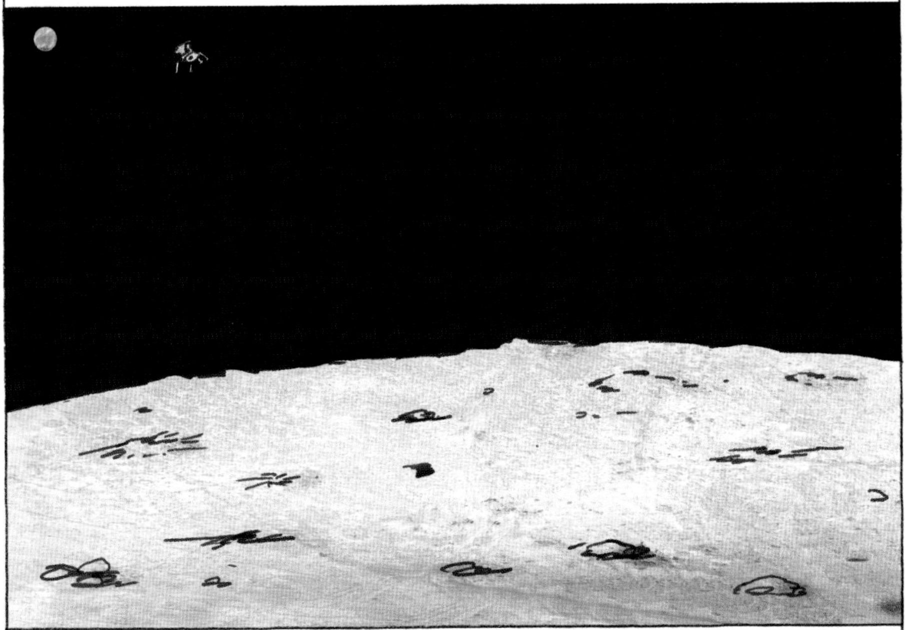

From the mission control center in Houston came the message "You're go for powered descent," which was astronaut-speak for "Things are good . . . go for it!"

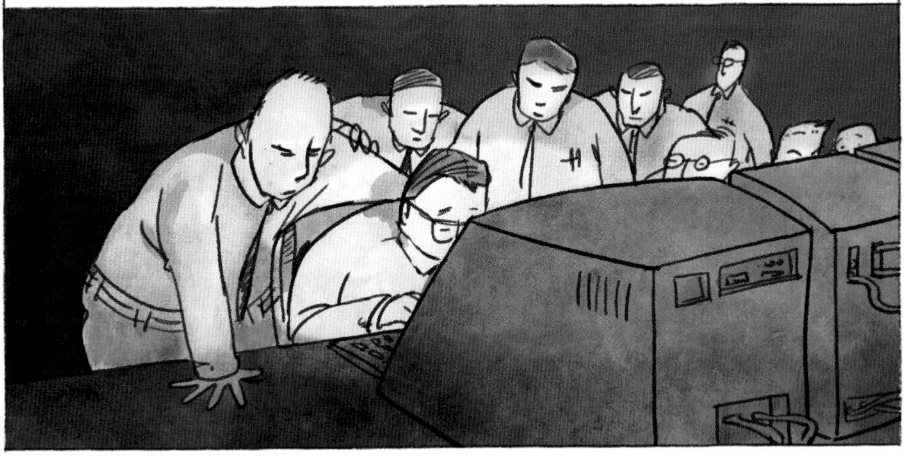

They headed down, and wouldn't you know, something went wrong . . . a light on Eagle's control panel flashed a warning: A computer was overloading. Engineers in Houston decided to ignore it . . .

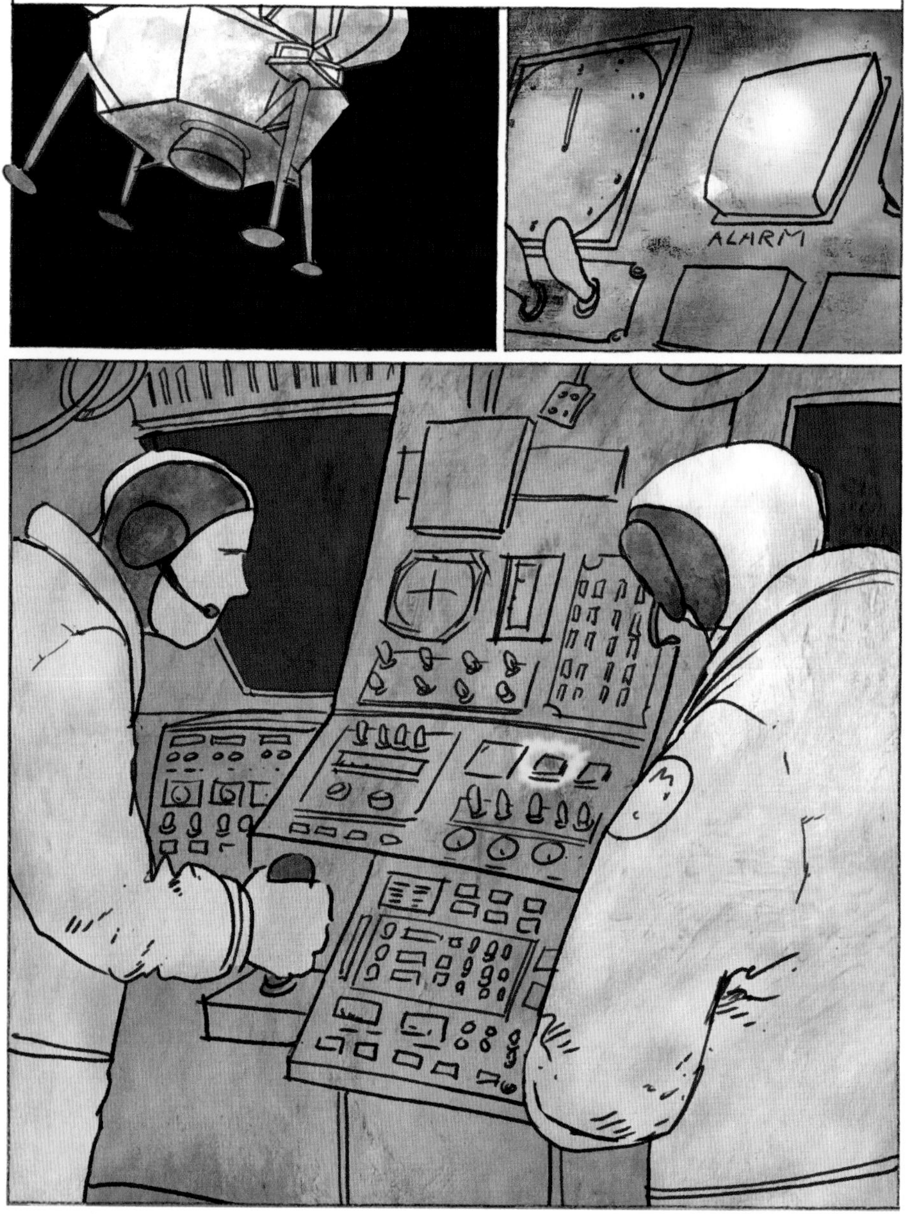
ALARM

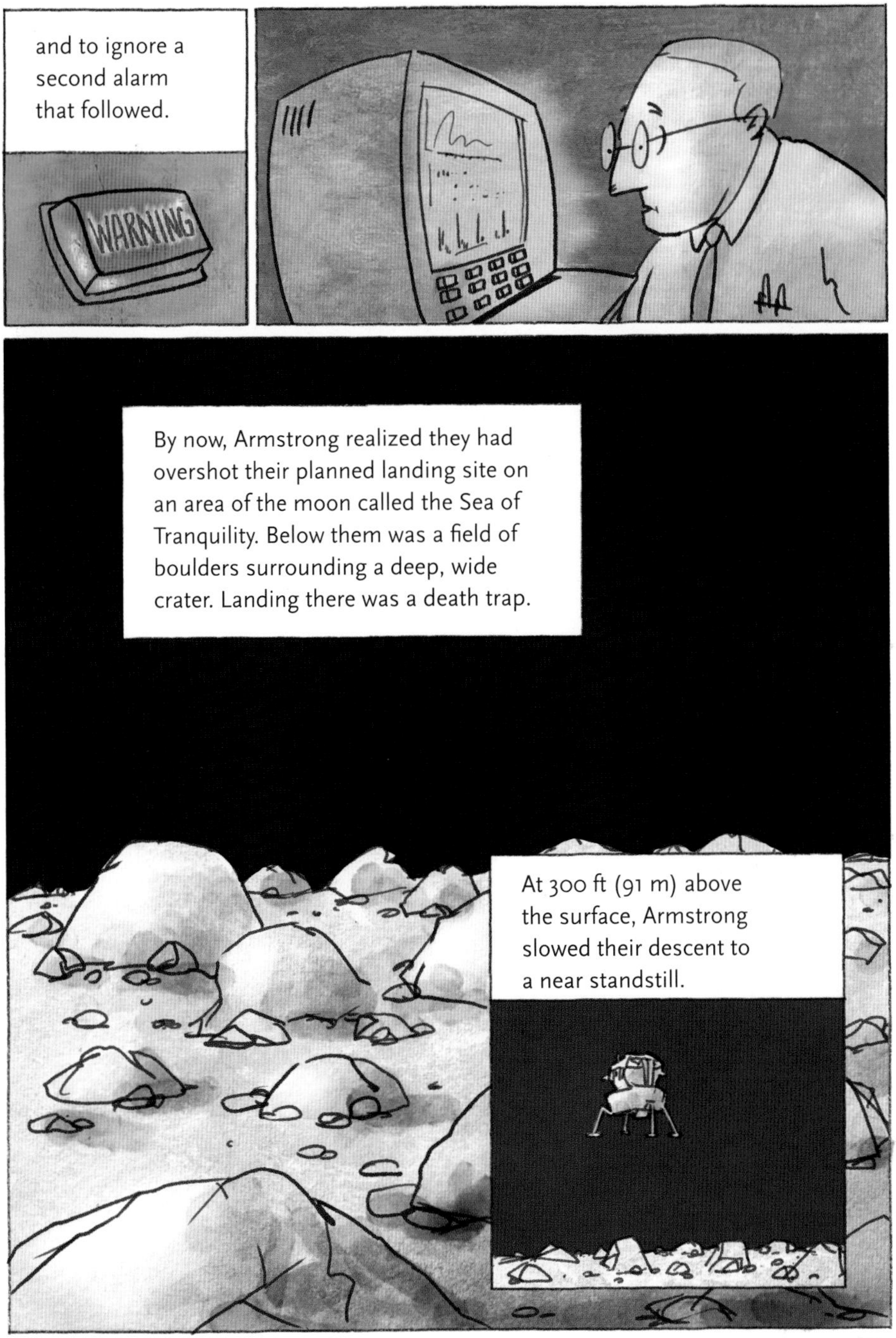
and to ignore a second alarm that followed.
WARNING
By now, Armstrong realized they had overshot their planned landing site on an area of the moon called the Sea of Tranquility. Below them was a field of boulders surrounding a deep, wide crater. Landing there was a death trap.
At 300 ft (91 m) above the surface, Armstrong slowed their descent to a near standstill.

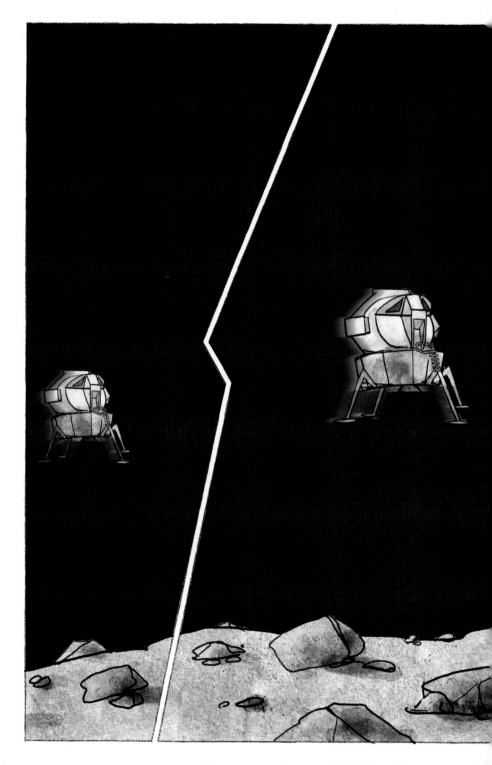

He had the idea to skim Eagle over the surface like a dragonfly over a pond. It was something NASA had never planned or practiced.

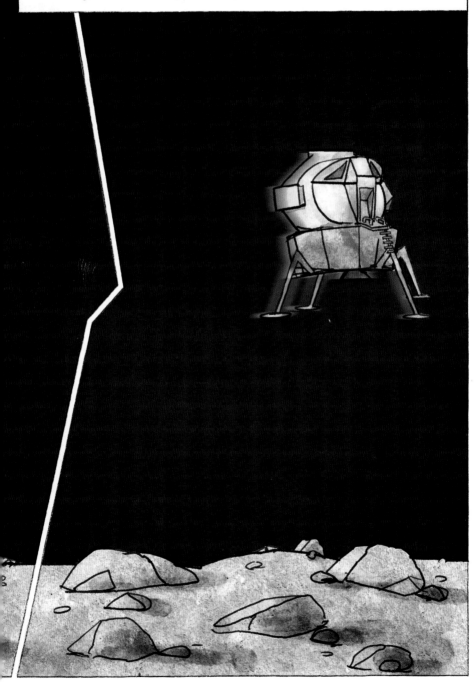

While Armstrong searched for a friendlier landing spot on the Sea of Tranquility, Aldrin called out the altitude of the lunar module in feet, the speed of descent in feet per second, and the horizontal speed in feet per second.

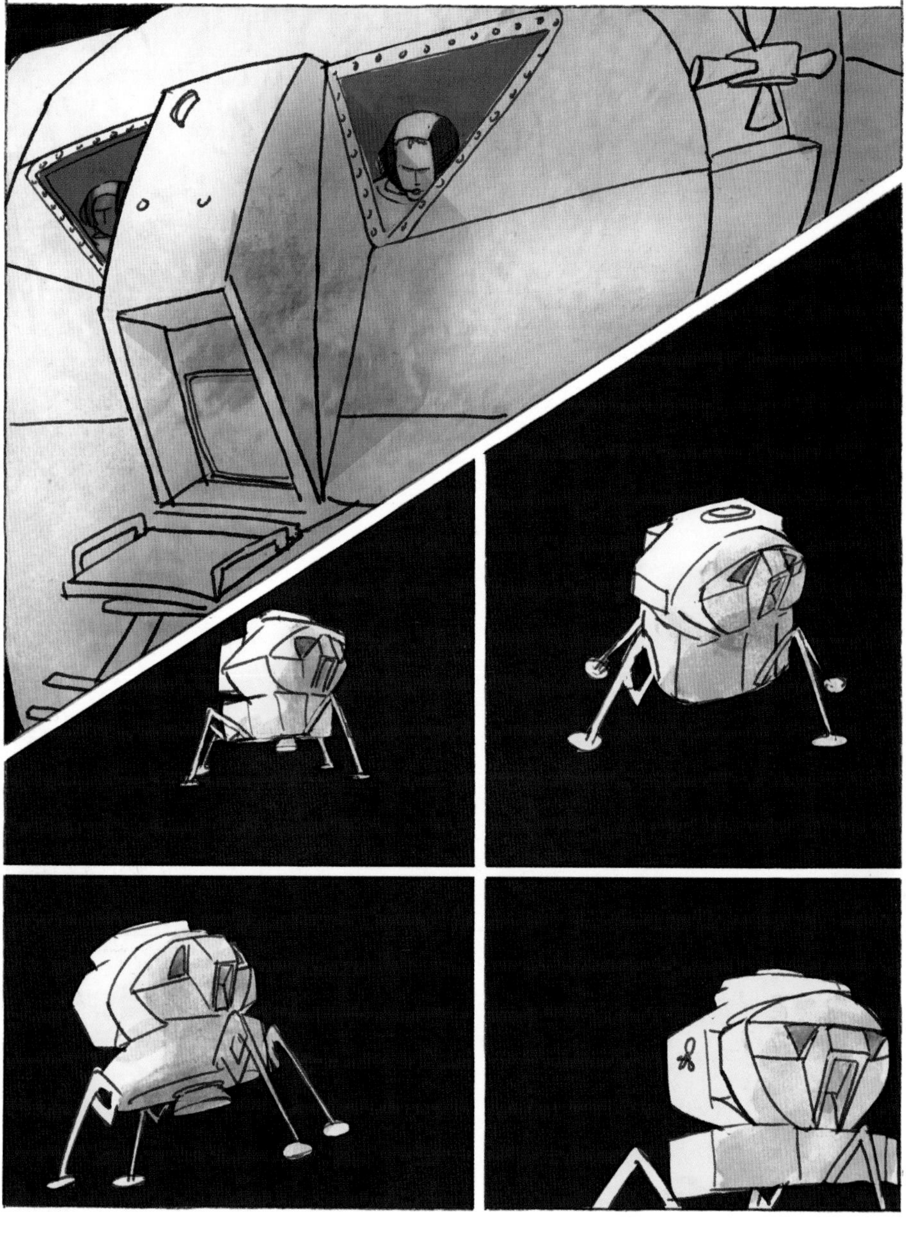

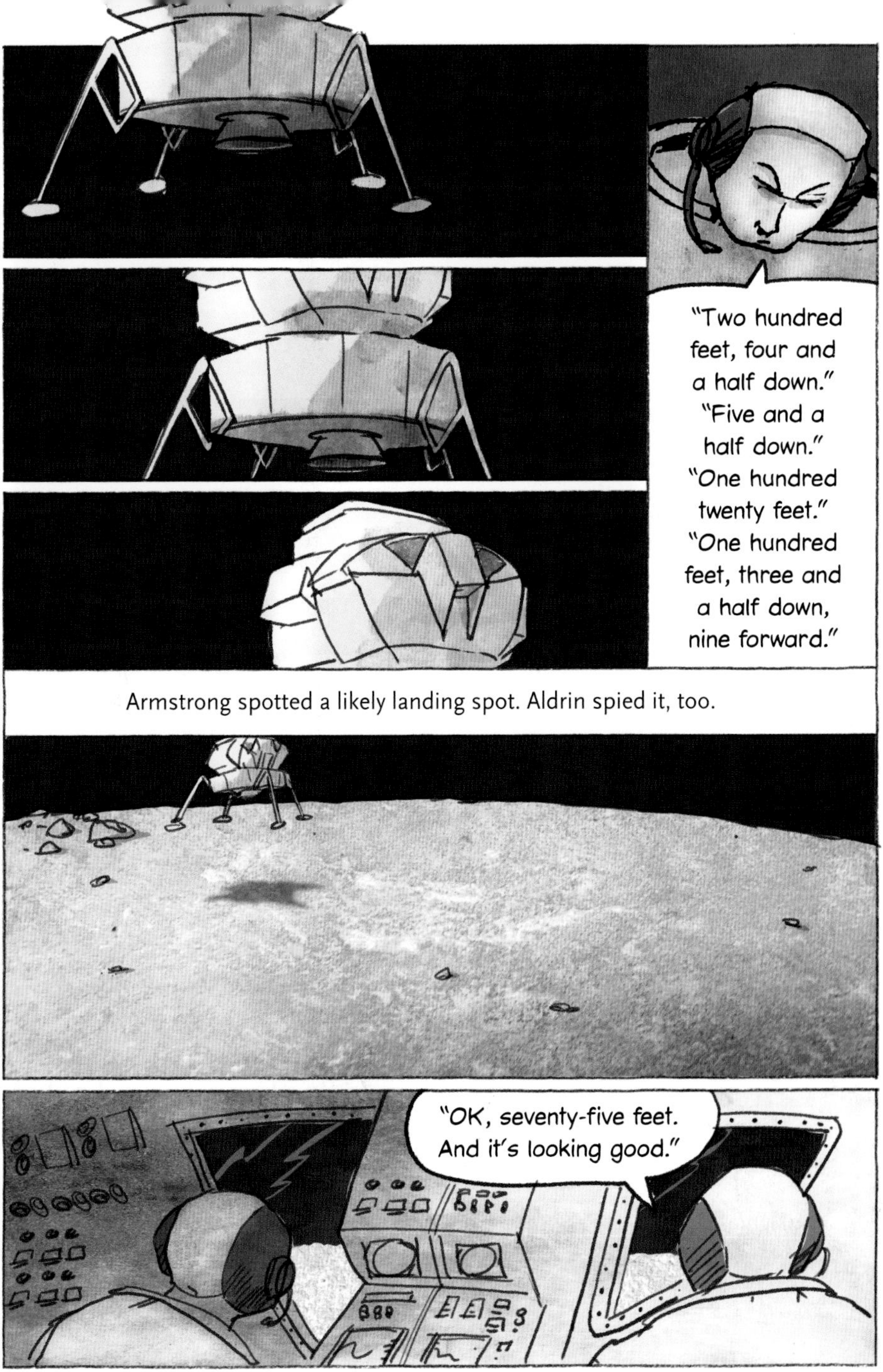
"Two hundred feet, four and a half down."
"Five and a half down."
"One hundred twenty feet."
"One hundred feet, three and a half down, nine forward."
Armstrong spotted a likely landing spot. Aldrin spied it, too.
"OK, seventy-five feet. And it's looking good."

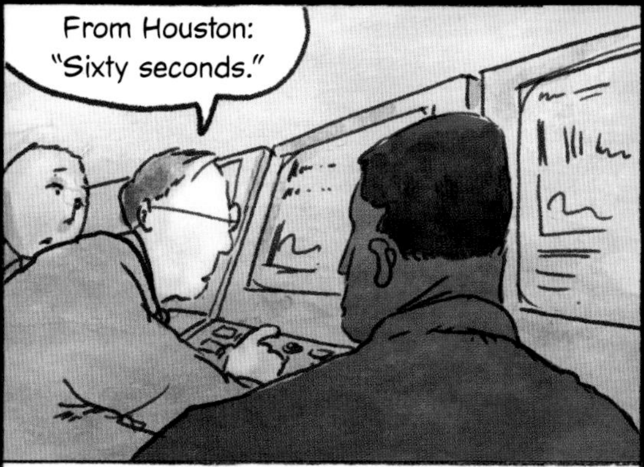
From Houston:
"Sixty seconds."

There was only sixty seconds of fuel left before power shut down. Mission control was frantic. Would Eagle run out of fuel and crash? Armstrong brushed off the worry. He was sure an unpowered drop of less than 50 ft (15 m) in moon's weak gravity wouldn't damage the lunar module.

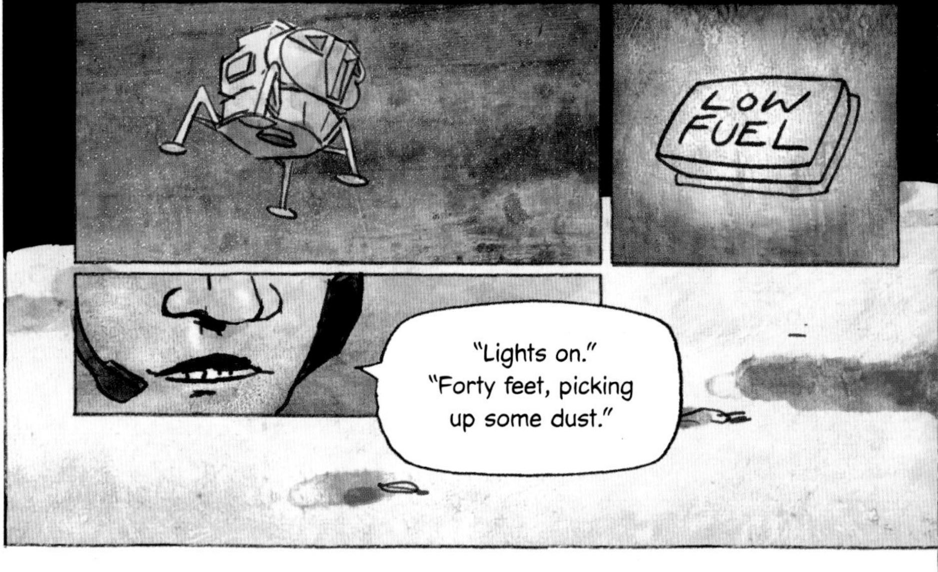
LOW
FUEL
"Lights on."
"Forty feet, picking up some dust."

From Earth: "Thirty seconds." "Contact light." "OK. Engine stop."
"Houston, Tranquility Base here. The Eagle has landed," said Armstrong.
It happened at 4:17:42 P.M. (EDT), on Sunday, July 20, 1969.

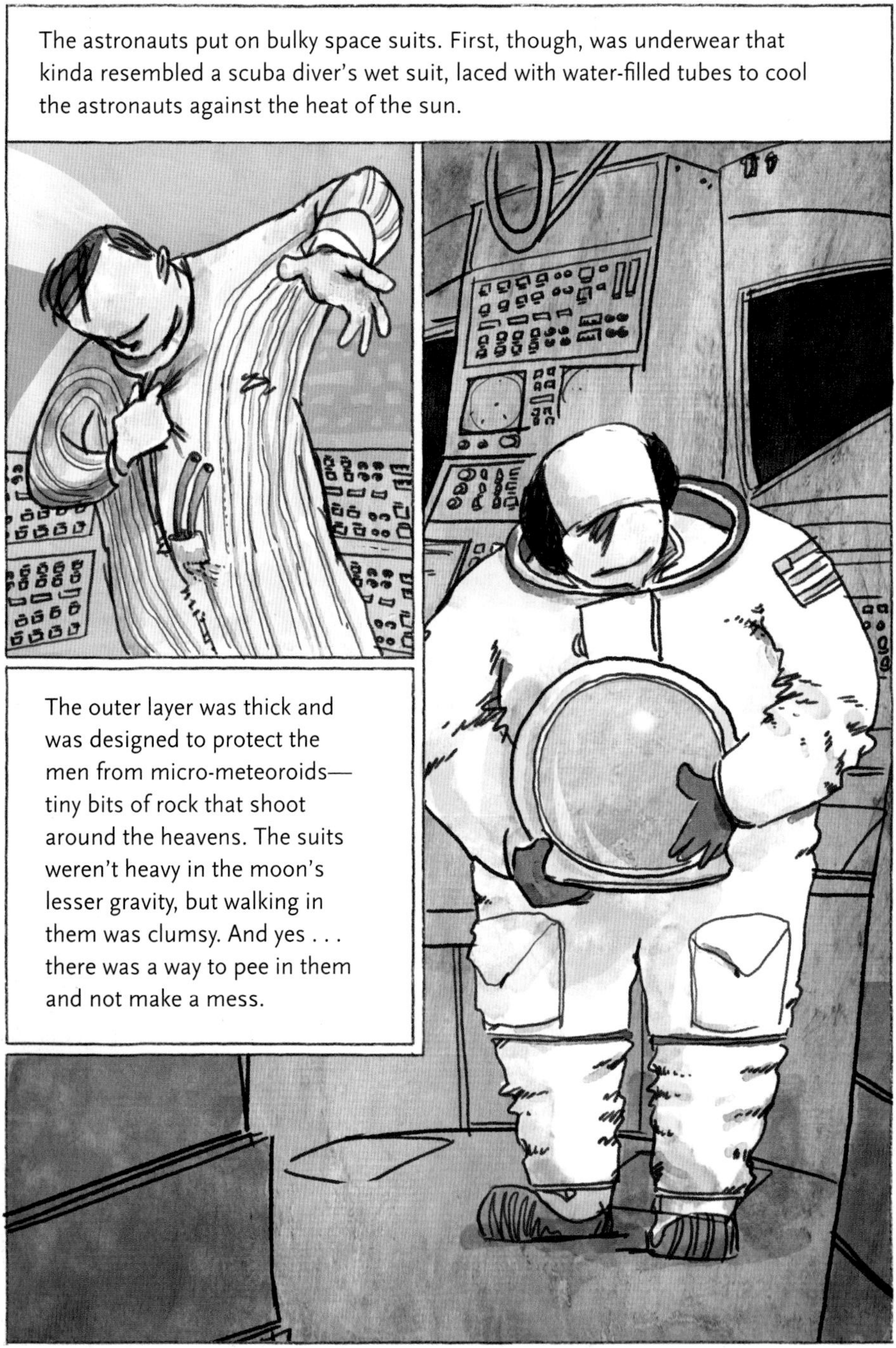
The astronauts put on bulky space suits. First, though, was underwear that kinda resembled a scuba diver's wet suit, laced with water-filled tubes to cool the astronauts against the heat of the sun.
The outer layer was thick and was designed to protect the men from micro-meteoroids—tiny bits of rock that shoot around the heavens. The suits weren't heavy in the moon's lesser gravity, but walking in them was clumsy. And yes . . . there was a way to pee in them and not make a mess.

Six hours after landing, Eagle's hatch opened, and Armstrong climbed out and down a ladder toward the lunar surface.

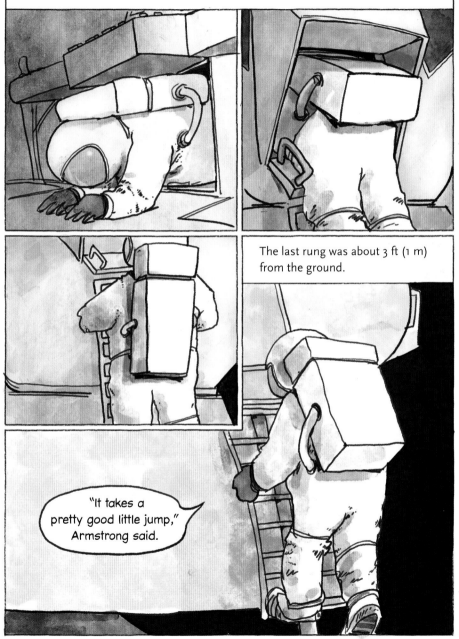

The last rung was about 3 ft (1 m) from the ground.

"It takes a pretty good little jump," Armstrong said.

He dangled his left foot off the rung and then stepped off, drawn to the surface by the moon's modest gravity. His boot struck the surface, and lunar dust blew out in a fine spray.

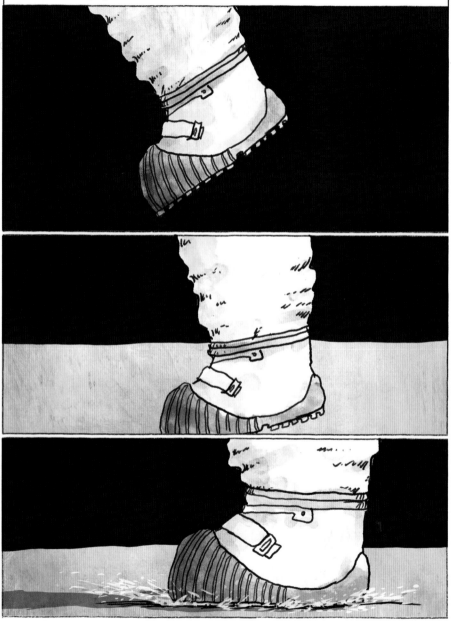

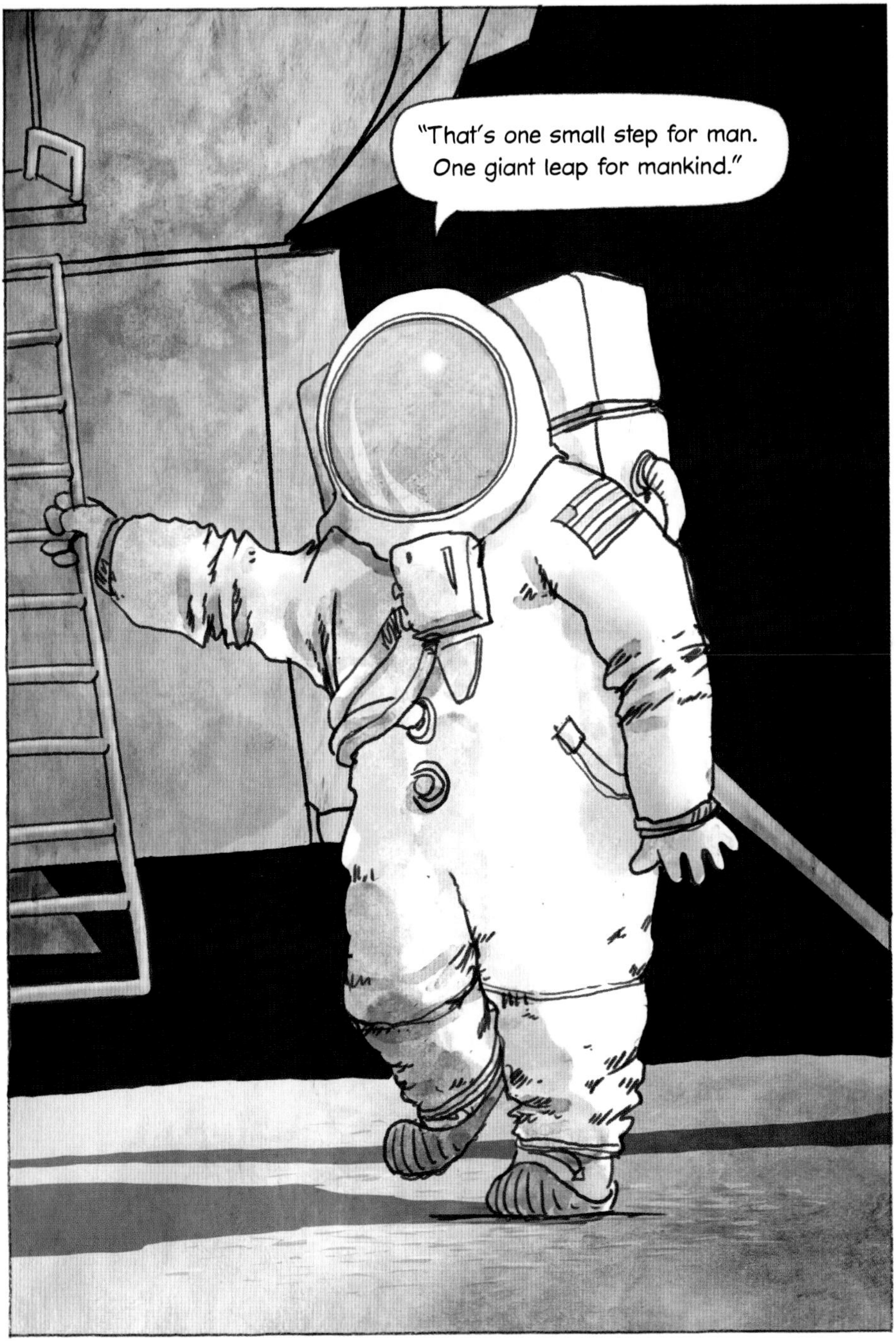
"That's one small step for man. One giant leap for mankind."

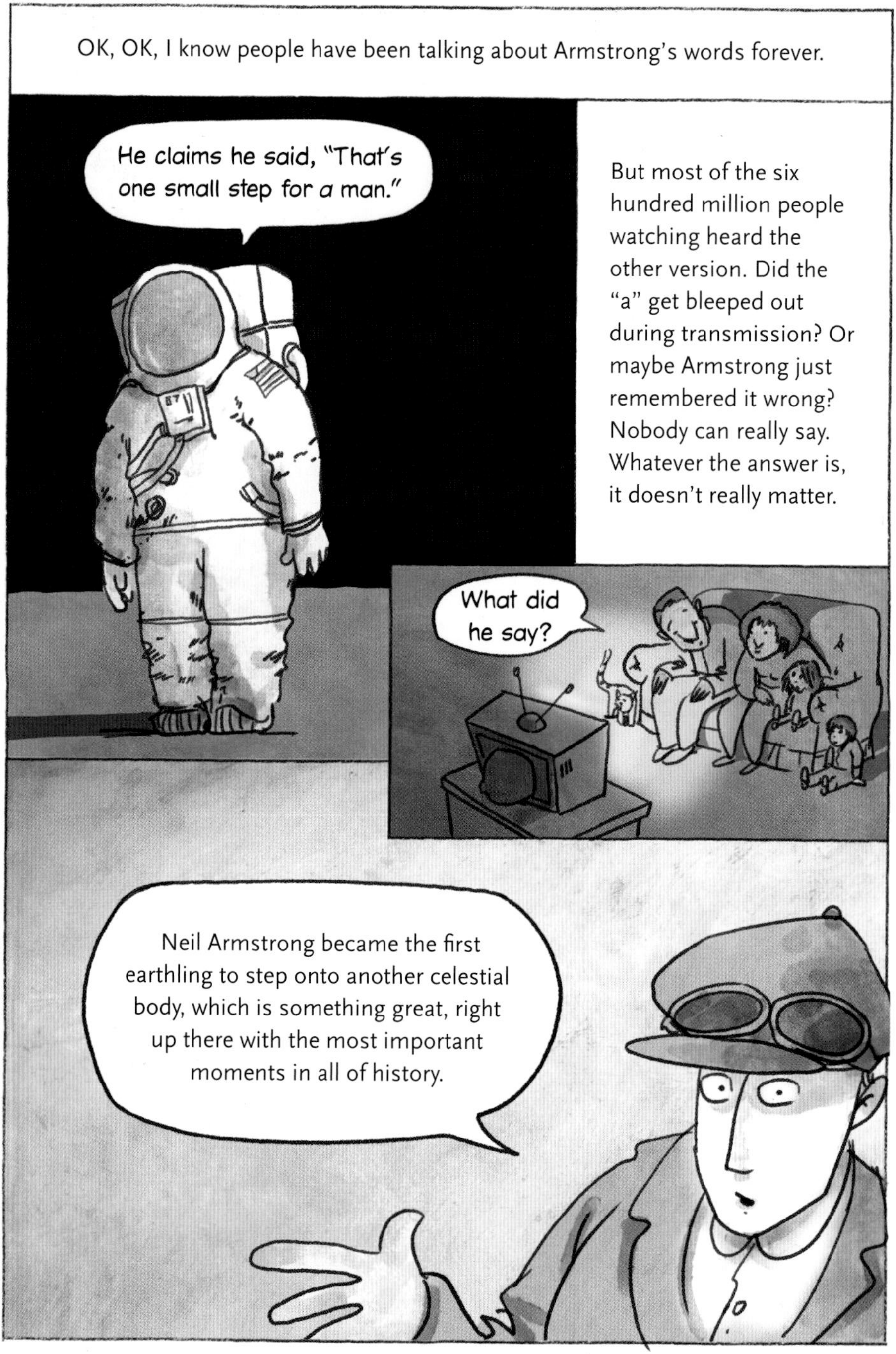
OK, OK, I know people have been talking about Armstrong's words forever.
He claims he said, "That's one small step for *a* man."
But most of the six hundred million people watching heard the other version. Did the "a" get bleeped out during transmission? Or maybe Armstrong just remembered it wrong? Nobody can really say. Whatever the answer is, it doesn't really matter.
What did he say?
Neil Armstrong became the first earthling to step onto another celestial body, which is something great, right up there with the most important moments in all of history.

Twenty minutes later, Buzz Aldrin joined him.

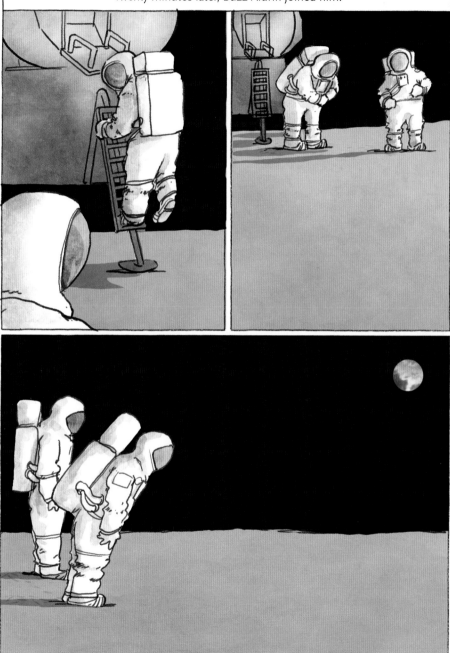

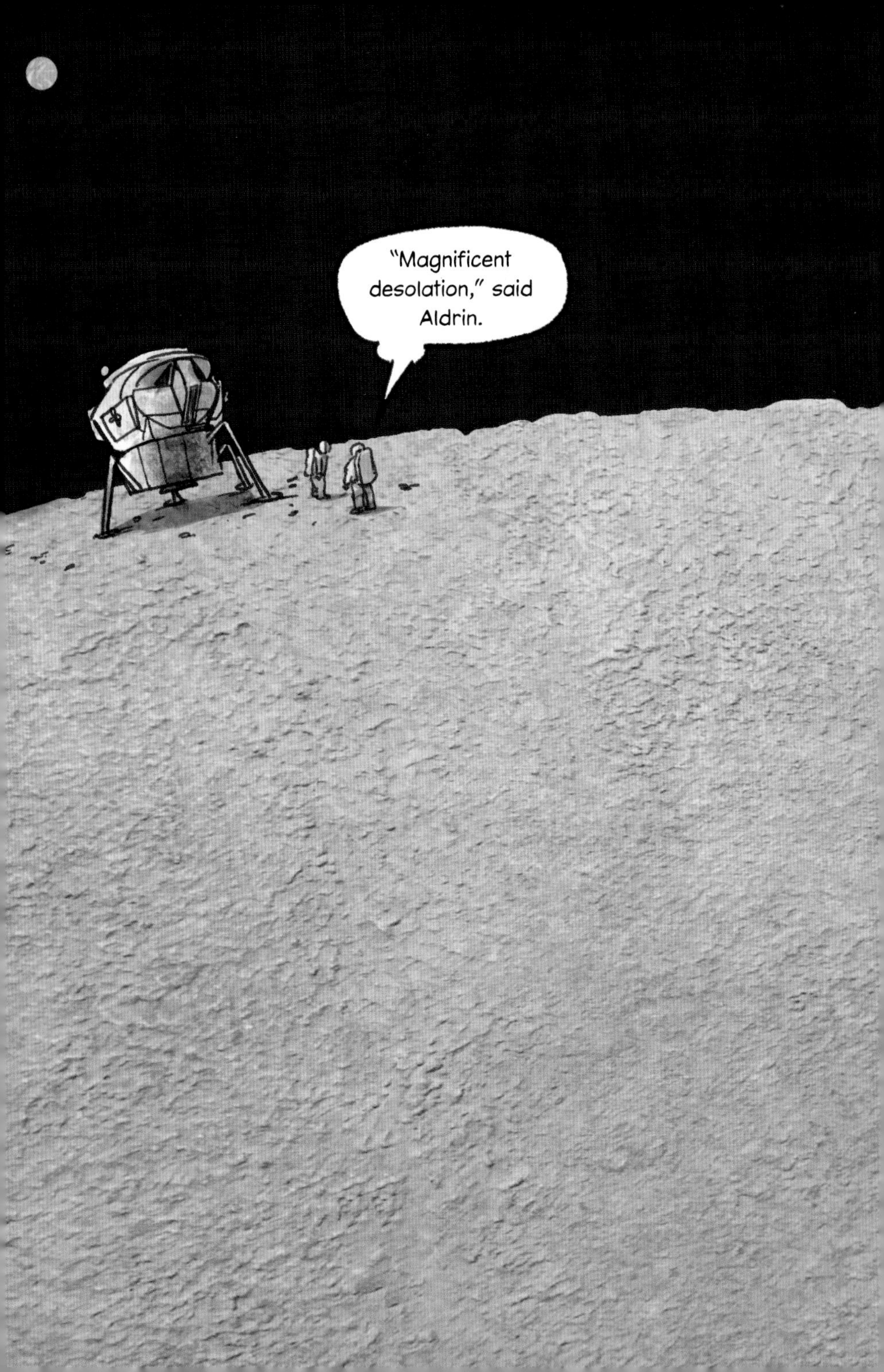
"Magnificent desolation," said Aldrin.

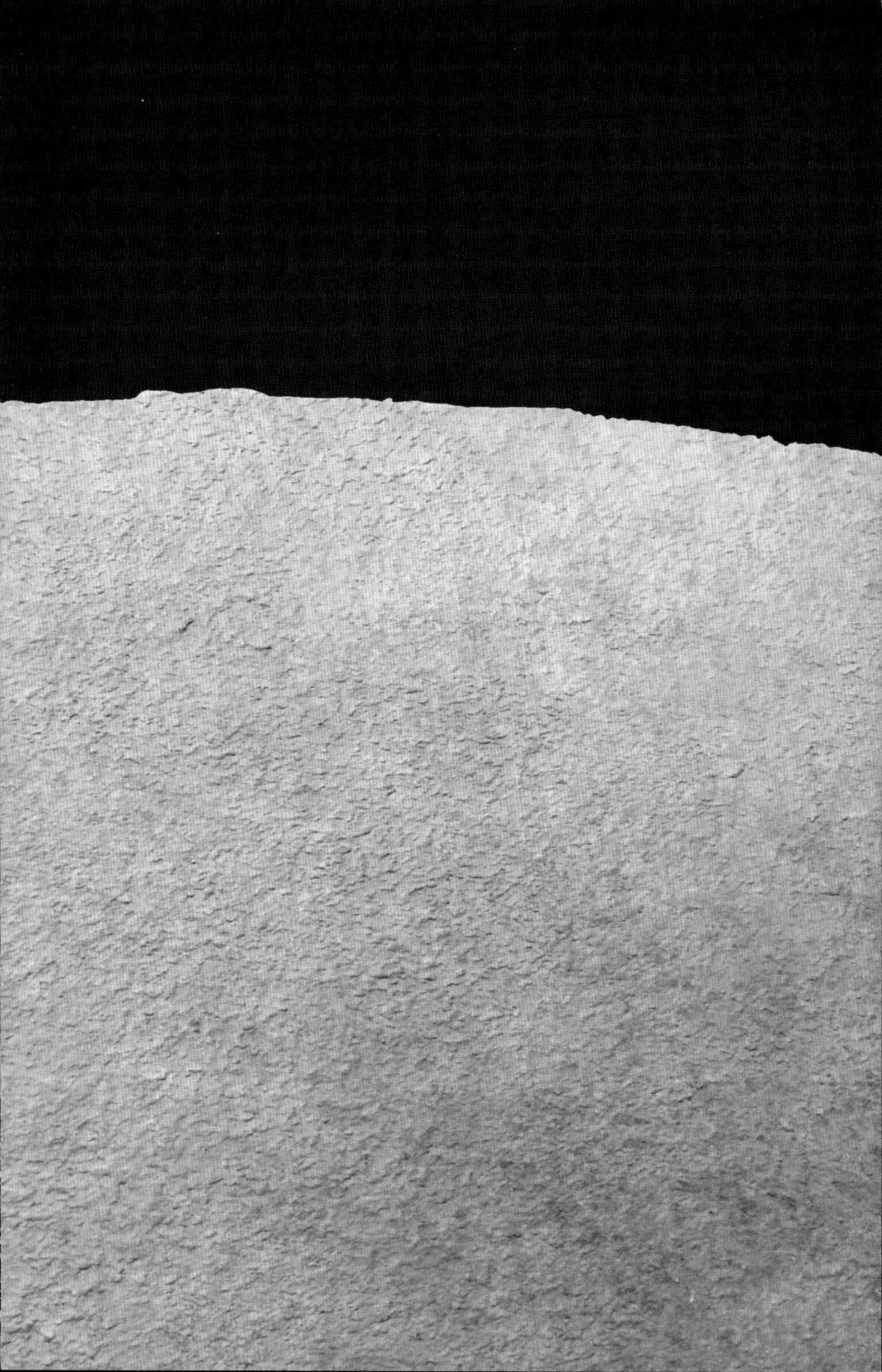

They read a plaque attached to a leg of the lunar module. "Here men from the planet Earth first set foot upon the moon. July 1969 A.D. We came in peace for all mankind."

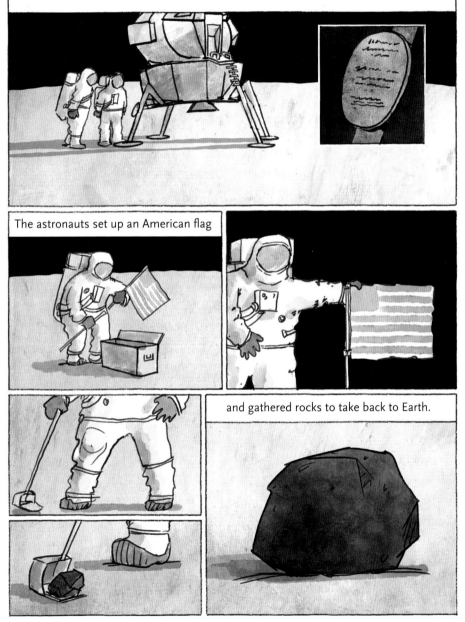

The astronauts set up an American flag

and gathered rocks to take back to Earth.

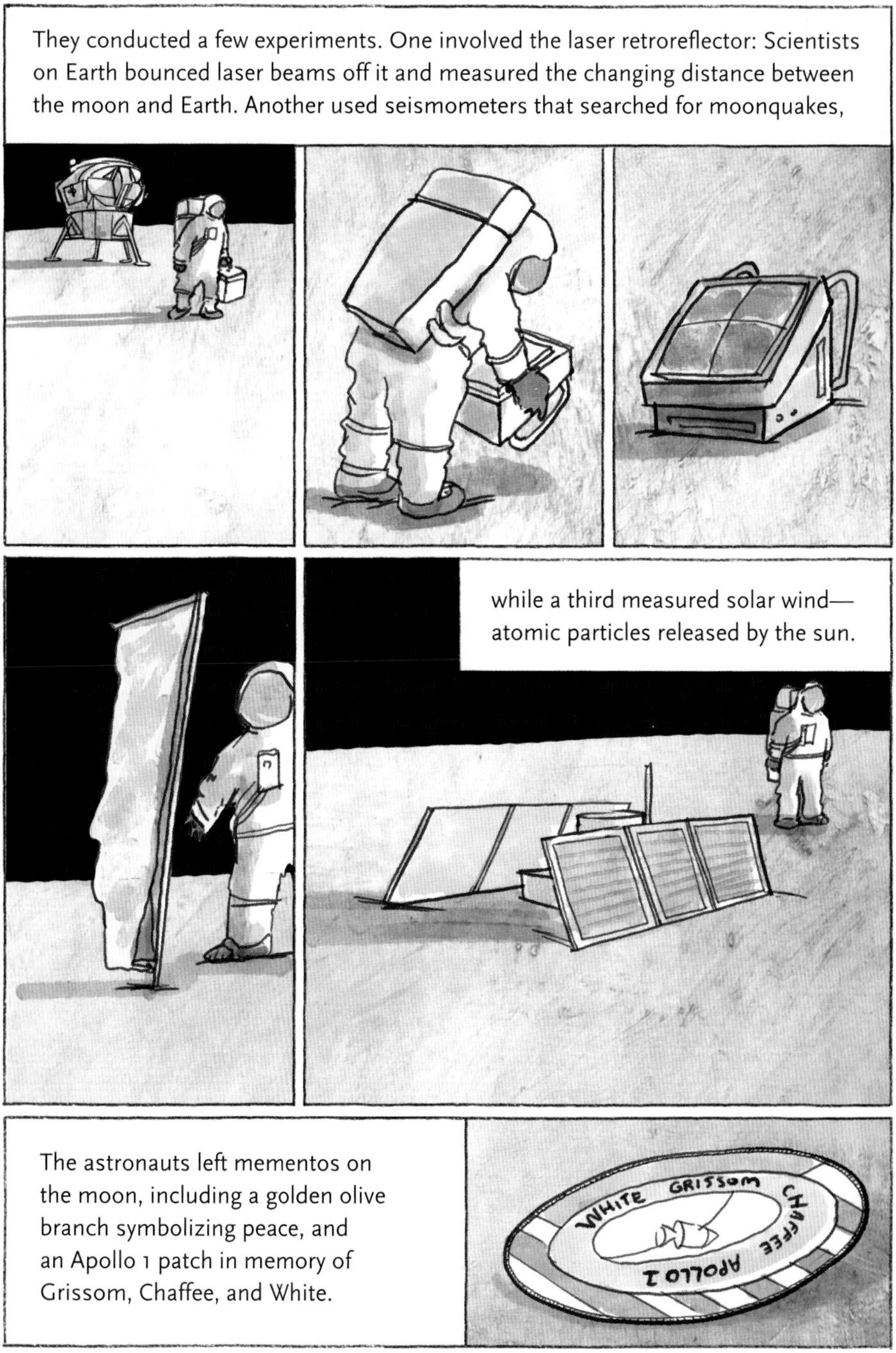
They conducted a few experiments. One involved the laser retroreflector: Scientists on Earth bounced laser beams off it and measured the changing distance between the moon and Earth. Another used seismometers that searched for moonquakes,
while a third measured solar wind—atomic particles released by the sun.
The astronauts left mementos on the moon, including a golden olive branch symbolizing peace, and an Apollo 1 patch in memory of Grissom, Chaffee, and White.
WHITE
GRISSOM
CHAFFEE
APOLLO I

Seven hours after their moonwalk, Armstrong and Aldrin prepared to leave.

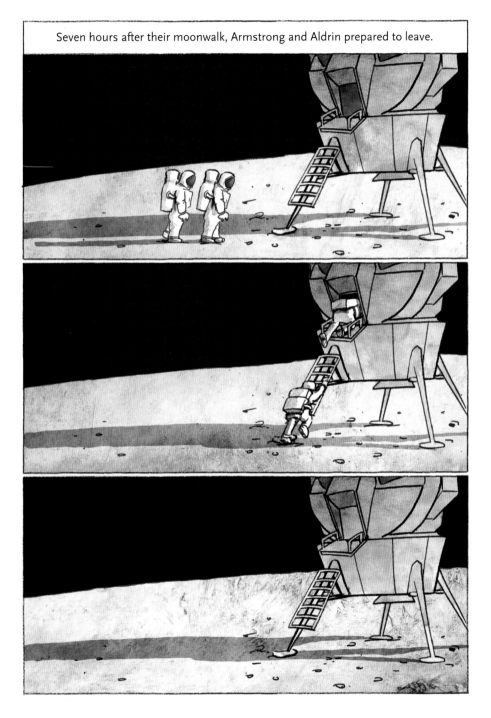

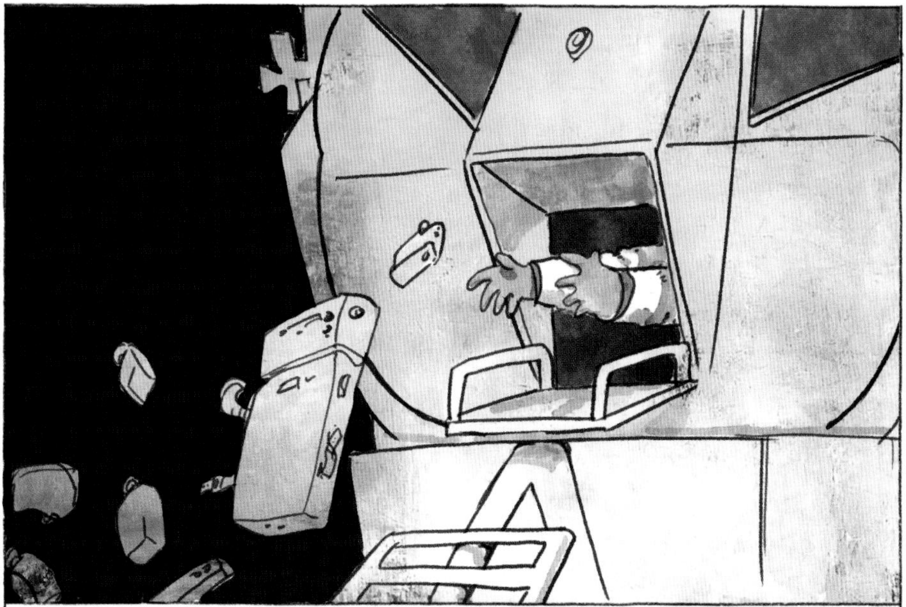

They lightened Eagle by discarding an impressive pile of junk: boots, a camera, canisters, scoops, a shovel, space suit parts, and an empty storage container. They left a bag of barf, too, so watch your step if you're ever on the Sea of Tranquility.

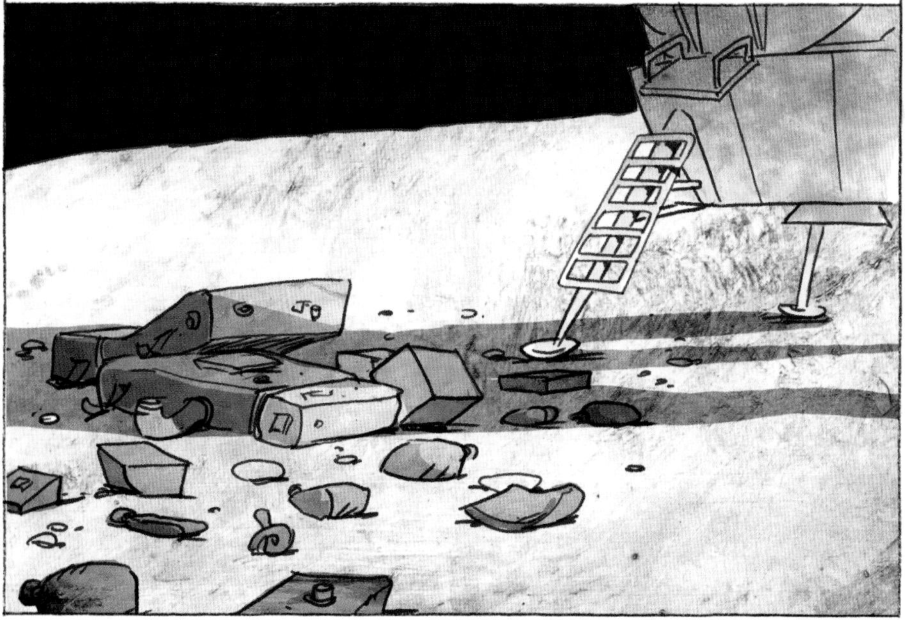

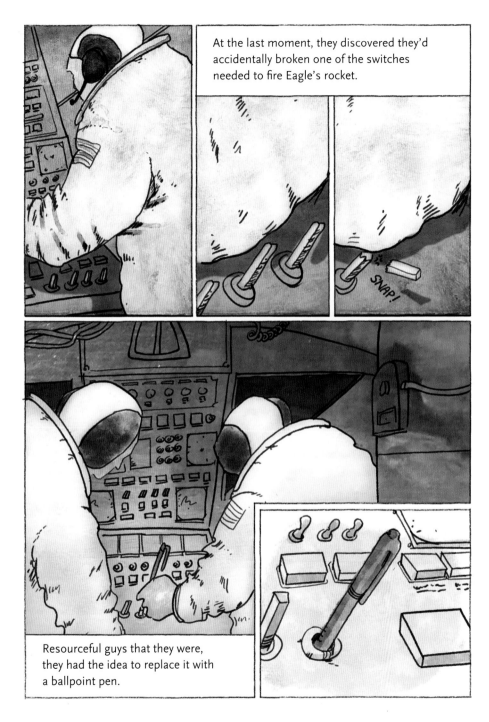

At the last moment, they discovered they'd accidentally broken one of the switches needed to fire Eagle's rocket.

SNAP!

Resourceful guys that they were, they had the idea to replace it with a ballpoint pen.

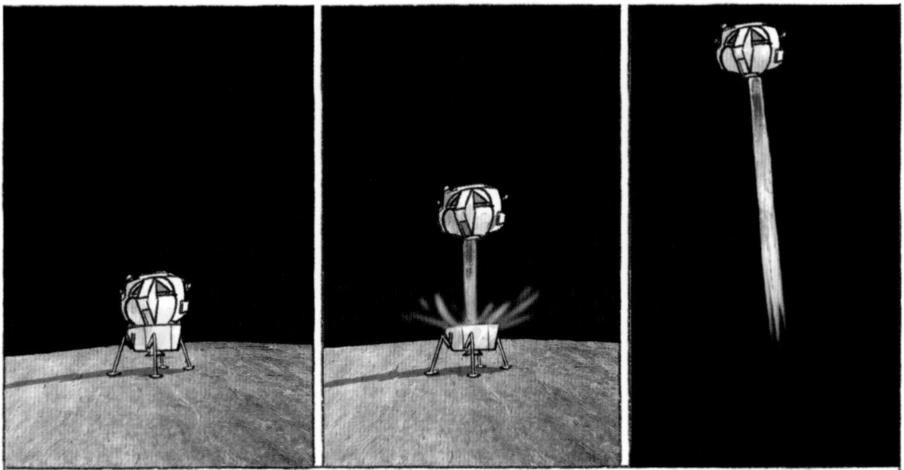

With the fix in place, they rocketed away, riding only the top of the lunar module into orbit. The bottom—including the legs and the descent engine—stayed behind.

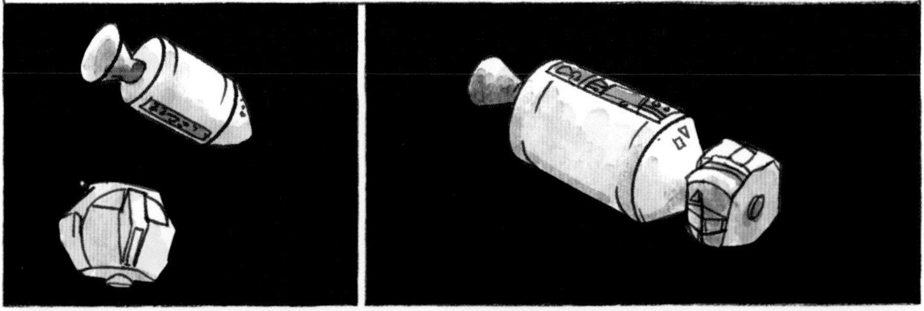

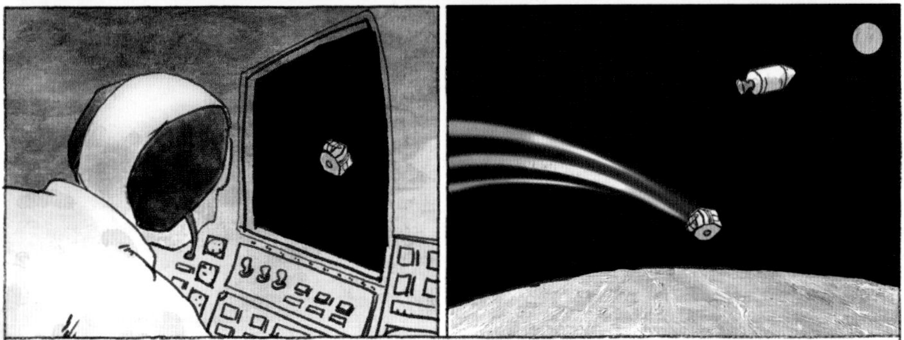

After rendezvousing with the orbiting Columbia, the ascent half of Eagle was discarded. Still within the grasp of the moon's gravity, it is assumed to have crashed at some unknown site.

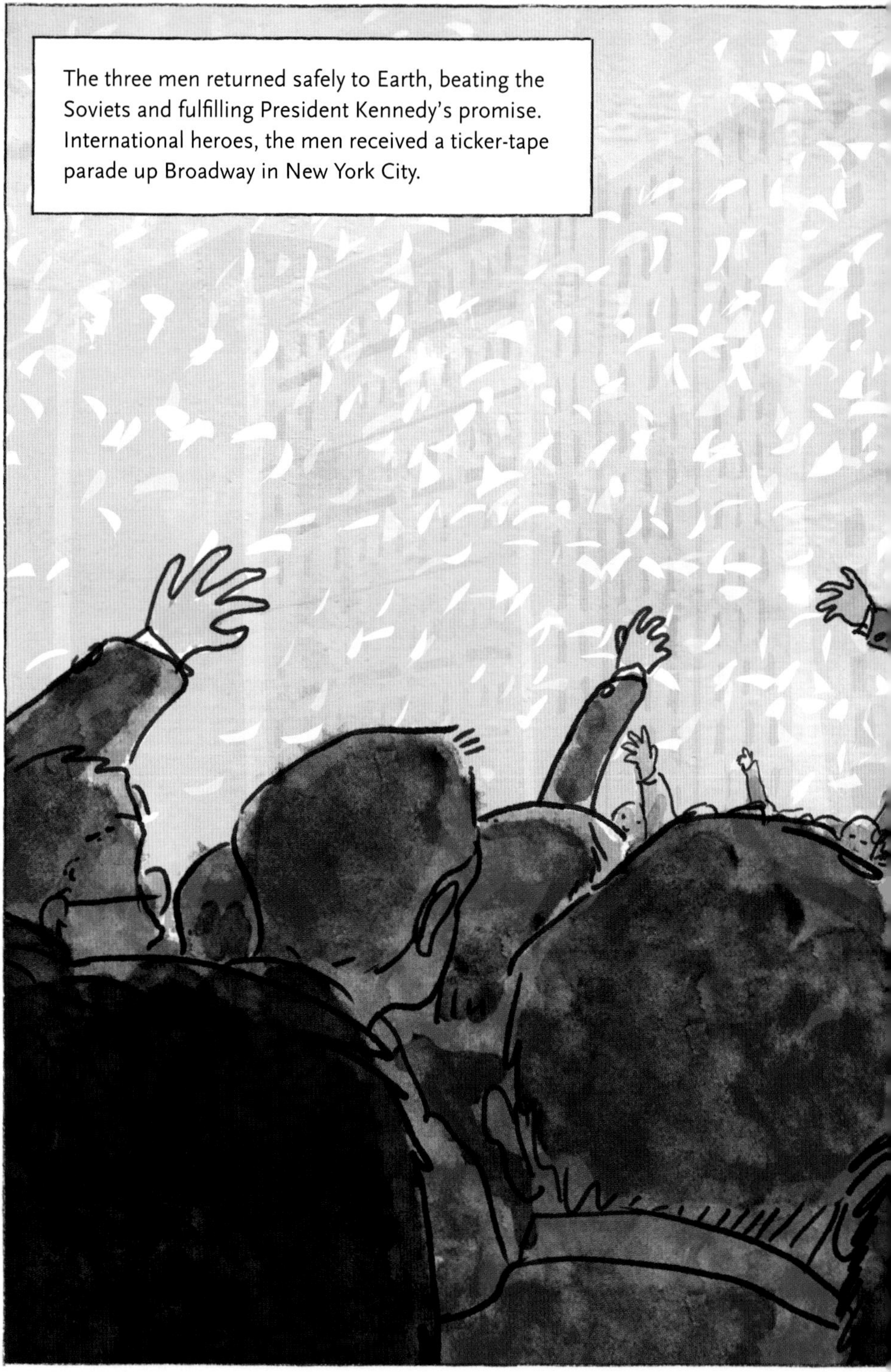
The three men returned safely to Earth, beating the Soviets and fulfilling President Kennedy's promise. International heroes, the men received a ticker-tape parade up Broadway in New York City.

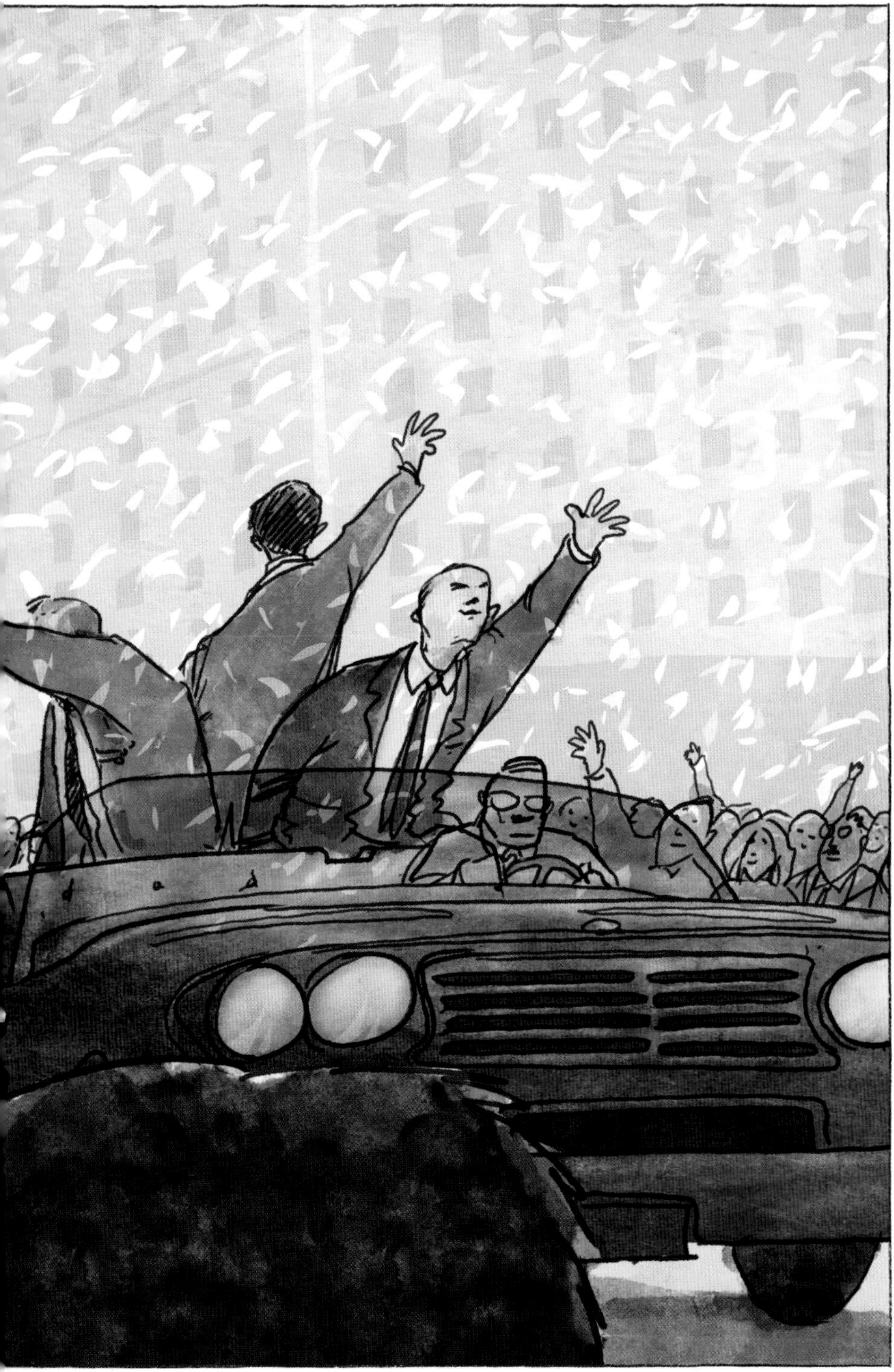

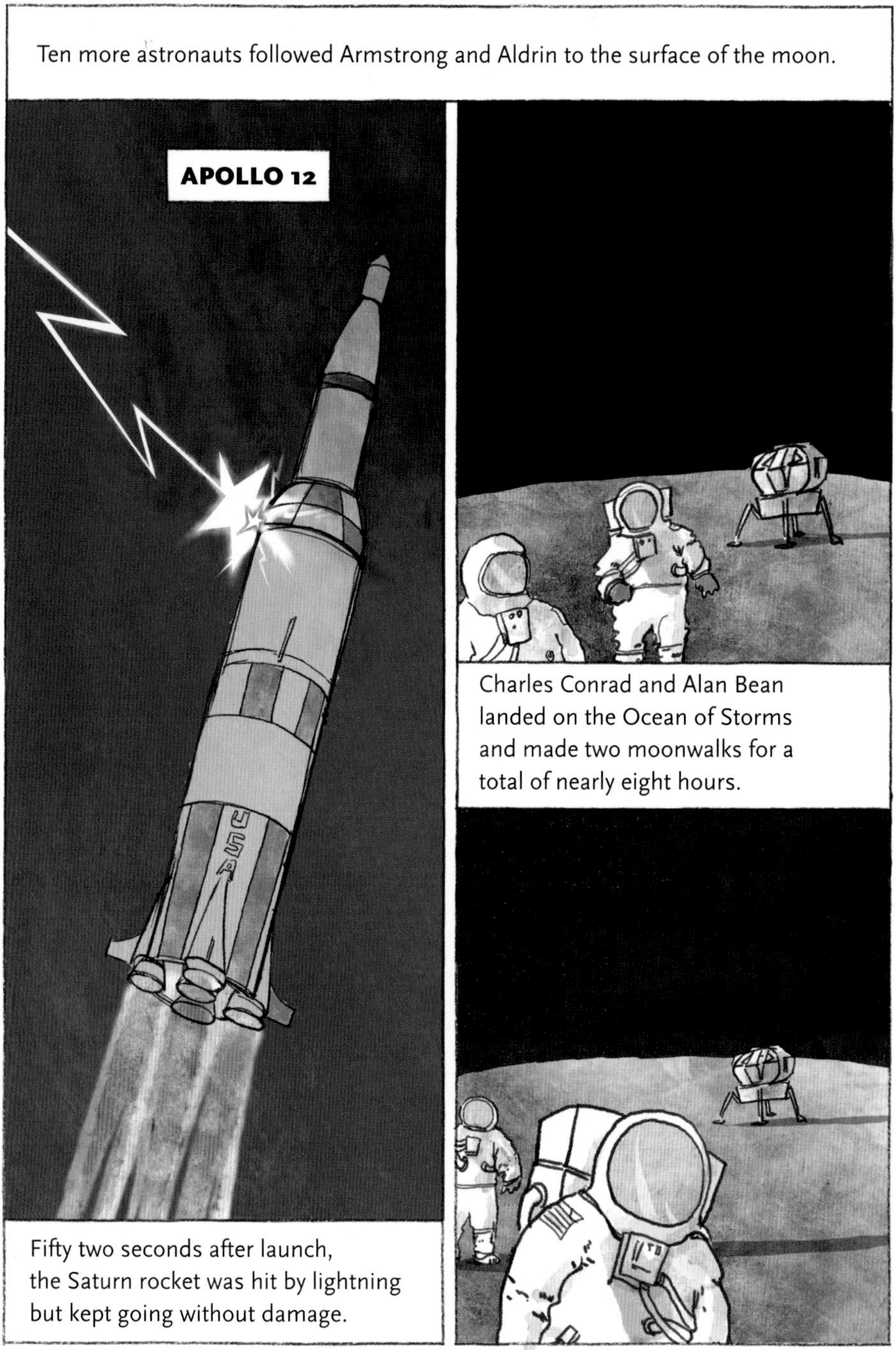
Ten more astronauts followed Armstrong and Aldrin to the surface of the moon.
APOLLO 12
USA
Fifty two seconds after launch, the Saturn rocket was hit by lightning but kept going without damage.
Charles Conrad and Alan Bean landed on the Ocean of Storms and made two moonwalks for a total of nearly eight hours.

APOLLO 13

An explosion in the service module nearly killed the crew and ended their moon mission. The ingenuity of the crew and ground engineers brought them safely home.

APOLLO 14

The lunar module landed in the uplands of the Fra Mauro crater. Alan Shepard—who had been America's first man in space—and Edgar Mitchell explored more than a half mile (0.8 km) from the lunar module.

Shepard hit a golf ball on the moon.

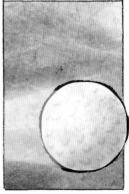

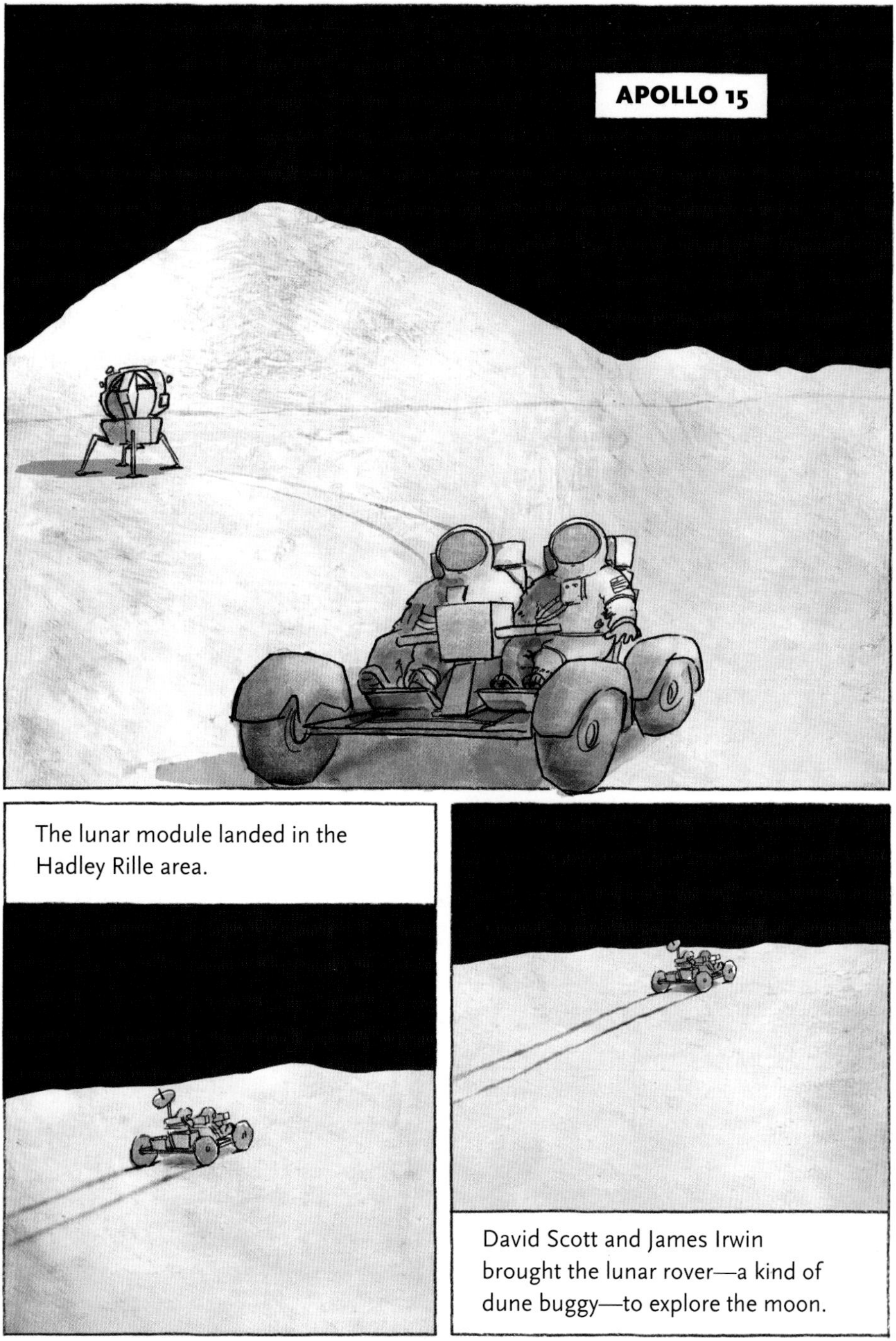
APOLLO 15
The lunar module landed in the Hadley Rille area.
David Scott and James Irwin brought the lunar rover—a kind of dune buggy—to explore the moon.

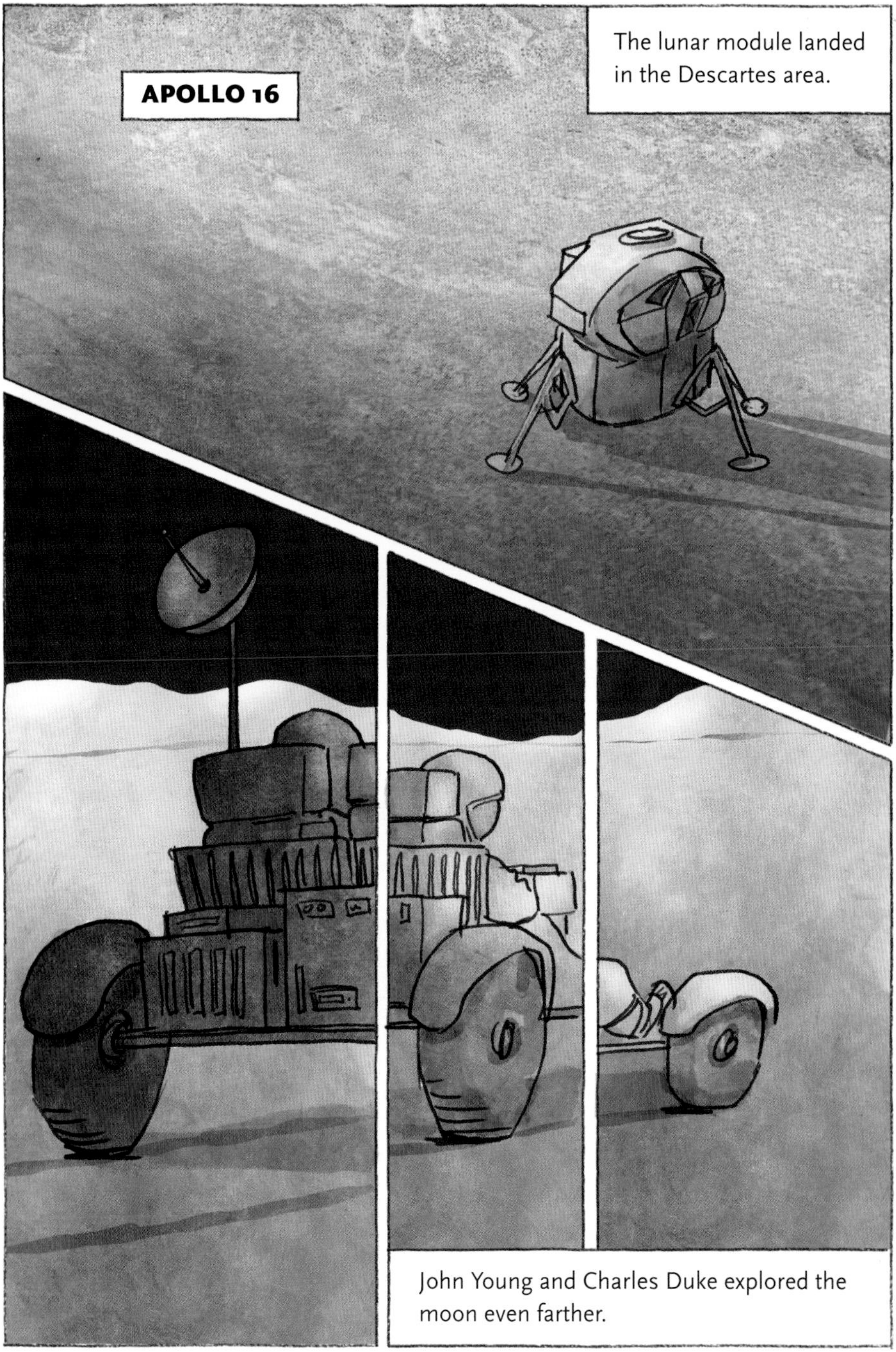
APOLLO 16
The lunar module landed in the Descartes area.
John Young and Charles Duke explored the moon even farther.

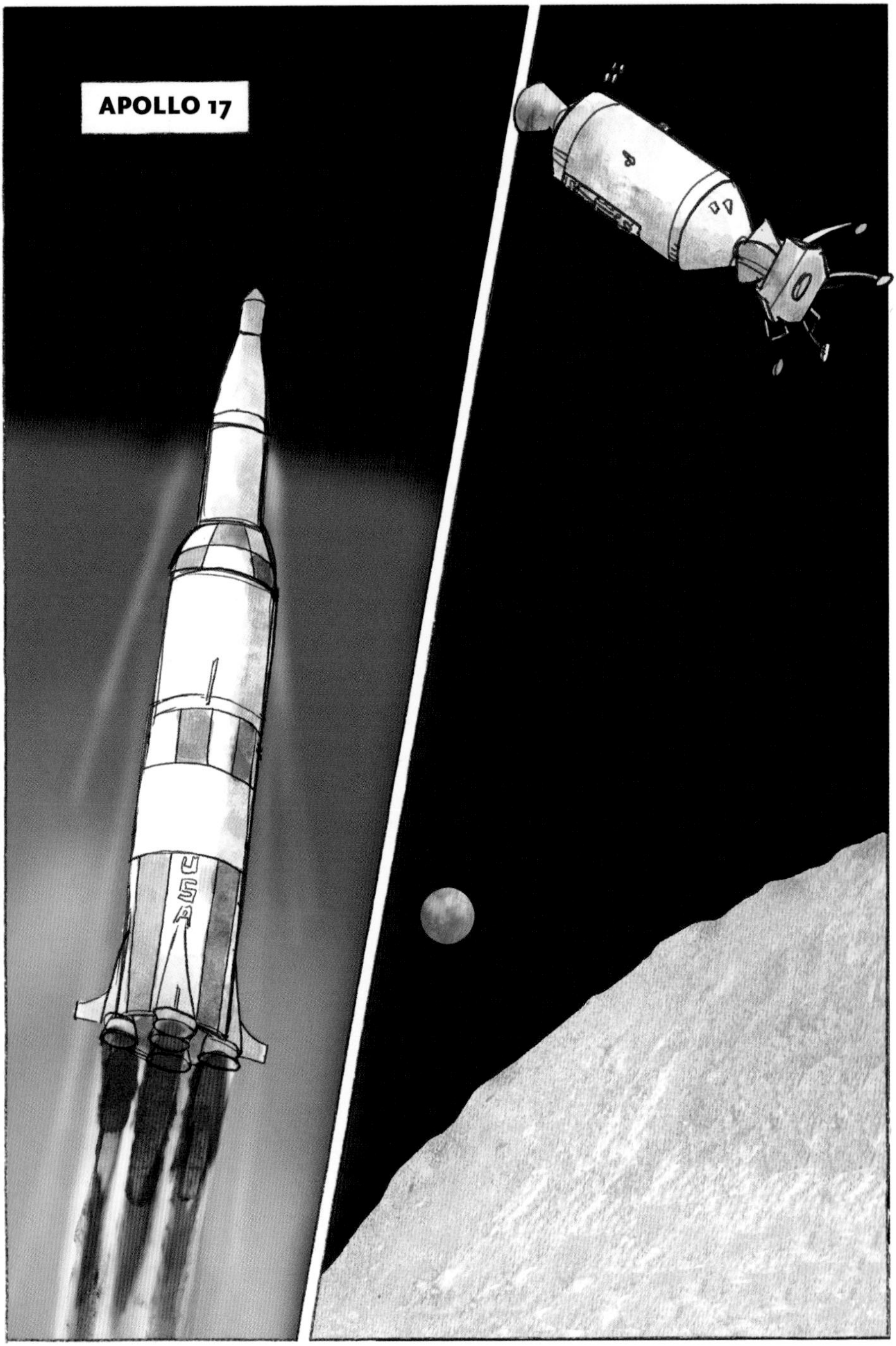
APOLLO 17
USA

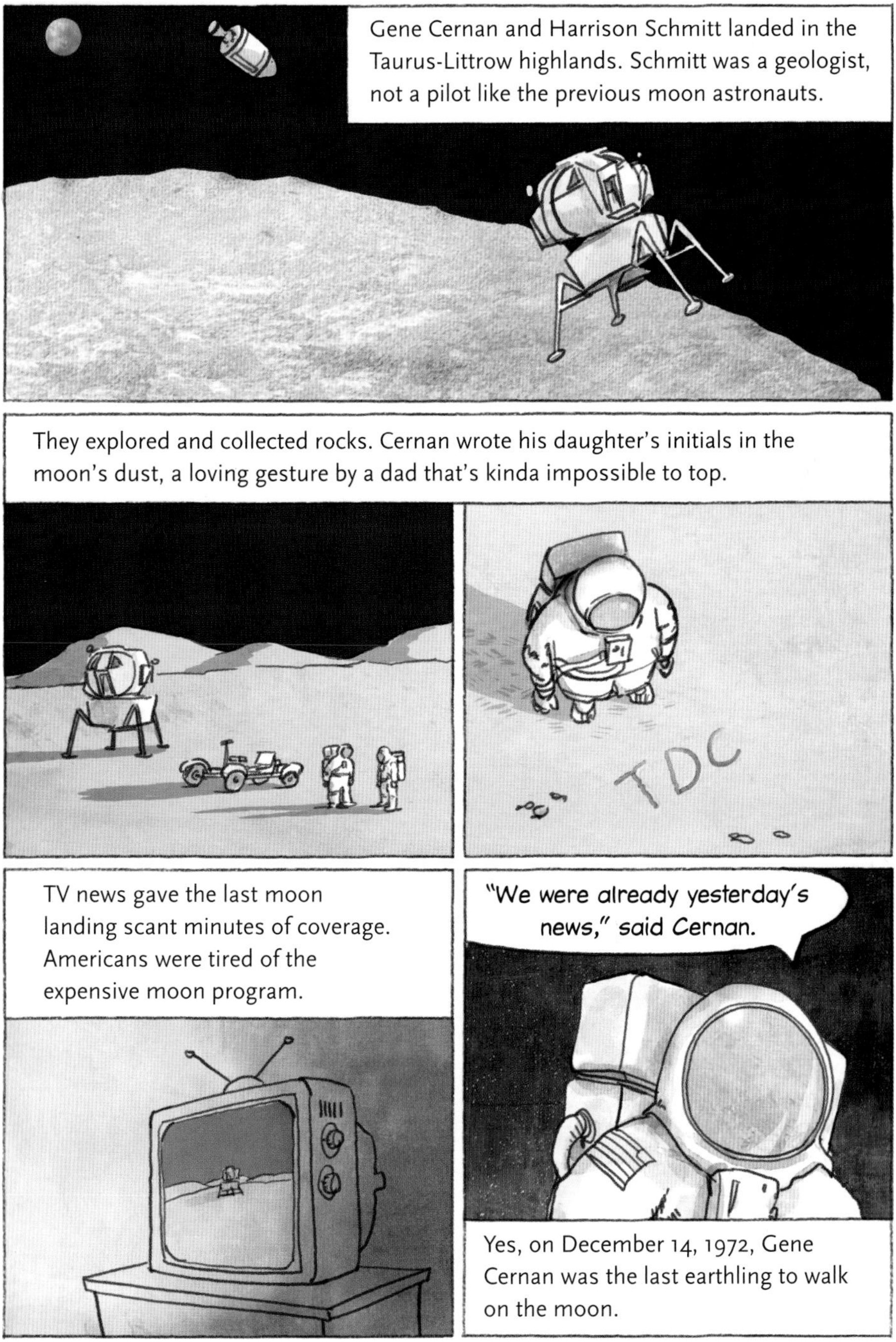
Gene Cernan and Harrison Schmitt landed in the Taurus-Littrow highlands. Schmitt was a geologist, not a pilot like the previous moon astronauts.
They explored and collected rocks. Cernan wrote his daughter's initials in the moon's dust, a loving gesture by a dad that's kinda impossible to top.
TDC
TV news gave the last moon landing scant minutes of coverage. Americans were tired of the expensive moon program.
"We were already yesterday's news," said Cernan.
Yes, on December 14, 1972, Gene Cernan was the last earthling to walk on the moon.

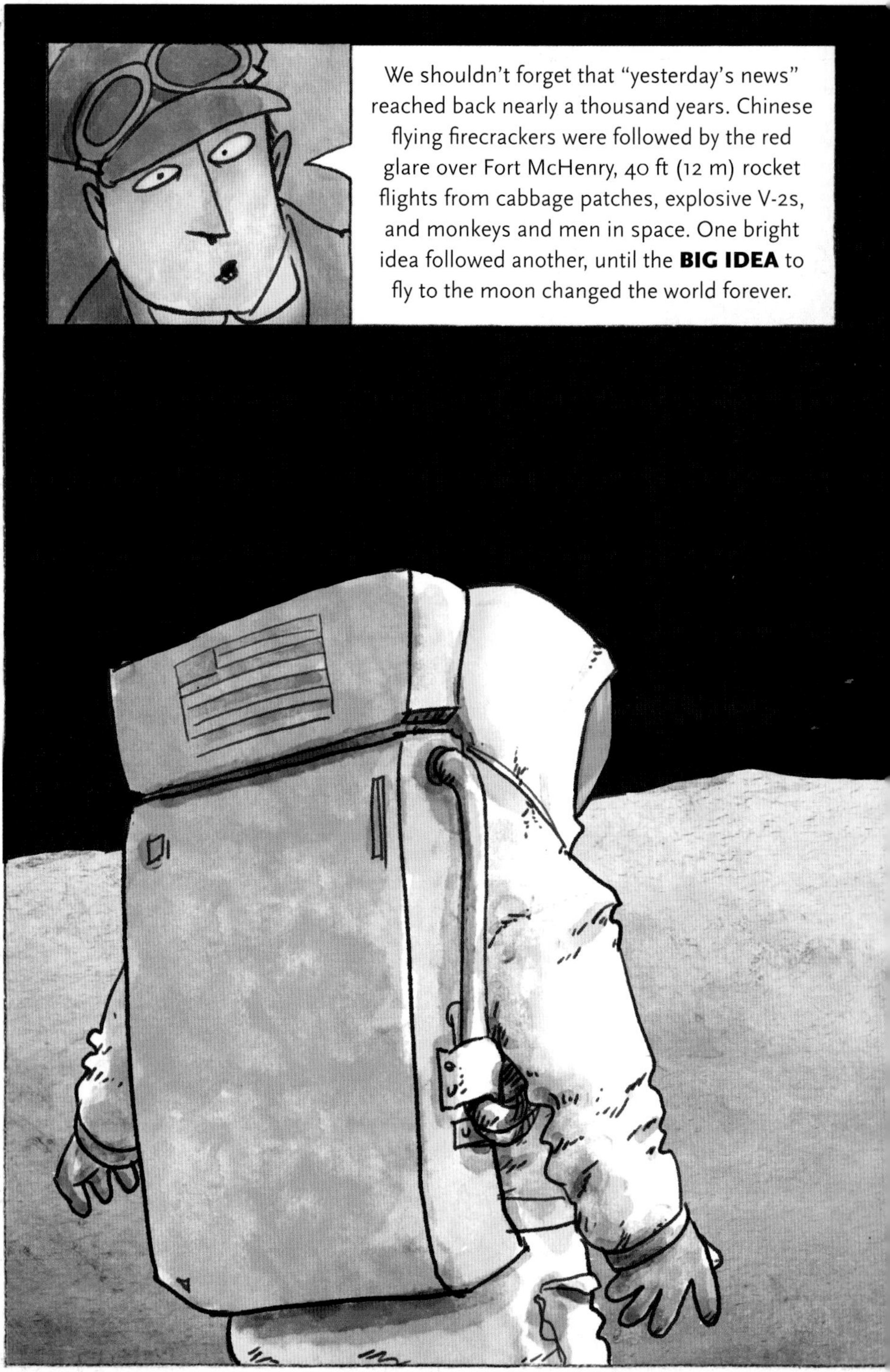

We shouldn't forget that "yesterday's news" reached back nearly a thousand years. Chinese flying firecrackers were followed by the red glare over Fort McHenry, 40 ft (12 m) rocket flights from cabbage patches, explosive V-2s, and monkeys and men in space. One bright idea followed another, until the **BIG IDEA** to fly to the moon changed the world forever.

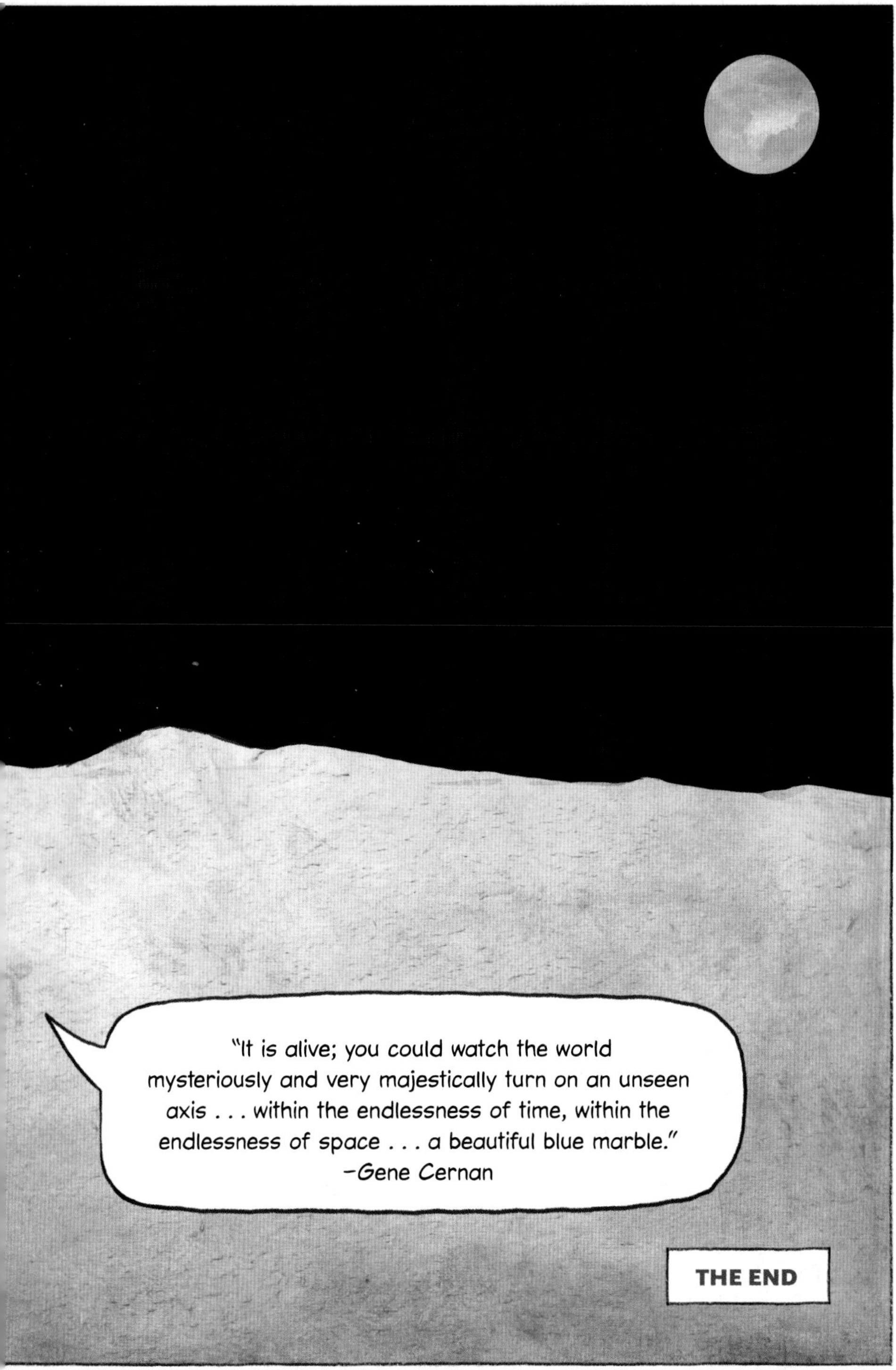
"It is alive; you could watch the world mysteriously and very majestically turn on an unseen axis . . . within the endlessness of time, within the endlessness of space . . . a beautiful blue marble." –Gene Cernan
THE END

SELECT ROCKET AND SPACEFLIGHT TIMELINE

Although the Americans and Soviets didn't share their ideas at the time, they did share the same drive and ambition to be first in space and on the moon. Some of the Soviet, and later Russian, achievements are listed in the timeline as well.

1865
The novel *From the Earth to the Moon* by Jules Verne is published. It tells the story of an organization that attempts to launch three people in a rocket for a moon landing.

1923
Die Rakete zu den Planetenräumen (*The Rocket into Planetary Space*) is self-published by German Hermann Oberth after its rejection as a doctoral thesis.

March 16, 1926
Goddard launches the first liquid-fueled rocket.

1927
In Germany, Verein für Raumschiffahrt (Society for Space Travel) is formed. It includes many top European rocket scientists.

1930
Oberth, with students including Wernher von Braun, launches his first liquid-fueled rocket.

1920 | 1930 | 1940

1903
Inspired by the writings of Jules Verne, first serious work is published that shows physical space exploration was theoretically possible: *Исследование мировых пространств реактивными приборами* (*The Exploration of Cosmic Space by Means of Reaction Devices*) by Russian Konstantin Tsiolkovsky.

1914
American Robert Goddard files for, and is subsequently awarded, US patents on multistage and liquid-fueled rockets.

1933–1945
V-2 rockets are developed by the Germans and used to attack Allies during World War II.

1933
Work begins in Germany on the Aggregat series of rockets, which leads to the V-2 rocket.

June 20, 1944
V-2 rocket (MW 18014) becomes the first man-made object to cross what would later be defined as the Kármán line, and hence makes the first spaceflight in history.

July 22, 1951
USSR sends first dogs into space
(Dezik and Tsygan).

October 4, 1957
USSR launches the first artificial
satellite—Sputnik. First signals from
space generated by humans (Sputnik)
are received on Earth.

November 3, 1957
First animal in orbit, the dog Laika, is
launched aboard the Soviet's Sputnik 2.

January 31, 1961
Ham, a chimpanzee, is first primate
to perform tasks in space.

June 16, 1963
Soviet Valentina Tereshkova becomes the
first woman in space in Vostock 6.

March 18, 1965
Soviet Alexei Leonov accomplishes first
extra-vehicular activity in space (any
action performed outside a spacecraft, in
this case a space walk).

July 20, 1969
The United States lands the first human
on the moon in Apollo 11, takes the first
moonwalk, performs the first space
launch from a celestial body other than
Earth, and brings back the first samples
from the moon.

1950 | 1960 | 1970

April 12, 1961
Soviet Yuri Gagarin performs first
human spaceflight and first human-
crewed orbital flight in Vostok 1.

May 5, 1961
Alan Shepard makes a suborbital
flight, becoming the first American
in space.

February 20, 1962
John Glenn makes America's first
orbital flight.

November 17, 1970
The USSR launches the first lunar
rover, Lunokhod 1.

December 15, 1970
The USSR's Venera 7 accomplishes
the first soft landing and sends the
first man-made signals from another
planet—Venus.

April 19, 1971
The USSR launches Salyut 1, the first space station.

December 2, 1971
The USSR's Mars 3 accomplishes the first soft landing on Mars and sends the first signals from Mars's surface.

July 15, 1972
The United States' Pioneer 10 is the first mission to leave the inner solar system and enter the asteroid belt.

October 22, 1975
On Venus, the USSR's Venera 9 takes the first photos from the surface of another planet.

February 7, 1984
American Bruce McCandless II takes the first untethered space walk during mission STS-41B.

January 28, 1986
The shuttle Challenger disaster is the first major American loss in space.

February 19, 1986
The USSR launches Mir, the first consistently inhabited long-term research space station.

February 14, 1990
The United States' Voyager 1 takes the first photograph of the entire solar system.

April 24, 1990
The Hubble Space Telescope is launched into orbit on American mission STS-31.

1970   1980   1990

September 17, 1976
The United States rolls out space shuttle orbiter Enterprise. It performs both manned and unmanned flight tests while mated atop a 747 aircraft.

September 5, 1977
The United States launches Voyager 1, a space probe whose primary mission is to fly by Saturn.

April 12, 1981
The United States' STS-1 makes the first orbital flight of the space shuttle program and is the first reusable manned spacecraft.

February 8, 1992
The United States' Ulysses makes the first polar orbit around the sun.

March 22, 1995
Russian Valeri Polyakov sets the record for the longest duration of a single stay in space: 437 days and 18 hours aboard Mir space station.

July 4, 1997
The United States' Mars Pathfinder becomes the first operational rover on another planet.

November 20, 1998
Built by the United States, Europe, Russia, Japan, and Canada, the International Space Station is the first multinational space station and the largest man-made object ever built in space.

May 29, 1999
A shuttle docks with the International Space Station for the first time during American mission STS-96.

2002
Elon Musk founds SpaceX, a private company, with the goal of eventually enabling humans to live on other planets.

August 10, 2015
On the International Space Station, lettuce becomes the first food eaten in space that was also grown there.

December 21, 2015
SpaceX accomplishes the first return-to-flight mission: Falcon 9 travels into space and returns to land back on Earth.

March 30, 2017
SpaceX achieves the world's first reflight of an orbital class rocket.

February 8, 2018
SpaceX launches Falcon Heavy, the world's heaviest rocket. It is able to carry 141,000 lb (63,957 kg) into low Earth orbit, thus paving the way for space travel beyond Earth.

2000   2010   2020

August 25, 2012
The United States sends Voyager 1 into interstellar space.

July 2015
The United States' New Horizons probe takes the first flyby photo of dwarf planet Pluto.

August 12, 2018
NASA launches Parker Solar Probe, carried aloft by a Delta IV Heavy rocket, to circle the sun, coming within 3.8 million miles (6.1 million km) of its surface.

For more historic moments:
www.timelines.ws/subjects/NASA.HTML

WHO WAS
RODMAN LAW?

Rodman Law (January 21, 1885–October 14, 1919) was a real daredevil: a career parachutist, building climber, and later silent-movie stuntman and actor. Taking chances must have run in the family, because his sister, Ruth Law, was a fearless pilot during the dangerous early days of aviation. Despite discrimination against women pilots, she became a famous, record-setting flyer. I bet she would have loved to fly to the moon!

Law was real, but as you can see, I am a cartoon. In fact, all of *Rocket to the Moon!* is a cartoon. So for those of you interested in flying to the moon, I suggest you enjoy these cartoons but find yourself realistic and accurate spaceship plans!

NOTES

Page 4—"You may light the fuse when ready, Sam," *New York Times*, March 14, 1913.

Page 6—Lagari Hasan Çelebi reportedly launched a gunpowder-powered rocket near Istanbul in 1633.

Page 11—"My interest . . . Jules Verne." DeGroot, Gerard. *Liberal Crusader: The Life of Sir Archibald Sinclair* (New York: NYU Press, 1993), p. 4.

Page 11—"Always had in . . . Jules Verne." Burrows, William. *This New Ocean: The Story of the First Space Age* (New York: Random House, 1998), p. 32.

Page 11—". . . ascending to Mars." Nelson, Craig. *Rocket Men: The Epic Story of the First Men on the Moon* (New York: Penguin, 2009), p. 94.

Page 16—"Interplanetary travel . . . the mysterious universe!" DeGroot, p. 13.

Page 20—"Germany has lost . . . in the right hands." Nelson, p. 105.

Page 31—"A man in Sputnik means control of the globe." DeGroot, p. 89.

Page 33—"Get the girl to check the numbers." "From Computers to Leaders: Women at NASA Langley." NASA Langley, NASA, March 27, 2014, www.nasa.gov/larc/from -computers-to-leaders-women-at-nasa-langley.

Page 33—"I want this human computer . . . I'm good to go" "'Hidden Figures': How Black Women Did The Math That Put Men On The Moon," NPR, www.npr .org/2016/09/25/495179824/hidden-figures-how-black-women-did-the-math-that-put -men-on-the-moon.

Page 38—"Here we go!" Nelson, p. 151.

Page 39—"Let the capitalist countries catch up with our country." DeGroot, p. 133.

Page 39—"There's nothing more important." Murray, Charles. *Apollo: The Race to the Moon* (New York: Simon & Schuster, 1989), p. 79.

Page 40— "I believe that . . . to the Earth." DeGroot, p. 142.

Page 53—"You lose crew . . . experimental aircraft." Murray, p. 225.

Page 55—"Apollo 8 was . . . on the moon." *Moon Shot*. Directed by Kirk Wolfinger. 1994. Burbank, CA: TBS Productions/Turner Home Entertainment. www.youtube.com /watch?v=jia78xRMTEc.

Page 55—"My wife was . . . from the moon." *Moon Shot*. Directed by Kirk Wolfinger.

Page 57—"Earthshine." *Moon Shot*. Directed by Kirk Wolfinger.

Page 59—"Armstrong was described as 'extraordinarily remote.'" Seymour, Gene. "Neil Armstrong, a hero who shunned fame," CNN, August 27, 2012.

Page 66—"Oh, boy, it looks good!" "John Glenn launch, Walter Cronkite 'Go, baby!' LIVE on TV, CBS, February 20, 1962" www.youtube.com/watch?v=GVB5dg7XX_g.

Page 69—"steering like crazy." Collins, Michael. *Carrying the Fire: An Astronaut's Journeys* (New York: Farrar, Straus & Giroux, 1974), p. 364.

Page 79—"Get me a napkin . . . God Almighty." Apollo 10 Onboard Voice Transcription, NASA, 1969, p. 348, www.jsc.nasa.gov/history/mission_trans/AS10_CM.PDF.

Page 80—"The most awesome . . . ever seen." Collins, p. 390.

Page 80—"It's a view worth the price of the trip." Collins, p. 390.

Page 82—"the weirdest-looking contraption ever to invade the sky." One Giant Leap for Mankind, NASA, www.nasa.gov/mission_pages/apollo/apollo11.html.

Page 84—"I could have jabbed a screwdriver through them without a lot of effort." Aldrin, Buzz and Malcolm McConnell. *Men From Earth* (New York: Bantam Books, 1989), p. 232.

Page 85—"The Eagle has wings." Apollo 11 Onboard Voice Transcription, NASA, 1969, p. 159, www.jsc.nasa.gov/history/mission_trans/AS11_CM.PDF.

Page 85—"You guys take care." Apollo 11 Spacelog, Phase 5: Descent to the Moon, 4:4:38:53, apollo11.spacelog.org/page/04%3A04%3A17%3A06.

Page 85—"See you later." Apollo 11 Spacelog, 4:4:38:56.

Page 87—"You're go for powered descent." Aldrin, p. 235.

Page 93–95—"Two hundred feet, four and a half down . . . Engine stop." Apollo 11 Onboard Voice Transcription, NASA, pp. 177–178.

Page 95—"Houston, Tranquility Base . . . Eagle has landed." Apollo 11 Onboard Voice Transcription, NASA, p.178.

Page 97—"It takes a pretty good little jump." Barbree, Jay. *Neil Armstrong: A Life in Flight* (New York: St. Martin's Press, 2014), p. 263.

Page 99—"That's one small step for man, one giant leap for mankind," Apollo 11 Spacelog, 4:13:24:48.

Page 102—"Magnificent desolation." Aldrin, p. 241.

Page 117—"We were already yesterday's news." DeGroot, p. 252.

Page 119—"It is alive . . . a beautiful blue marble." French, Francis. *In the Shadow of the Moon: A Challenging Journey to Tranquility, 1965–1969* (Lincoln: University of Nebraska Press, 2007), p. 388.

BIBLIOGRAPHY

Books

Aldrin, Buzz and Malcolm McConnell. *Men From Earth*. New York: Bantam Books, 1989.

Barbree, Jay. *Neil Armstrong: A Life in Flight*. New York: St. Martin's Press, 2014.

Breuer, William B. *Race to the Moon: America's Duel with the Soviets*. Westport, CT: Praeger, 1993.

Burrows, William E. *This New Ocean: The Story of the First Space Age*. New York: Random House, 1998.

Collins, Michael. *Carrying the Fire: An Astronaut's Journeys*. New York: Farrar, Straus & Giroux, 1974.

DeGroot, Gerard J. *Dark Side of the Moon: The Magnificent Madness of the American Lunar Quest*. New York: New York University Press, 2006.

Farmer, Dora Jane and Gene Hamblin. *First on the Moon*. Boston: Little, Brown and Company, 1970.

French, Francis and Colin Burgess. *In the Shadow of the Moon: A Challenging Journey to Tranquility, 1965–1969*. Lincoln: University of Nebraska Press, 2007.

Mailer, Norman. *Of a Fire on the Moon*. Boston: Little, Brown and Company, 1969.

Miller, Ron. *The Dream Machines: A Pictorial History of the Spaceship in Art, Science and Literature*. Malabar, FL: Krieger Publishing, 1993.

Murray, Charles and Catherine Bly Cox. *Apollo: The Race to the Moon*. New York: Simon & Schuster, 1989.

Nelson, Craig. *Rocket Men: The Epic Story of the First Men on the Moon*. New York: Viking, 2009.

Articles

Blitz, Matt. "The True Story of 'Hidden Figures' and the Women Who Crunched the Numbers for NASA." *Popular Mechanics*. popularmechanics.com/space/rockets/a24429/hidden-figures-real-story-nasa-women-computers (accessed February 12, 2018).

NASA. "At Long Last." www.hq.nasa.gov/office/pao/History/SP-4204/ch21-6.html (accessed December 4, 2017).

NASA. "Brief History of Rockets." www.grc.nasa.gov/www/k-12/TRC/Rockets/history_of_rockets.html (accessed November 6, 2017).

NASA. "Building KSC's Launch Complex 39." www.nasa.gov/sites/default/files/167394main_BuildingKSC-08.pdf (accessed December 4, 2017).

NASA. "Crawler-Transporter." science.ksc.nasa.gov/facilities/crawler.html (accessed December 4, 2017).

NASA. "Former Astronauts Recall Historic First Moon Landing." July 25, 2014. www.nasa.gov/content/former-astronauts-recall-historic-first-moon-landing (accessed November 28, 2017).

NASA. "July 20, 1969: One Giant Leap for Mankind." July 20, 2017. www.nasa.gov/mission_pages/apollo/apollo11.html (accessed November 28, 2017).

NASA. "Launch Complex 39-A & 39-B." science.ksc.nasa.gov/facilities/lc39a.html (accessed November 4, 2017).

NASA. "Robert Goddard: A Man and his Rocket." www.nasa.gov/missions/research/f_goddard.html (accessed April 10, 2018).

NASA. "Wide Awake on the Sea of Tranquillity." July 9, 2014. nasa.gov/exploration/home/19jul_seaoftranquillity.html (accessed December 6, 2017).

NASA History Program Office. "A Brief History of Animals in Space." history.nasa.gov/animals.html (accessed January 3, 2018).

New Mexico Museum of Space History. "Konstantin Tsiolkovesky: The Father of Astronautics and Rocket Dynamics." nmspacemuseum.org/halloffame/detail.php?id=27 (accessed November 7, 2017).

New Mexico State University; New Mexico Space Grant Consortium. "Lunar Legacy Project." spacegrant.nmsu.edu/lunarlegacies/artifactlist.html (accessed December 7, 2017).

New York Times. "Skyrocket Bursts With Man on Board." March 14, 1913. www.nytimes.com/1913/03/14/archives/skyrocket-bursts-with-man-on-board-law-near-death-when-he-attempts.html.

NPR. "'Hidden Figures': How Black Women Did The Math That Put Men On The Moon." September 25, 2016. npr.org/2016/09/25/495179824/hidden-figures-how-black-women -did-the-math-that-put-men-on-the-moon (accessed January 15, 2018).

Smithsonian National Air and Space Museum. "Apollo Urine Collection and Transfer." airandspace.si.edu/multimedia-gallery/5159hjpg (accessed December 6, 2017).

Smithsonian National Air and Space Museum. "Location of Apollo Lunar Modules." airandspace.si.edu/explore-and-learn/topics/apollo/apollo-program/spacecraft/location /lm.cfm (accessed December 8, 2017).

Smithsonian National Air and Space Museum. "Scientific Experiments." airandspace .si.edu/exhibitions/apollo-to-the-moon/online/science/scientific-experiments.cfm (accessed February 12, 2018).

Space.com. "NASA's Mighty Saturn V Moon Rocket Explained." November 9, 2012. www.space.com/18422-apollo-saturn-v-moon-rocket-nasa-infographic.html (accessed December 4, 2017).

Space.com. "The Scoop on Space Poop: How Astronauts Go Potty." www.space .com/22597-space-poop-astronaut-toilet-explained.html (accessed December 5, 2017).

Whitehouse, Dr. David. "First Dog in Space Died Within Hours." BBC News. news.bbc .co.uk/2/hi/science/nature/2367681.stm (accessed April 11, 2018).

Television

Discovery Channel. *MythBusters*. "Crash and Burn." November 11, 2009. Season 7. Episode 17.

Movie

Moon Shot. TBS Productions/Turner Home Entertainment. 1994. www.youtube.com /watch?v=jia78xRMTEc (accessed November 27, 2017).

Websites

Garrett, Russ and Matthew Ogle. Spacelog. Apollo 11. apollo11.spacelog.org /page/04:04:17:06/ (accessed March 22, 2018).

Hermann Oberth Raumfahrt Museum. www.oberth-museum.org/index_e.html (accessed November 7, 2017).

NASA. "Apollo 10 Onboard Voice Transcription." June 1969. www.jsc.nasa.gov/history /mission_trans/AS10_CM.PDF (accessed December 5, 2017).

NASA. "Apollo 11 Onboard Voice Transcription." August 1969. www.jsc.nasa.gov/history /mission_trans/AS11_CM.PDF (accessed April 10, 2018).

PBS NOVA Online. "To The Moon." July 13, 1999. www.pbs.org/wgbh/nova/tothemoon/ (accessed April 10, 2018).

Thamtech, LLC. "First Men on the Moon." www.firstmenonthemoon.com (accessed November 29, 2017).

AUTHOR'S NOTE

I'm not the first to say that BIG IDEAS stand on the shoulders of earlier, lesser-known big ideas. But repeating it doesn't make it any less true. Or less exciting! The BIG IDEAS That Changed the World series celebrates the hard-won succession of ideas that ultimately remade the world.

Reminding ourselves that big ideas are born from other ideas is especially appropriate when celebrating the fiftieth anniversary of the moon landing. I recall watching the event on television with my folks. It was a pivotal moment in American and world history, and the astronauts were the clear focus. But a long line of fascinating people and ideas over many years and even centuries contributed to Neil Armstrong's step onto the Sea of Tranquility. Those stories were the inspiration for this book.

The rocket's development and usage were mostly in the hands of men, particularly white men. President Kennedy's 1961 pledge to land a man on the moon primarily fell to people possessing scientific and technical skills that were openly and tacitly denied to most women and people of color. There were exceptions of course, such as Katherine Johnson, a mathematician for NASA. So it is encouraging to see that today, NASA is being advanced by a diverse group of people. The world changes as the ideas have grown. As the series develops, it is certainly my intent to include the diverse group of people from all walks of life who have contributed to the ideas that comprise our world today.

BIG IDEAS are not an end point but just one stop on a continuum of ideas, big and small, which stretches across time. Whether an inspired success or a tragic failure, the ideas are a trail I'll follow in this series. And like other trips, the pleasure will not be in the destination but in the journey.

INDEX